New Directions in Philosophy and Cognitive Sc

Series Editors: **John Protevi**, Louisiana State University and **Michael Wheeler**, University of Stirling

This series brings together work that takes cognitive science in new directions. Hitherto, philosophical reflection on cognitive science – or perhaps better, philosophical contribution to the interdisciplinary field that is cognitive science – has for the most part come from philosophers with a commitment to a representationalist model of the mind.

However, as cognitive science continues to make advances, especially in its neuroscience and robotics aspects, there is growing discontent with the representationalism of traditional philosophical interpretations of cognition. Cognitive scientists and philosophers have turned to a variety of sources – phenomenology and dynamic systems theory foremost among them to date – to rethink cognition as the direction of the action of an embodied and affectively attuned organism embedded in its social world, a stance that sees representation as only one tool of cognition, and a derived one at that.

To foster this growing interest in rethinking traditional philosophical notions of cognition – using phenomenology, dynamic systems theory, and perhaps other approaches yet to be identified – we dedicate this series to "New Directions in Philosophy and Cognitive Science."

Titles include:

Jay Schulkin (*editor*)
ACTION, PERCEPTION AND THE BRAIN

Rex Welshon
NIETZSCHE'S DYNAMIC METAPSYCHOLOGY
This Uncanny Animal

Forthcoming titles

Miranda Anderson
THE RENAISSANCE EXTENDED MIND

Massimiliano Cappucio and Tom Froese (*editors*)
ENACTIVE COGNITION AT THE EDGE OF SENSE-MAKING

Maxime Doyon and Thiemo Breyer
NORMATIVITY IN PERCEPTION

Matt Hayler
A PHENOMENOLOGICAL ANALYSIS OF TECHNOLOGY USE

John Shook and Tibor Solymosi (*editors*)
NEUROSCIENCE, NEUROPHILOSOPHY AND PRAGMATISM
Understanding Brains at Work in the World

Also by Rex Welshon

NIETZSCHE'S PERSPECTIVISM (*co-authored with Steve Hales*, 2000)

PHILOSOPHY, NEUROSCIENCE, AND CONSCIOUSNESS (2011)

THE PHILOSOPHY OF NIETZSCHE (2004)

New Directions in Philosophy and Cognitive Science
Series Standing Order ISBN 978–0–230–54935–7 Hardback
                           978–0–230–54936–4 Paperback
(*outside North America only*)

You can receive future titles in this series as they are published by placing a standing order. Please contact your bookseller or, in case of difficulty, write to us at the address below with your name and address, the title of the series and one of the ISBNs quoted above.

Customer Services Department, Macmillan Distribution Ltd, Houndmills, Basingstoke, Hampshire RG21 6XS, England

Nietzsche's Dynamic Metapsychology

This Uncanny Animal

Rex Welshon
University of Colorado at Colorado Springs, USA

palgrave
macmillan

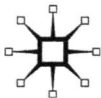

First published 2014 by
PALGRAVE MACMILLAN

Palgrave Macmillan in the UK is an imprint of Macmillan Publishers Limited, registered in England, company number 785998, of Houndmills, Basingstoke, Hampshire RG21 6XS.

Palgrave Macmillan in the US is a division of St Martin's Press LLC, 175 Fifth Avenue, New York, NY 10010.

Palgrave Macmillan is the global academic imprint of the above companies and has companies and representatives throughout the world.

Palgrave® and Macmillan® are registered trademarks in the United States, the United Kingdom, Europe and other countries

ISBN 978-1-349-33803-0   ISBN 978-1-137-31703-2 (eBook)
DOI 10.1057/9781137317032

This book is printed on paper suitable for recycling and made from fully managed and sustained forest sources. Logging, pulping and manufacturing processes are expected to conform to the environmental regulations of the country of origin.

A catalogue record for this book is available from the British Library.

A catalog record for this book is available from the Library of Congress.

Transferred to Digital Printing in 2014

For the late Louis Cicotello, friend and desert rat: sublime always

Contents

List of Figures

Series Editors' Foreword

Almost all of us can recall the exhilarating Nietzsche of our first fevered readings – monster and provocateur, poet and aphorist, genealogist and essayist – the one who has kept countless undergraduates thinking and debating long into the night.

Rex Welshon reminds us, though, of the existence of a sober Nietzsche – or perhaps better, a sober reading of Nietzsche. Via his careful reconstruction, Welshon lets us see how we can use Nietzsche to pose insightful questions to many of the presuppositions of contemporary philosophy of mind and cognitive science.

This sympathetic and probing work pushes Nietzsche to very interesting places, namely, into connection with the various forms of embodied cognitive science our series seeks to highlight and explore. Fully aware of the dangers of anachronism, further aware of the difficulties Nietzsche writing strategies pose, and prepared to criticize Nietzsche's positions when needed, Welshon guides us through the vast and heterogeneous corpus of Nietzsche's works to the spots where we find a naturalist and yet non-representationalist Nietzsche, one who can truthfully be called a dynamic "embodied-embedded" thinker.

Acknowledgments

I would like to thank various audiences for critical comments that have been incorporated into this book. I would like to thank the College of Letters, Arts, and Sciences Dean's Office and the Philosophy Department of the University of Colorado Colorado Springs for their collegiality and supportive ways. I would like to thank the Palgrave Macmillan editors for their patience and the production staff for their expert handling of the manuscript. Finally, I would like to thank my wife, Perrin, and our children, Anna and Calvin, for insisting that there is more to a flourishing life than writing about it.

Introduction

In the last fifteen years, Nietzsche scholarship has become sober. Most of the allegations against Nietzsche deriving from various politically charged controversies surrounding him and his work – that he is a fascist, *ad hominimem* attacks against his work premised on his insanity, the worry that his anti-religious proclivities make his work unsavoury – have been shown to be mistaken, and the dust-up about his alleged post-modernism has faded. Recent scholarly work on Nietzsche is characterized instead by a commitment to detailed examinations of particular facets of Nietzsche's thought and particular books, and, above all, to sustained argument on behalf of and opposed to particular claims he appears to be making. This recent work abjures the zing of Nietzsche's style and the shocking extremes of expression to which he is prone, replacing them with the kind of careful explanation and scrutiny characteristic of the contemporary professor outfitted with all the gizmos found in the philosopher's toolbox. This book – an examination of Nietzsche's metapsychological views and his philosophy of mind (or, in one sense of the term, his philosophical psychology) – is an instance of this type.

For many philosophers, Nietzsche's views on psychology and philosophy of mind are not nearly as compelling as his views on truth, metaphysics, religion, and morality, and the interest that does attach to Nietzsche's psychological views derives from their role in these more famous attacks. For Nietzsche himself, however, the converse is closer to the truth: his attacks on metaphysics, truth, religion, morality, and other famous questions of philosophy are secondary to his fascination with human psychology. He admires psychology above all other sciences (*BGE* 23) and notes that he is unique in the history of philosophy for being the first psychologist among philosophers (*EH* IV: 6). Richard

1

Schacht's comment that "it is above all upon 'man' – upon human nature, human life, and human possibility – that his attention focuses" (Schacht 1983: 267) is correct, for the challenges that Nietzsche's naturalizing proclivities pose to then-existing philosophical psychology and the role those challenges play in his dismantling of metaphysical and epistemological pretensions cannot be overestimated. Moreover, many of Nietzsche's psychological and meta-psychological insights still have the power to surprise us with their incisiveness, and some of his claims about our nature can still unnerve us with their disturbing implications. Apart, then, from the role they play in his other projects, Nietzsche's philosophical reflections on the mind, on drives, on consciousness, on subjectivity, on agency and volition, and his psychological observations on the inglorious recesses of the human psyche are more than rich enough to merit sustained treatment.

In previous work (Hales & Welshon 2000; Welshon 2004), I have detailed some of what I think about Nietzsche's philosophy of mind, meta-psychology, and psychology of cognition. This book presents an opportunity to expand, deepen, and, on occasion, amend and correct those discussions and to supplement them with investigations into other topics – such as his views on perception, emotion, and interoception, his claims about the subject and its perspectivity, and willing – that are constitutive of Nietzsche's meta-psychology. This book also presents an opportunity to discuss relations between Nietzsche's views and certain contemporary views in cognitive science and philosophy of mind that stress the dynamic embodiment and embeddedness of human psychological processes and abilities. I argue, among other things, that Nietzsche's frequent emphasis on our animality, our bodies, and our emotions comprise an important philosophical precursor to the dynamic embodied-embedded cognitive science movement widespread in contemporary psychology and philosophy of mind. Of course, Nietzsche's views were stated more than a hundred years ago and without the benefit of the technological advances in intracranial imaging technologies and mathematical modelling that have accompanied the emergence of these branches in cognitive and affective neuroscience. But one of the reasons his views remain so interesting is that they skip right over the last eighty years of computationalist, internalist, and behaviourist philosophy of mind to intersect – in some cases without loss – the contemporary extended mind hypothesis and its various offshoots. Nietzsche argued that identifying psychological states and properties with states and properties of entities of the sort studied by physics is hopeless. So, even if, as I think, he is a naturalist, his is a naturalism whose closest contemporary counterpart is one that does not expect computationalist neuroscience to successfully describe the contours of the mind's structure, but one that suggests that the brain is a massively complex dynamical system coupled with the body and the body's surrounding environment. I develop this aspect of Nietzsche's thought throughout the book.

It is admittedly awkward to suggest that Nietzsche's meta-psychology anticipates contemporary developments in cognitive neuroscience, much less that he anticipates particular contemporary claims by particular cognitive neuroscientists. After all, these contemporary developments are soaked in theoretical commitments – computationalism, representationalism, dynamicism, connectionism, emergentism, non-reductionism, and other 'isms' – that Nietzsche not only did not know about, but that are incompatible with his avowed hostility towards theories of every kind. It is certainly true that Nietzsche rarely offers axioms, theorems, or many experimental hypotheses to confirm. Nor does he offer any kind of 'theory' in the sense used by contemporary literature professors and their critics. In fact, with the exception of offering occasional stabs at empirical conjectures, Nietzsche abjures empirical theories in his work and actually warns against interpreting him as if his business is the production of new philosophical theories (TI "Epigrams and Arrows" 26). That he has little patience for theories is not a criticism of him, of course, but a comment on our expectation that he conduct his business as we do ours. Philosophers nowadays can barely talk without reaching into a basket of favoured theoretical commitments, and most of us simply cannot help ourselves when it comes to what may be found on the shelves in today's philosophical hardware store. As much as I would like to be able to express particular views without taking advantage of these philosophical tools, they cannot be avoided entirely.

That Nietzsche works differently than today's professional philosopher is hardly news. But it is mistaken to infer on the basis of his different strategies and styles that he is unrecognizable as a philosopher. He offers plenty of arguments; those arguments revolve around a cluster of classical (and not-so-classical) philosophical issues; his diagnoses of the weaknesses of others' arguments are often philosophical in nature; and his positive proposals are on more than a few occasions stated in ways that are congruent with proposals made by other philosophers. But his style – in and out of topics quickly, as if they were glacial streams – is so energetic that often he is already on to the next thought before the reader fully understands the implications of the previous ones. Nowhere is this quick-dip approach more regularly practiced than in his observations about the issues discussed under the rubrics of psychology, philosophical psychology, and philosophy of mind. Offering psychological and physiological explanations of what are traditionally thought to be problems in the philosophy of mind and reflecting on psychological matters are among Nietzsche's favourite pastimes. Against what he thinks is traditional philosophical morality, he argues that there are no objectively true moral propositions, that there are no self-warranting moral intuitions, that there is no moral reality independent of human projects, and that moral values are entirely the creation of humans. And against traditional kinds of philosophical psychology, he argues that there are no souls, that there are no philosophical subjects, that the roles of reason and the conscious will are far less influential than has typically been thought, and that any categories invoked to explain human psychological processes, states, abilities, capacities, and human action cannot be inconsistent with scientific advances. But all of these arguments, explanations, and insights are routinely offered up in passages that are just as likely also to contain a juicy historical aside, a snippet of cultural critique, a blast against religion, a weird dietary recommendation, or a discussion of some arcane issue in metaphysics or epistemology. All one can do as an interpreter is acknowledge Nietzsche's unique style, admitting that emulation would be embarrassing and that something will always remain for another reading.

In this book, I am interested primarily in what might be called Nietzsche's metapsychology or, alternatively, his philosophy of mind. The terms 'metapsychology' and 'philosophy of mind' are typically used to refer to the philosophical undertaking of fixing the basic categories at use in psychological explanation. Metapsychology is thus distinct from psychology across a number of dimensions. Metapsychology is typically not thought to be an empirical science, whereas most psychology at least thinks of itself as an empirical science. Again, metapsychology is typically not concerned with understanding particular psychological phenomena such as memory across the lifespan, working memory, or schizophrenia. Its focus is directed instead towards the ontological, explanatory, and conceptual foundations of empirical psychology. Metapsychology thus merges across a number of dimensions with philosophy of mind, and issues arising in the latter are often implicated in discussions of the former.

In Chapter 1, I argue that Nietzsche is a naturalist, but that his is a peculiar naturalism. He is a philosophical naturalist in at least three ways. First, he argues that the domains of entities, processes, systems, states, properties, and events at use in psychology should map to the domains of entities, processes, systems, states, properties, and events at use in other natural sciences. Second, he assumes and sometimes argues for the claims that the ontology of psychology must be consistent with, first, a physics properly purged of atomistic mechanism, second, a biology carefully safeguarded against Darwinist excesses, and, third, a dynamicist physiology. And, third, he assumes and occasionally argues that the methods of philosophy must, to use Brian Leiter's phrase, be "methodologically continuous" with those found in science (Leiter 2002, 2013). Having introduced the distinctions between kinds of naturalisms and having alerted readers to the peculiarity of Nietzsche's brand of naturalism, discussion turns to the claim, sometimes made on his behalf, that his kind of naturalism is best understood as a species of positivism. I argue to the contrary that, for various reasons, Nietzsche is not well interpreted as a positivist, even if there are positivist elements to his negative assessments of other philosophers and even if there are some positivist elements to his own views. But whatever positivist elements may exist in his own views are benign and shared by many others, both in the philosophical and scientific traditions, who are not positivists.

In Chapter 2, I argue that Nietzsche adopts a general physiological outlook that aligns with contemporary dynamic embodied-embedded views of the mind. To say that his physiological outlook aligns with these views of the mind is to say that his physiological outlook is, at minimum, consistent with these views of the mind. But it is also to say also that his physiological outlook implies these dynamic embodied-embedded views of the mind. To launch this argument, I introduce various concepts from nonlinear dynamics and embodied-embedded cognitive science. Next, I argue, with Gregory Moore (Moore 2002), that Nietzsche was influenced by the work of two then-contemporary physiologists, Wilhelm Rolph and Wilhelm Roux, both of whom stress the dynamicism of physiology in general and human physiology in particular. I use the dynamic physiological outlook that Nietzsche adopted as the basis of an argument that shows why teleology is entirely superfluous in physiological explanations and largely superfluous even in psychological explanations. Eschewing teleology is not, admittedly, something that Nietzsche always successfully does, and I acknowledge that he is not fully consistent on these matters. However, I do try to quarantine the most offensive passages and I argue, as does John Richardson (Richardson 2004), that the vast majority of Nietzsche's most glaringly teleological claims can be given deflationary interpretations and that the vast majority of his other various claims can thus be inoculated against teleological interpretations. The chapter concludes with discussions of

Nietzsche's fondness for evolutionary arguments against philosophers and religious types and his insightful, if fragmentary, understanding of biological and physiological functions, adaptive phenotypes, and adaptations. Along the way, I argue – concurring with Maudemarie Clark (Clark 2013) and disagreeing with Richard Schacht (Schacht 2013) – that Nietzsche can be exonerated of the charge of being a Lamarckian.

In Chapter 3, discussion first turns to sensory perception and interoception, which are kinds of basic conscious experience. Nietzsche's views about sensory perception and interoception (the perception of intra-organismic events, states, and processes such as hunger, thirst, pain, pleasure) are, I argue, remarkably prescient of contemporary dynamic embodied-embedded views of these phenomena. I begin the chapter with a distinction between unconscious, subconscious, and conscious states and processes, arguing that Nietzsche's views about the subconscious cortical work-up of sensory information into conscious sensory perception and conscious interoception assume both that basic consciousness is completely embodied and that embodied consciousness is embedded in an environment with which we are causally coupled in a dynamic network of nonlinear feedforward and feedback loops. Implications of this view are discussed. I then turn to perspectivism, which, for purposes of this book, is interpreted as a genetic claim about the operational constraints with which our belief formation mechanisms engage the extra-organismic world. Genetic perspectivism contrasts with epistemological perspectivism, which, as Steve Hales and I have argued (Hales & Welshon 2000), is a claim about the unavoidable indexicality of belief justification. Here, I develop genetic perspectivism, showing the important role that perception and interoception play in Nietzsche's thinking about belief formation, but showing also that it is a mistake to interpret genetic perspectivism as a thesis that invokes only perception and interoception. I argue instead, as does Christoph Cox (Cox 1997), that the organism's affective engagement with the extra-organismic world is every bit as important for understanding genetic perspectivism as are perception and interoception. The chapter concludes with a discussion of Nietzsche's falsification thesis. As with perspectivism, falsification is sometimes interpreted as a genetic claim and sometimes as an epistemological claim. I argue that it is best understood as an epistemological claim about the alethic properties of beliefs and that, as such, it is a contentious claim. I suggest that interpretive errors with the falsification thesis are easy to make and that Nietzsche himself is guilty of some of them.

In Chapter 4, I discuss Nietzsche's fundamental explanatory category for psychology, the drive. I argue that drives are dispositions that contain as proper parts occurrent internal states that frequently come loaded with affective/qualitative character and are goads to behaviour. I show that this view of drives is consistent with and anticipates recent work in affective neuroscience, in particular that it anticipates Panksepp's empirical hypotheses concerning mammalian seeking systems, a complex of neural pathways that, like Nietzschean drives, are partly perceptual, partly affective, partly evaluative, and partly cognitive. I show that the affective character of the internal states that are constituent elements of drives and the causal efficacy of those occurrent internal states are not distinct, but that the affect is, instead, that in which the internal state's causal efficacy consists. I then turn to a discussion of Nietzsche's claim that thought is a kind of drive. This highly implausible claim is unpacked and defended as far as I think it can be defended.

In Chapter 5, I discuss Nietzsche's critical assessment of reflective and reflexive consciousness. Having introduced basic consciousness in Chapter 3 and the category of drives in Chapter 4, I turn in Chapter 5 to an interpretation of what Nietzsche has to say about more complex kinds of conscious states. I start by distinguishing between basic and reflective conscious states, arguing that the best interpretation of Nietzsche's several criticisms of consciousness is that his target is reflective conscious states rather than basic conscious states. I contrast Nietzsche's views about more complex kinds of conscious states with the higher-order theory of consciousness, a popular contemporary view. I argue that Nietzsche is not a higher-order theorist for all kinds of conscious states even if he does concur with higher-order theories on the structure of reflective conscious states. I then argue that the distinction between basic and reflective conscious states allows us to see what is wrong with the higher-order theory and what is right about Nietzsche's claims that all conscious states are phenomenal and that some of them are not only phenomenal but epiphenomenal. In the second and third sections, Nietzsche's assessment of the phenomenality and epiphenomenality of reflective conscious states are analysed. In the second, I suggest that the phenomenality of reflective consciousness is revealed in the temporal and causal mis-sequencing we are prone to when we take introspection as a reliable method for gaining knowledge of our own thoughts and feelings. Nietzsche thinks to the contrary that introspection is an unreliable guide and that knowledge of ourselves and our psychological states are both severely limited by the ineliminable perspectivity of the ways that our beliefs are formed. In the third section, I discuss Nietzsche's infamous claim that reflective consciousness is epiphenomenal. I show that he actually makes two distinct claims concerning epiphenomenality, one more plausible than the other.

In Chapter 6, I discuss Nietzsche's views on the self, the will, and power. Nietzsche repeatedly claims that there is no self, but he just as repeatedly criticizes others for their mistaken views of the self as a way of introducing his own views about the structure and betterment of the self. I distinguish three issues at play in philosophical discussions of the self: ontological issues surrounding the composition, nature, and structure of the self; phenomenological considerations about the perspectival nature of subjectivity, the ownership of psychological states, and the experience of agency; and epistemological claims about *de se* knowledge. Since Chapter 5 already discusses Nietzsche's deep suspicion about claims of *de se* knowledge, attention turns in Chapter 6 to the other two issues. In the first section, I argue that Nietzsche is best interpreted as being a supervenience-based non-reductive physicalist about the self and that his particular sub-species of the view is an emergentist view according to which the self is a structure that emerges from the dynamic internal milieu of conscious, subconscious, and unconscious drives. Benefits of this view are discussed. In the second section, discussion turns to the will and willing. Consistent with Leiter's phenomenological interpretation of Nietzsche's views about the will (Leiter 2002), I argue that Nietzsche's willingness to attribute a kind of directing causation to intentions is plausibly understood as a downward emergent cause on a set of implementing causes. Unfortunately, defending this interpretation of Nietzsche requires defending downward directing causation as needed and possible. A potentially devastating argument – the causal exclusion argument – undermines the possibility that any emergent process, state, or property, whether the self, reflective consciousness, or intentions, has any causal efficacy. I argue that the exclusion argument is unsound and that Nietzsche's views about the self and intentional action are therefore viable. In the final section, I argue for a deflationary understanding of power and will to power. On this understanding, power as a psychological explanatory category refers to the ongoing processes of self-discipline and self-overcoming that a strong person is capable of exercising over the welter of drives that comprise her.

Throughout the book, I interweave findings from contemporary perceptual, cognitive, and affective neurosciences that help confirm Nietzsche's philosophical speculations. I do this for two reasons: first, these findings are inherently interesting, and, second, that they are as recent as they are suggests just how impressive Nietzsche's ability to follow the thread of a dynamic approach to human psychology really is. Nietzsche really struggled with expressing his own version of a dynamic embodied and embedded view of the human mind. In part, these struggles are a consequence of the impoverished scientific frameworks with which he was familiar and the language used by the philosophers and scientists of his day. It is only in the 20th century that dynamic modelling came into its own, and it is only in the last twenty years or so that the internalist computationalism dominant in empirical psychological science has begun to weaken. The current landscape of dynamic, embodied, and embedded philosophy of mind and metapsychology is one that Nietzsche would have found quite attractive, so I have used the descriptive power of these contemporary ways of thinking about the human mind to expose the isomorphic contours of his thinking about these matters. Of course, not only would he find the contemporary scene amenable, he would also contribute to it various corrections, suggestions, new hypotheses, and criticisms. One of the privileges and curses of Nietzsche's genius was to understand the failures and shortcomings of his own time so profoundly and to see so far ahead into the future that it is only now, from the perspective of that future, that we are beginning to understand some of what he was then saying.

1

Naturalism, Science, Positivism

Nietzsche is to be taken at his word when he says that he wants to 'translate man back into nature' (BGE230). This task, which he admits may be 'strange and insane' (BGE230), is nevertheless a directive to anyone devoted to gaining knowledge of human psychology. Knowledge must turn its back once and for all on the errors, falsifications, and mystifications about human psychology that most of the contributors to the philosophical tradition have routinely supplied. We must instead 'stand before the *rest* of nature, with intrepid Oedipus eye and sealed Odysseus ears, deaf to the siren songs of old metaphysical bird catchers who have been piping to him all too long, "you are more, you are higher, you are of a different origin!"'(BGE230). Since we have to be *of* nature if we are to stand before the *rest* of nature, our psychology must likewise be explicated using only naturalistic resources rather than the spiritual dualist drivel that the philosophical and religious salesmen have been peddling for centuries.

Although it has become increasingly popular to portray Nietzsche as a philosophical naturalist, and although this interpretive strategy gets his views right in many ways, his philosophical naturalism is in more than a few ways unusual. In fact, his views about nature, science, and the place of humans in nature are really quite peculiar. In what, then, does philosophical naturalism consist, in what way is Nietzsche a naturalist, and in what way is his version of naturalism peculiar? These are the topics of this chapter. In Section I, we discuss Nietzsche's ambivalent relation to the science of his day. In Section II, his arguments against the real world and positivism are discussed. Section III continues that investigation by arguing that he is not a positivist.

10

I Naturalism, scientists, and science

It has to be apparent to anyone who reads his work that Nietzsche repeatedly contrasts the natural with the supernatural and non-natural. His animus against religion and philosophy is fuelled in large part by his belief that their attempts at explaining our psychological complexity by invoking supernatural and non-natural entities such as the soul and supernatural and non-natural mechanisms such as sin and the will systematically mislead us away from the only places where accurate psychological explanations might be found. Of course, dismissing the supernatural and the non-natural for their misleading tendencies presupposes that the natural is understood, for otherwise it is not possible to know what makes souls, sins and wills supernatural or non-natural rather than natural. It would be helpful were Nietzsche to define 'naturalism' or at least 'nature.' He never bothers, so it must be done for him. We shall understand the term 'nature' to refer to all of the causally efficacious phenomena (objects, properties, processes, states, events, systems) that are found in the spatio-temporal world, including all of the physical, geological, chemical, biological, physiological, psychological, sociological, and other entities, features, and products of the earth. We shall then understand the term 'naturalism' to refer to the philosophical position that affirms that the domain of the causally efficacious is exhausted by nature so understood.

The type of naturalism just introduced is *substantive* naturalism. Substantive naturalism affirms that philosophy and empirical science should share the same substantive domain – that is, they should both quantify over the kinds of things, properties, processes, and events studied by the natural, psychological, and social sciences. Substantive naturalism is distinct from two other kinds of naturalism. *Ontological* naturalism is the view that philosophy and empirical science should share the same ontology, where an ontology is the set of categories (e.g., object, property, process, event, state, and system) that an empirical view is prepared to quantify over. The distinction between substantive and ontological naturalism can be clarified by noting that even if ontological naturalism is accepted, it does not follow that a particular substantive domain consistent with it must be accepted. One could, for example, grant that all substantive scientific theories must accept that there are processes and events and yet disagree about which processes and events count as natural and which are counted as not natural. *Methodological* naturalism is the view that philosophy and empirical science have the same explanatory goal of discovering knowledge, and that philosophy and empirical science share the same types of methods and explanations. Nietzsche's naturalism is, it will be argued, substantive and ontological, but only fitfully methodological, which is just to say that he thinks philosophers and scientists should share ontology and substantive domains, and, with qualifications, method types and explanation types as well.[1]

Equipped with his naturalistic viewpoints, predispositions, and hunches, Nietzsche slices his way through large tracts of philosophical jungle, exposing and cutting away the metaphysical growths, epistemological curiosities, and psychological monstrosities found there. In this, his naturalizing project is not all that dissimilar from Willard Van Orman Quine's naturalizing project. Both dislike the overgrown and fetid rainforests that philosophers often find amenable, preferring instead starker, more austere topographies – the desert in Quine's case, and, in Nietzsche's, the alpine mountains. True, Quine's typical strategy is to unleash logic, philosophy of language, and philosophy of science against the anti-naturalist excesses of the philosophical tradition. Although Nietzsche occasionally sounds like Quine – as when he deploys semantic arguments against the category of substance and the philosophical subject (e.g., in BGE 17) and when he argues with Aristotle on the law of non-contradiction (KSA 12 9[97] = WP 516) – most of his arguments against anti-naturalism employ resources from non-behaviorist psychology and history, two resources that Quine steadfastly shuns.

Still, Nietzsche shares with Quine the beliefs that the progression of knowledge is a joint venture between scientists and philosophers, that each must contribute to the views of the other, and that each suffers when advances made by the other are ignored. There is nothing inconsistent about Nietzsche's naturalistic philosophizing if he accepts what advances in science can give him. Of course, he does not think that the science of his day has much to give him, but he does find a few things in it that can help him develop his projects. Likewise, there is nothing inconsistent about Nietzsche's philosophical naturalism if he proposes that a particular ontology – one based on will to power, for example – should be shared between science and philosophy; or if he suggests that particular methods or explanations – genealogy and physiological reduction, for example – would, if implemented, be useful across science and philosophy; or if he emphasizes a particular meta-psychological category – the drive, for example – as a particularly illuminating explanatory category for psychological explanation. These matters are investigated in due course.

Just as Nietzsche incorporates certain scientific advances into his naturalizing project only with caution, he is prepared to accept that his contributions to science and philosophy may, upon subsequent empirical and philosophical investigation, turn out to be false or over-reaching. However, his relations to scientists contemporaneous with him and his relations to some of the scientific theories of his day are ambivalent. The degree of this ambivalence indexes the peculiarity of his naturalism.[2] Indeed, his assessment of the science of his day is so ambivalent, and his reasons so telling, that his relations to many aspects of contemporary science would likely be just as troubled. Against scientists themselves, Nietzsche repeatedly suggests that their views, hypotheses, and arguments are contaminated by decadence and asceticism, and against the disciplines of science, he argues that some rely on unwarranted ontological and epistemological assumptions. So, while it may be that the scientific and philosophical communities have the last word on his proposals, they do so only within the constraints imposed by his ambivalence towards scientists, science, and philosophy as these are typically practiced.

Nietzsche admires many aspects of science and many character traits of scientists. He agrees with science's insistence that we 'abandon belief in simple causalities precisely where everything seems so easy to comprehend and we are the fools of appearance. The "simplest" things are *very complicated* – a fact at which one can never cease to marvel!'(D 6). Likewise, he praises Greek and Roman culture above all for being 'erudite,' for being able to host 'all the scientific *methods*... natural science, in concert with mathematics and mechanics' (A 59). Scientific methods above all come in for repeated praise because they induce the mental hygiene necessary for eliminating superstition. These methods – natural science, mathematics, and mechanics – are, he says, 'what is essential, as well as being the most difficult, as well as being that which has habit and laziness against it longest' (A 59). He therefore recommends that everyone learn at least one science (HH 635).

One feature of these methods that makes them admirable is their reliance on the senses. *Twilight of the Idols*, '"Reason" in Philosophy' 3 puts the matter directly:

We possess scientific knowledge today to precisely the extent that we have decided to *accept* the evidence of the senses – to the extent that we have learned to sharpen and arm them and to think them through to their conclusions. The rest is abortion and not-yet-science: which is to say metaphysics, theology, psychology, epistemology.

Unlike metaphysics, epistemology, and theology, utilizing experience-based scientific methods yields theories that do not pretend to discover a real world lurking behind the apparent world. Thus, these methods help us avoid the upside-down division between the real and apparent worlds that fuels the upside-down ontology, imaginary epistemology, mirror psychology, and false kinds of causality found in religion and philosophy. As a result, the danger that science and scientific method pose to metaphysicians, dogmatic moralists and religious peddlers is so acute that both method and results must be attacked: 'it is all over with priests and gods if man becomes scientific! – *Moral*: science is the forbidden in itself – it alone is forbidden. Science is the *first* sin, the germ of all sins, *original* sin' (AC 48).

A number of substantive scientific hypotheses and findings also receive Nietzsche's praise. During the 1870s and 1880s, he read extensively on biology, physiology, and physics and was fascinated by, among others, Friedrich Lange's *History of Materialism*, the anti-materialist work of Roger Boscovich (an astronomer-physicist-mathematician-philosopher), and Ernst Haeckel's and Wilhelm Roux's writings on evolution and biology. The more particular influences of Haeckel and Roux are discussed in greater detail in the next chapter, but here Nietzsche's agreement with arguments that Boscovich and Lange make against materialism, mechanism, and atomism, which were influential doctrines in 19th century physics, may be mentioned.

Materialism is the view that matter exhausts existence. *Matter*, in turn, is the substance of what exists. Traditionally, matter is ascribed properties of extension, hardness, impenetrability (or indivisibility), mobility, and inertia. *Atomism* is the compatible but distinct view that matter reaches a minimum extension in microscopic bits that are impenetrable, indivisible, changeless, and without structure. *Materialist atomism* is then the conjunctive view that material atoms and aggregations of material atoms and their properties exhaust existence. *Mechanism* is that particular type of materialist atomism according to which the explanation of the behavior of atoms and aggregations of them must be accomplished using only mechanical terms. A *mechanical explanation*, in turn, is an explanation that provides a mathematical analysis for phenomena that makes them predictable law-abiding events of matter in motion. Rejecting mechanism entails rejecting the exhaustiveness of mathematical explanations that refer only to matter in motion.[3]

Nietzsche opposes materialism, atomism, and mechanism alike. His opposition to materialism and atomism is influenced by arguments developed by Roger Boscovich, who offers both a critique of materialistic atomism and a rival dynamicist account of what matter is if it is not material. In *Beyond Good and Evil* 12, Nietzsche notes that 'as regards materialistic atomism: it is one of the best-refuted theories there are...thanks chiefly to the Dalmation Boscovich who...has taught us to abjure the belief in the last part of the earth that "stood fast" – the belief in "substance", in "matter", in the earth-residuum and particle atom.' According to Boscovich, materialist atomism makes atoms nothing more than corpuscles or little ball bearings, impenetrable and indivisible. Since such corpuscular atoms occupy the basal level of explanation in physics, all other physical properties and relations must be explicable in terms of these properties and relations (if any). Unfortunately, when atoms are thought of in this way, the phenomenon of impact becomes nonsensical. For, suppose we have two ball bearings moving at different velocities, and the faster one impacts the slower one from behind. At the moment of impact, the slower one appears to accelerate instantaneously and change its velocity. But instantaneous acceleration is contrary to the law of continuity, which states that nothing passes from one state to another without passing through all the intermediate states. So, either the law of continuity must be abandoned or this particular model of impact must be abandoned. Boscovich opts for the latter alternative.

The dynamicist account of matter that Boscovich offers as a replacement for materialist atomism conceives of atoms as non-extended inertial points surrounded by repulsive forces. On this alternative, velocity change does not occur instantaneously at the moment of impact between two atoms. Instead, velocity change occurs continuously as a result of a repulsive force that operates at small distances. As the distance between atoms decreases, the repulsive force increases, and, at infinitesimal distances the repulsive force approaches infinity. The slower atom's acceleration is thus a continuous change that results as the faster atom approaches it. Thus is the principle of continuity salvaged for every level above the atomic. Yet, on this view, atoms can have no extension, for were they extended, then they would be divisible. But, by hypothesis, atoms are indivisible. Hence, they are non-extended and have no spatial volume. Having no spatial volume, Boscovichian atoms have no mass in the Newtonian sense of the term and, hence, exert no Newtonian force. Rather, Boscovichian atoms are nothing more than centers of forces surrounded by a field of other such centers of forces. The affinity between this view and certain of Nietzsche's ontological views is apparent and has been discussed by others.[4]

If the work of Boscovich provides Nietzsche ammunition for arguing against atomistic materialism, the work of Friedrich Lange equips him to do battle with a much more pervasive framework in the history of philosophy, namely, mechanical materialism. The impact that Lange's *History of Materialism* (1866) has on Nietzsche's ontological, epistemological, and methodological views is significant.[5] He read and re-read Lange for almost ten years and continuously drew philosophical sustenance from the *History*. Lange was an early proponent of an evolutionary approach to epistemology and psychology, both of which Nietzsche develops. More pertinent here is that much of Nietzsche's knowledge of Newtonian physics – and perforce, materialism and mechanism – probably comes from reading Lange.[6] Nietzsche gleaned enough about mechanistic materialism from Lange's *History* to think about alternative views of force and to think that he too could produce proposals concerning dynamically coupled systems. As will be shown here, these alternative views of what a force is and the proposals describing dynamically coupled systems together form the basis of many of Nietzsche's naturalist claims and so provide a substantive backdrop for his psychological views. In comparison, most of the physics of his day shies away from dynamic views and tries instead to explain everything mechanistically. Nietzsche is hostile towards the entirety of this mechanistic project, objecting both to the mathematization inherent in mechanistic explanations and to the assumption that enduring material objects comprise their domain. Here is how he puts it: a mechanistic explanation 'wants nothing but quantities; yet force is to be found in quality. Mechanistic theory can thus only *describe* processes, not explain them' (KSA 12 2[76] = WP 660). Since mechanism at best *describes* phenomena and an explanation requires something more than a description, he concludes that the set of mechanistic *explanations* is empty.

Suppose that Nietzsche is correct that the most a mechanistic framework can accomplish is a description of substances and matter. Mechanism would be in even worse shape if those descriptions of processes and events employed concepts that *mis*-described those processes and events. And Nietzsche affirms exactly this. One source of mismatch is that mechanistic concepts comprise nothing more than a mathematical calculus applied to dynamic processes. Even if such concepts and categories are handy to us as we think about dynamic processes, they presuppose entities – enduring material objects and mathematical features – that, Nietzsche claims, are fictions. He makes this point succinctly in *Gay Science*, arguing that mechanistic science 'permits counting, calculating, weighing, seeing, and touching, and nothing more' (GS 373), a restriction that follows from a decision to 'operate only with things that do not exist: lines, planes, atoms, divisible time spans, divisible spaces' (GS 112). Since mechanistic concepts mis-describe dynamic processes and events from the start, mechanistic descriptions also fail to describe what they are invoked to describe. So, he concludes that not only is the set of mechanistic explanations empty but that the set of mechanistic descriptions of *processes* and *events* is also empty.

If Nietzsche is correct that mechanism cannot even describe processes or events, then mechanism as a descriptive undertaking is severely restricted in its scope, shrinking to substance and matter and their properties. However, he has other arguments that even this restricted domain of substance and matter is empty, and still other arguments that at the basal level all that exists are dynamic events, processes, and systems (KSA 11 38[12] = WP 1067; KSA 12 10[138] = WP 639; KSA 13 11[134] = WP 559; KSA 13 14[79] = WP 635; KSA 13 14[86] = WP 636; KSA 13 14[152] = WP 515, among others). When these arguments are conjoined with those already reviewed, it falls out directly that mechanism does not describe, much less explain, anything *at all*. Hence, he concludes generally that the set of mechanistic *descriptions* turns out to be just as empty as the set of mechanistic explanations.

If neither explanation nor description, what are mechanistic accounts? Nietzsche suggests that they are translations:

a translation of this world of effect into a *visible* world – a world for the eyes – [this] is the concept of 'motion.' Here the implication is always that *something* is moved, and whether in the fiction of a lump atom or even of its abstraction, the dynamic atom, we still conceive of a thing which effects – that is, we haven't left behind the habit that senses and language seduce us to. Subject, object, a doer for every doing, the doing separated from what does it: let's not forget that this is mere semiotics and does not refer to something real. Mechanics as a theory of *motion* is itself already a translation into the sensual language of man.

We need unities in order to be able to count: we should not therefore assume that such unities exist. We have borrowed the concept of unity from our concept of "I" – our oldest article of faith. If we didn't consider ourselves to be unities, we would never have created the concept of "thing".... Thus, in order to sustain the mechanistic theory of the world, we always have to include a proviso about the use we are making of two fictions: the concept of motion (taken from the language of our senses) and the concept of the atom = unity (originating in our psychological "experience"). Its prerequisites are a *sensual prejudice* and *a psychological prejudice*. (KSA 13 14[79] = WP 635)

According to this passage, mechanism is a conceptual framework that results when the sensual prejudice – that what is experienced through the senses is the criterion of existence – and the psychological prejudice – that our subjective unity is the criterion of objective unity – collude to spit out two fictions, motion and the atom that moves. Once atoms and atomic motion are assumed, mechanism can be launched. But, as Nietzsche points out, that mechanism requires atoms that move does not entail that there are any atoms or, if there are, that they move. (Note also that mechanism is a result of the sensual prejudice that what is experienced is the criterion of existence. We return to this argument below, in the next section's discussion of positivism.)[7]

Despite his hostility to science's mechanistic and reductionist predilections, Nietzsche is usually careful not to dismiss science outright. In the section of *The Gay Science* immediately following his criticism of mechanism, he suggests that there may be infinite perspectives to adopt when studying the phenomena that science studies (GS 374). In this way, his criticism of science can be seen to be an instance of his general attitude about most things, namely, that we are well advised to refrain from dogmatic over-assertion on behalf of our philosophical commitments. That attitude is a direct implication of Nietzsche's perspectivism. Perspectivism does not require deriding specific perspectives, such as science; it just insists that they are not the *only* perspective to take on a subject and that different perspectives may enrich our lives in ways other than those found in science. The mistake for Nietzsche is thinking that the perspective of science is the only perspective worth taking. More on this in Chapter 3.

Nietzsche's view of science's proper function is at odds not only with what the scientists of his day thought but with what most contemporary scientists think. For him, the idea of bias-free observation and neutral investigation are non-starters symptomatic of a set of attitudes towards our environment and ourselves that are, he claims, decadent, where by 'decadent' we understand, with him, 'contrary to life.' If perspectivism is correct, then bias is inescapable and objective neutrality is a pretence. Indeed, discovering objective truths is not even one of the functions of science; the function of science is, rather, to make discoveries about ourselves, our perspectives, and our needs and desires. In *The Gay Science* he writes,

Let us introduce the refinement and rigor of mathematics into all sciences as far as this is at all possible, not in the faith that this will lead us to know things but in order to *determine* our human relation to things. Mathematics is merely the means for general and ultimate knowledge of man. (GS 246)

This is an unusual way of thinking about science.[8] But it is a view that he holds to over many years, as evidenced by *Daybreak*48, published in 1881: 'Only when he has attained a final knowledge of all things will man have come to know himself. For things are only the boundaries of man.'

Quine and other 20th century philosophers and cognitive scientists have followed Nietzsche's lead here. One of the central points of Quine's naturalized epistemology is the impossibility of avoiding cognitive bias.[9] The contrary thought – that bias can be avoided if we just get our epistemological house in order – is a central pillar of the traditional epistemological project, which is permeated by foundationalist thinking. Foundationalism affirms that knowledge is two-fold: first, a set of foundational sentences or beliefs at the base of knowledge and, second, a much larger set of non-foundational sentences or beliefs that blossoms from those foundations by applying various conceptual tools and logical relations to them. One of the salient points of Quine's criticism of foundationalism is that the foundational observation sentences are not, contrary to what is claimed on their behalf by foundationalists, free from perspectival bias. Not even observation sentences confront the tribunal of experience individually – they do so only in big bunches, and the meanings of observation sentences are not isolable independently of a whole host of other sentences and their meanings. As a consequence, semantic meaning, even at the level of basic observation, is holistic, and given that holism, the foundationalist's attempt to determine the meaning of individual observation sentences must fail. Meaning holism and Quine's celebrated rejection of the analytic/synthetic distinction together entail rejecting foundationalist epistemology and admitting that the traditional epistemological ideals of objectivity and objective knowledge are bankrupt. All knowledge is situated at a time and in a place, and all knowledge is pervaded by pragmatic considerations, by bias, by perspectives. The key question for naturalized epistemology is not, 'How do we eliminate bias?' but 'Which biases are worth having and which are not?' As will be argued in Chapter 3, this is a reasonable interpretation of Nietzsche's epistemological perspectivism as well.

Scientists of Nietzsche's day come in for repeated ridicule for ignoring just this point. He accuses them of being quiet hedgehogs burrowing in their molehills (D 41) and of colluding with asceticism, decadence, and Christianity (GS III 23–27). Scientists, unlike philosophers, are *not* characterized by their work: their impersonal attention to minute details in the construction of experiments, in tiny differences of collected data, and their strict adherence to mechanical and mathematical methods together make scientists impersonal observers disengaged from their own scientific activity. This attitude is, Nietzsche thinks, pathological. First, by restricting attention to experiments, data collection and data inter- pretation, scientists abstract themselves from the value of the work they participate in. The vaunted notion of scientific objectivity thus results in a kind of pervasive non-reflexivity about the value of scientific work for human life. Second, by making of themselves objective observers of phenomena, scientists try to drain themselves of affective and evalua- tive engagement with nature. However, trying to drain oneself of affec- tive and evaluative engagement with nature is, he thinks, a decadent response to the world's unpredictability (see the extended discussion at BGE 207). Nietzschean philosophers, for whom nothing is impersonal (BGE 6), know this and do not try to deny their engagement.

More particularly, Nietzsche criticizes the biologists of his day for their over-reliance on Darwinian thinking. While many of his criticisms of Darwinian evolutionary thinking are not pertinent to the concerns of this book, certain issues will become relevant. According to Nietzsche, Darwin relied on the existence of a 'struggle for existence' and the resulting drive for 'self-preservation' in that struggle (GS 349) to drive evolutionary development. Nietzsche holds to the contrary that the struggle for existence is a small part of evolutionary development and that a much more significant casual force than self-preservation is self- expansion and appropriation. Predictably, his criticism of the struggle for existence and of self-preservation is introduced by arguing *ad hominem* against philosophers, Spinoza more than anyone else, whose own poor health made self-preservation peculiarly salient. He uses the example of Spinoza to argue then against Darwin and other biologists:

> That our modern natural sciences have become so thoroughly entangled in this Spinozistic dogma (most recently and worst of all, Darwinism with its incomprehensibly one-sided doctrine of the 'struggle for existence') is probably due to the origins of most natural scientists: In this respect they belong to the "common people"; their ancestors were poor and undistinguished people who knew the difficulties of survival only too well at first-hand. The whole of English Darwinism breathes something like the musty air of English

overpopulation, like the smell of the distress and overcrowding of small people. (GS 349)

For Nietzsche, quite the opposite seems more likely to be true: 'the general aspect of life is *not* a state of crisis or hunger, but rather richness, luxuriance, even absurd extravagance – where there is a struggle it is a struggle for *power*... . Malthus should not be mistaken for nature' (TI 'Expeditions' 14). This theme will be developed throughout this book.

II   Things-in-themselves, the 'real' world, and positivism

Exploring whether Nietzsche's views may be gathered under the umbrella of positivism helps us further understand the contours of his naturalism.[10] He is not a positivist on what is probably the most prevalent understanding of the term. Nor is he a positivist on any but a perverse understanding of the term.

Part of the energizing force behind the debate about Nietzsche's alleged positivism is that the terms 'positivism' and 'positivist' are more often used pejoratively against pugnacious apologists of science than they are as terms that pick out an identifiable set of doctrines. For those who think that Nietzsche's views are beyond aggressive apologetics, the mere thought of labeling any of his views as 'positivist' is offensive. This kind of concern with positivism and positivists in turn reveals that part of the debate about Nietzsche's positivism is a disagreement over how the word 'positivism' is to be defined, and is, thus, fairly uninteresting: words being the social creatures they are, legislating their use is difficult, especially when stakes are high and when understanding what they are being used to describe is of some moment. Still, some substantive issues are in play even in this definitional skirmish, and these substantive issues play a role in appreciating the subtlety of Nietzsche's views about science and naturalism. These issues also introduce certain topics that are revisited in subsequent chapters.

The word 'positivism' first appeared in the 19th century in the work of Auguste Comte, although views consistent with positivism stretch back to antiquity and were widely available in the post-Kantian and post-Humean philosophical worlds. Comtean positivism, much like the more famous logical positivism of the 20th century, is a set of claims about the respective roles of sensory experience and reason in gaining and justifying empirical knowledge, the exhaustiveness of empirical knowledge, the role of sensory experience in determining the meaning of the words and sentences of language, and what role, if any, logic and mathematics play in empirical sciences. Positivism in this way of thinking about it presupposes and is a development from empiricism. Empiricism typically consists of some or all of the following claims:

1. All beliefs are *generated* either immediately or eventually from sensory experience – the causal (genetic) claim of empiricism
2. All beliefs are *justified* either immediately or eventually by sensory experience – the warrant claim of empiricism
3. All beliefs are such that their *truth or falsity is determined* either immediately or eventually by sensory experience – the alethic claim of empiricism
4. All *knowledge* satisfies 1.–3. – epistemological empiricism
5. The *meaning* of all words and sentences is either immediately or eventually a set of sensory experiences – semantic empiricism[11]
6. The *referent objects* of all singular terms, predicates, and sentences are sets of sensory experiences – ontological empiricism

Many of these empiricist elements (one exception is 6.) are constituent planks in the Comtean positivist program.

In addition to these empiricist elements, Comtean positivism contains other elements that concern social science, political organization, and social reform. Insofar as these are constituents of his views, Comte's positivism is an instance of the grand teleological histories popular in the 19th century, according to which human history is an ongoing progression towards a lofty, and in some cases, trans-human, goal. On Comte's version of progressive history, humanity has already gone through two stages – the theological and the metaphysical – and is on the cusp of the third and greatest stage – the positive. A characteristic feature of the theological stage is the search for primary and final causes, that is, the search for causes that get human history off the ground and goals towards which humanity is aiming. In the theological stage, supernatural agents and their absolute plans and desires provide both primary and final causes; in the metaphysical stage, those supernatural agents are replaced by equally absolute transcendental abstract concepts and entities; and in the positive state, the demand for primary and final causes is abandoned. In their absence, the need for absolute truth and absolute knowledge disappear, and both are replaced with relativistic truth and knowledge.

If this grand philosophical history were to exhaust Comtean positivism, Nietzsche would be an adherent, for he too conceives of humanity as engaged in a prolonged disillusionment with the transcendental, the supernatural, and the absolute. Nietzsche is less optimistic than Comte about our eventual liberation, about the role that intellectuals and scientists play in organizing society so as to achieve that liberation, and about the idea that society should even be organized to achieve the liberation of all (see e.g., KSA 12 9[44]). But his diagnosis of our disenchantment with the theological and metaphysical and his prescription that we re-engage ourselves as natural beings directly parallel Comte's three stages. (Perhaps that is too strong: it may be better to say that Nietzsche's views parallel Comte's only up to a point. Identifying the point at which Nietzsche diverges from Comte clarifies how Nietzsche is not a Comtean positivist.)

Nowhere is Nietzsche's agreement with Comte's philosophical history clearer than in the justly famous passage from *Twilight of the Idols* called 'How the "Real World" at Last Became a Myth.' The passage may be quoted in full:

1. The real world – attainable to the wise, the pious, the virtuous man – he lives in it, *he is it.*
   (Oldest form of the idea, relatively sensible, simple, and convincing. Transcription of the proposition, "I, Plato, *am* the truth.")

2. The real world – unattainable for the moment, but promised to the wise, the pious, the virtuous man ("to the sinner who repents").
   (Progress of the idea: it grows more refined, more insidious, more incomprehensible – *it becomes a woman*, it becomes Christian ...)

3. The real world – unattainable, indemonstrable, cannot be promised, but the very thought of it – a consolation, an obligation, an imperative.
   (Fundamentally, the same old sun, but shining through mist and skepticism; the idea grown sublime, pale, northerly, Königsbergian.)

4. The real world – unattainable? Unattained, at any rate. And if unattained also *unknown.* Consequently also no consolation, no redemption, no duty: how could we have a duty to something unknown?
   (Gray morning. The first yawn of reason. The cockcrow of positivism.)

5. The "real world" – an idea which is no longer of any use, not even a duty any longer – an idea grown useless, superfluous, *consequently*, a refuted idea: let us abolish it!
   (Broad daylight; breakfast; return of cheerfulness and *bon sens*; Plato blushes for shame; all free spirits run riot.)

6. We have abolished the real world: what world is left? the apparent world perhaps? But no! With the real world we have also abolished the apparent world.

> (Noon; moment of the briefest shadow; end of the longest error; high point of humanity; INCIPIT ZARATHUSTRA.)

In this history, stages 1 through 3 parallel the theological and metaphysical stages of Comte's history and stage 4 represents Comtean positivism. From this we may immediately infer that Nietzsche endorses some of what Comte endorses. Of course, Nietzsche's own history adds two stages subsequent to Comtean positivism, and the arguments implicit in these two subsequent stages locate the ways in which Nietzsche's own views diverge from Comte's.

The difference between stage 4 and stage 5 is that the former makes an epistemological claim that the real world is unknown, while the latter infers from that epistemological claim an ontological conclusion that the real world is refuted. The argument contained in these two numbered items is, then, the following:

P1: The real world is unknown (from stage 4)

P2: If the real world is unknown, then the real world is useless

P3 (IC): The real world is useless (P1, P2)

P4: If the real world is useless, then the real world is refuted

Hence, the real world is refuted (P4, P3)

The form of the argument lurking beneath Nietzsche's instance of it is the following:

P1*: X is unknown

P2*: If X is unknown, then X is useless

P3* (IC*): X is useless

P4*: If X is useless, then X is refuted

C*: X is refuted

Such arguments are too sweeping. Consider another instance that reveals one problem with the form:

P1': The neuroanatomical location of odor is unknown

P2': If the neuroanatomical location of odor is unknown, then the neuroanatomical location of odor is useless

P3' (IC'): The neuroanatomical location of odor is useless

P4': If the neuroanatomical location of odor is useless, then the neuroanatomical location of odor is refuted

Hence, the neuroanatomical location of odor is refuted

What is mistaken about this argument is that the move from P2* to P3* (and hence from P2 to P3 and P2' to P3'), is an instance of the fallacy from ignorance. So, if Nietzsche is to be absolved of committing a fallacious argument from ignorance when he uses the argument form to move from P2 to P3 in *Twilight of the Idols*, then there better be something about his premises that saves his argument.

Either there is something special about what Nietzsche calls 'the real world' that makes its unknown status alone sufficient to render it useless or there is a missing premise that licenses the move from P2 to P3. Nietzsche is not a dunderhead, so perhaps there is something that he fails to mention because he considers it already known. If the following clause is added to P2, the result is a premise that licenses the move from premise to interim conclusion:

P2+: If the real world is unknown *and it is necessary that the real world be known to exist if it is to have any uses*, then the real world is useless

P2+ makes explicit the necessary condition that if the real world is not known to exist, then the real world has no utility.

It bears noting that Nietzsche's claim here in 'How the "Real World" at Last Became a Myth' is that the real world is not known to exist, not that the real world is known not to exist or that the real world is unknowable. Let us be clear about the difference between these claims.

¬K(R): The real world is not known to exist;

and

K(¬R): It is known that the real world does not exist

are distinct claims. Their distinctness can be seen by conditionalizing them in distinct orders. The following is true:

(a) K(¬R) → ¬K(R)

and the latter is false:

(b) ¬K(R) → K(¬R)

The former, (a), is true because if it is known that the real world does not exist, then it is true and justified that that the real world does not exist. On the other hand, the latter, (b), is false: even if it is not known that the real world exists, it is not the case, as the consequent asserts, that it is known that the real world does not exist. For it is consistent with the real world's existence being unknown that the real world nonetheless exists. We might, for example, be perverse in such a way that we can never believe that the real world exists or, believing it, we might be perverse in some other way such that we can never be warranted or justified in our belief that the real world exists. Or, of course, it might be that the real world does not exist, so that even if it is believed that the real world exists and even if our belief that the real world exists is warranted, it just so happens that the real world does not exist. So much follows from any of a number of standard understandings of knowledge, truth, belief, warrant and justification.[12]

Note again the wording of Stage 4 – 'The real world – unattainable? Unattained, at any rate. And if unattained also *unknown*.' For the argument here to succeed, we do not need to know that the real world does not exist for the real world to have no uses. We need only not to know that the real world exists for it to have no uses. It is also at this stage that positivism is introduced. Why? Because, as Nietzsche notes, so long as we have no knowledge of the real world's existence, the real world's claim to be the ground of moral duties and imperatives collapses. For, so long as the real world is not known to exist, whatever its unique features may be they can play no role in being the ground of or warrant for our moral duties. So the clause added in P2+ is exactly what Nietzsche requires to prevent the argument in Stage 3 through Stage 4 from committing a fallacy of ignorance.

It is a separate question why Nietzsche thinks that the real world needs to be known in order for it to have any uses or, alternatively put, why Nietzsche thinks that the real world's being unknown is sufficient for it to have no uses. And it is still another question why Nietzsche thinks that the only uses for the real world or things-in-themselves are being a consolation, redemption, or a ground for moral duty. Answering these questions begins by acknowledging that the target of this argument in Stage 3 is, as is commonly allowed, Immanuel Kant. Nietzsche notes that 'the real world – unattainable, indemonstrable, cannot be promised, but the very thought of it – a consolation, an obligation, an imperative.'

This passage is a direct reference to Kant, who argued in *Critique of Pure Reason* that only the world of appearances/phenomena – entities that exist only because they are apprehended – are known, whereas the real world of things-in-themselves/noumena – things that exist independently of any apprehension – are unknown. However, it is an important Kantian claim that, despite their being unknown, the domain of things-in-themselves/noumena can and in fact must be *thought*. Kant has at least five reasons for thinking this is so, most of them directly relevant for understanding Nietzsche's naturalism, and all but one of them left unmentioned in this passage from *Twilight of the Idols*.

The thing-in-itself/noumenon is needed in Kant's philosophy, first, because without it, "we should be landed in the absurd conclusion that there can be appearances without anything that appears" (CPR, Bxxvii). Another way of putting the point using causal language makes the second Kantian point: the thing-in-itself/noumenon is the represented of which appearances/phenomena are representations (CPR, A190/B235). Third, since we can know only that which is given in intuition (where intuition is uncategorized sensory experience) and since space and time are forms of intuition, there is something that humans do not and cannot know, namely the nature of the world's denizens once the categories and forms of intuition under which they fall are stripped from them. The name Kant gives to such an unintuited, uncategorized denizen is 'thing-in-itself/noumenon.' Fourth, the thing-in-itself/noumenon vs. appearance/phenomenon distinction helps Kant distinguish his *transcendental* idealist views from the *empirical* idealist views of Georg Berkeley. Fifth, and the immediate target of Nietzsche's Stage 3, Kant held that morality is a set of demands only on free rational agents. If so, then there has to be a domain populated by free rational agents. That domain is not that of appearances/phenomena, since that domain of objects is governed by natural law. The only possible domain for free rational agents to populate is the noumenal realm. Despite our lack of knowledge about the noumenal realm, it can be thought about because, as argued in *Critique of Practical Reason*, we are in fact bound by moral duty and it is only in the noumenal realm that we find moral subjects – free rational agents. And, because our existence as free rational agents is not reducible to our existence as law-governed empirical subjects, moral truths present themselves to us as imperatives rather than descriptions of our (rational and moral) behavior.

We investigate the first four reasons for Kant's inclusion of the thing-in-itself/noumenon shortly, but it is the final Kantian reason that merits immediate discussion because this is the reason Nietzsche actually cites in Stage 3. Nietzsche is not forthcoming here about the argument behind the claim that the real world (i.e., the noumenal realm) is a ground for our moral duties only if known to exist. But an argument is not far away. It is a widely accepted thesis that 'ought' implies 'can.' Nietzsche here marks a parallel implication, viz., 'ought' implies 'know.' Various distinct claims may be distilled out of this slogan – among them that one cannot have a duty to X if one does not know that one has a duty to X, and that one cannot have a duty to X if one does not know why X is a duty in the first place. Nietzsche is after a different target. His reason for holding that the unknown real world is sufficient to render it useless is that the only non-religious use (for consolation and redemption) that the real world might have – as the ground of moral duty – presupposes that we are among its inhabitants. For only if we know that we are free rational agents – that is, only if we know that we are noumenal subjects – will morality have any hold on us. If it turns out that we are not inhabitants of the noumenal realm, then we are wholly natural subjects and, as such, we are bound only by the laws of causation and not at all by the categorical imperative. Even if we are inhabitants of the noumenal realm but don't know that we are, a similar result follows. In this case, the categorical imperative appears only as an imperative binding on some rational being(s), but since each of us is such that we do not know that we are members of the population of rational beings, none of us can affirm that the categorical imperative is binding on us. If so, then not knowing that the real world exists is all that is needed for the real world to be useless as a ground for moral duty for us. And if so, then knowing that the real world does not exist is not additionally necessary. Therefore, failing to know that the real world does not exist does not undermine Nietzsche's argument here that the real world is useless as a ground for moral duty.

Nietzsche's other arguments against the thing-in-itself do not focus on its role as a warrant for moral duty. These other arguments engage Kant's epistemological and ontological reasons for thinking that the thing-in-itself is necessary. If Nietzsche's arguments against these other claims are successful, and if in the process he is able to show that we can know that the real world does not exist, it would be a boon to his argument against the real world's utility in *TI*. For if no sound epistemological or ontological reasons for the necessity of a real world of things-in-themselves are to be had, then all of the other philosophically minded arguments for its existence also collapse, thus showing that since it is completely unsupportable, the real world's existence *cannot* be known. If so, then the real world of things-in-themselves is not only unknown but unknow*able*.

Both in his published works and in his *Nachlass*, Nietzsche argues for three separate conclusions concerning the thing-in-itself: first, that we can have no knowledge that there are things-in-themselves; second, that the thing-in-itself is an absurdity; and, third, that there are no things-in-themselves. An amusing argument for the first conclusion occurs in *Human, All too Human* 9:

> It is true, there could be a metaphysical world; the absolute possibility of it can hardly be contested. We see all things through the human head and cannot cut this head off; and yet the question remains as to what part of the world would still be there if one had in fact cut it off. ... That other possibility still remains, but we cannot even begin to do anything with it, much less to allow happiness, salvation, and life to hang from the spider threads of such a possibility.– For we could assert nothing at all about the metaphysical world except its otherness, an otherness inaccessible to and inconceivable for us; it would be a thing with negative characteristics.– Even if the existence of such a world were to be proven ever so well, any knowledge of it would certainly still be the most irrelevant of all knowledge: even more irrelevant than knowledge of the chemical composition of water must be to a sailor endangered by a storm.

To make this passage more persuasive to hard-bitten philosophers, it is probably necessary to replace the colorful image of cutting off our heads with the less colorful but more accurate description that we cannot know the nature (or perhaps even the existence) of the world independent of our sensory experience because all knowledge is gained and justified immediately or eventually by sensory experience. But the point is the same either way, namely, that we are prevented by our cognitive constraints from knowing what the metaphysical world might be like were we not to have those cognitive constraints.[13] This is not really a criticism of Kant, since Kant readily accepts the point. But Nietzsche infers from this claim that lacking knowledge of what he calls the 'metaphysical' world entails that its mere possibility is not sufficient to hang our happiness, salvation, and our life on.

Elsewhere, Nietzsche argues directly that the metaphysical world and the thing-in-itself are absurdities and that the thing-in-itself either does not or cannot exist. For instance, in a note from 1885–1886, he claims that:

> The "thing-in-itself" [is] nonsense. If I remove in thought all the relationships, all the "properties" [*Eigenschaften*], all the "activities" [*Thätigkeiten*] of a thing, the thing does not remain behind: because

thingness was only a *fiction added* by us, out of the needs of logic, thus for the purpose of defining, communication (to bind together the multiplicity of relationships, properties, activities). (KSA 12 10[202] = WP 558)

This passage and others like it (e.g., KSA 12 2[85] = WP 557; KSA 12 9[40] = WP 560; TI, '"Reason" in Philosophy' 5, 6), argue that the thing-in-itself makes no sense because there is nothing to a thing except the properties that comprise it and the activities that property-comprised thing enters into.[14] On such a bundle theory of things, no *thing* remains after its properties and (except in the case of a universe with only one atomically simple thing in it) its relations are stripped. But the thing-in-itself is exactly that which is supposed to remain after all properties and relations are removed. Hence, the thing-in-itself does not make any sense. This is not quite a *reduction ad absurdum* of the thing-in-itself, but it is close enough to a *reductio* for Nietzsche to affirm that the thing-in-itself is nonsense. He offers a closely related line of thought in another note:

> even supposing there were an in-itself, an unconditioned thing, it would for that very reason be unknowable! Something unconditioned cannot be known; otherwise it would not be unconditioned! Coming to know, however, is always "placing oneself in a conditional relation to something" – one who seeks to know the unconditioned desires that it should not concern him, and that this same something should be of no concern to anyone. (KSA 12 2[154] = WP 555)

In sum, Nietzsche's attitude towards the thing-in-itself is similar to that of many of Kant's own contemporaries (and many current philosophers), an attitude expressed by a quip attributed to F. H. Jacobi, who claimed against the thing-in-itself that 'without this presupposition I could not enter into the system and with this presupposition I could not remain there.'

III   Beyond positivism and idealism

The 'Homeric laugh' (HAH 16) that Nietzsche reserves for things-in-themselves echoes throughout *Gay Science, Beyond Good and Evil, Genealogy of Morals,* and *Twilight of the Idols.* But what implications his disdain for things-in-themselves and the real world have on his thinking about sensory experience, science, causation, logic, mathematics, and the nature of the world and its inhabitants forms the nub of the dispute between those who are prepared to call him a positivist and those who recoil from doing so. A showcase argument for the claim that Nietzsche is a positivist is the intricately structured *Beyond Good and Evil* 15:

> To study physiology with a clear conscience, one must insist that the sense organs are *not* phenomena in the sense of idealistic philosophy; as such, they could not be causes! Sensualism, therefore, at least as a regulative hypothesis, if not as a heuristic principle.
>
> What? And others even say that the external world is the work of our organs? But then our body, as a part of this external world, would be the work of our organs! But then our organs themselves would be – the work of our organs! It seems to be that this a complete *reductio ad absurdum,* assuming that the concept of a *causa sui* is something fundamentally absurd. Consequently, the external world is *not* the work of our organs–?

Interpreters have found this passage confounding, for it raises exceptionally thorny issues about sensations, phenomenalism, conceptualization, and scientific knowledge. Worse, it seems to have certain implications that are inconsistent with others of Nietzsche's views. For our purposes, the issues of interest is this: does *BGE* 15 entail that Nietzsche is a positivist, or does it entail that he is not a positivist, or does it entail neither?

One way into the difficulties posed by this passage is to consider the *reductio* argument of the second two-thirds of the passage (after 'What?') in a little more detail. Here, Nietzsche presents a direct argument against phenomenalism. *Phenomenalism* is the reductionist ontological claim, identified above as ontological empiricism, that objects are nothing but collections or sets of actual and possible sensations.[15] Ontological empiricism – phenomenalism – is a paradigmatic example of idealism, the claim that ideas are all that exist. So, Nietzsche says, suppose we grant that material objects are nothing but sets of actual and possible sensations caused by our sensory organs. Our sensory organs are material objects. If so, then our sensory organs are nothing but sets of actual and possible sensations caused by our sensory organs. If so, then our sensory organs are their own causes. If so, then our sensory organs are *causa sui* (i.e., entities that cause themselves). But *causa sui* are fundamentally absurd. Hence, it is not the case that our sensory organs are their own causes and phenomenalism is false.

Nietzsche thinks this argument is not only valid but sound. What implications, then, does his opposition to phenomenalism have on the highly condensed argument contained in the first three sentences of the passage? And, then, what implications does his opposition to phenomenalism have on his adherence to or divergence from positivism? To begin, the argument of the first three sentences must be presented as clearly as it can be, for, as stated, it is enthymematic (no mention of sensualism, used in the conclusion, makes any appearance in the premises). Here's a first stab at regimentation:

> 1: If it is not the case that the sense organs are phenomena in the sense of idealistic philosophy, then one can study physiology with a clear conscience
>
> 2: If the sense organs are phenomena in the sense of idealistic philosophy, then it is not the case that they are causes
>
> C: Sensualism is true, therefore, at least as a regulative hypothesis, if not as a heuristic principle.

Unstated in this argument but implicit is Nietzsche's premise that sense organs are causes and not phenomena in the sense of idealistic philosophy.

Fleshing Nietzsche's reasoning out and adding a premise connecting the study of physiology to sensualism yields the following:

> P1: If it is not the case that the sense organs are phenomena in the sense of idealistic philosophy, then one can study physiology with a clear conscience
>
> P2: If the sense organs are phenomena in the sense of idealistic philosophy, then it is not the case that the sense organs are causes
>
> P3: The sense organs are causes
>
> P4: It is not the case that the sense organs are phenomena in the sense of idealistic philosophy (P2, P3)
>
> P5: One can study physiology with a clear conscience (P4, P1)
>
> P6: The sense organs are causes and one can study physiology with a clear conscience (P3, P5)
>
> P7: If the sense organs are causes and one can study physiology with a clear conscience, then sensualism is true, at least as a regulative hypothesis, if not as a heuristic principle
>
> Therefore, sensualism is true, at least as a regulative hypothesis, if not as a heuristic principle. (P7, P6)

Again, with the missing premises added, the argument is valid.[16] So, if all of the premises are true, then Nietzsche's advocacy of sensualism in the third sentence of *Beyond Good and Evil* 15 as a regulative hypothesis must be consistent with his rejecting phenomenalism in the passage's penultimate sentence.

One does not see the word 'sensualism' in epistemological contexts much these days, but in the 19th century the word was familiar, roughly co-extensive with 'sensationalism,' the genetic empiricist claim identified earlier that all beliefs are generated either immediately or eventually from sensory experience.[17] Nietzsche rarely subscribes to the genetic empiricist claim.[18] Nor, at least here, does he subscribe to the warrant or alethic claims of empiricism either. He advocates instead that sensualism be adopted as a *regulative* hypothesis. The genetic empiricist claim is too strong and easily falsified, for if even one belief is not generated immediately or eventually from sensory experience, then the claim is mistaken. Adopting sensualism as a regulative hypothesis, on the other hand, is to adopt it only 'as a guideline which directs the course of inquiry without anticipating its outcomes.'[19] This way of putting the matter is exactly right: genetic empiricism is for Nietzsche a guiding principle and not an epistemological doctrine. It is thus that affirming sensualism and rejecting phenomenalism are consistent with one another, for sensualism as a regulative principle is consistent with the falsity of genetic empiricism and the falsity of the phenomenalist reduction of all objects to sets of actual and possible sensations. After all, the best guide to knowledge acquisition may be to hold that beliefs are caused by sensory experience even if it turns out upon investigation that some beliefs are not caused by sensory experience and even if it turns out that no objects reduce to sets of actual and possible sensations.

For these reasons, Nietzsche says at *Gay Science* 372 – a passage entitled 'Why We Are No Idealists' – that 'formerly, philosophers were afraid of the senses. Have we perhaps unlearned this fear too much? Today we are all sensualists, we philosophers of the present and the future, *not* in theory but in *praxis*, in practice.' That looks like an outright rejection of phenomenalism. But it is coupled with a note of caution:

We today are inclined to make the opposite judgment (which actually could be equally wrong), namely that *ideas* are worse seductresses than our senses, for all their cold and anemic appearance, and not even in spite of this appearance: they have always lived on the "blood" of the philosopher, they always consumed his senses and even, if you believe us, the "heart."

Taken as a whole, this passage adds up to opposing idealism as an ontological claim, being wary of genetic empiricism as a causal claim, and, consistent with *Beyond Good and Evil* 15, upholding sensualism as a regulative or practical principle. Given that the truth of genetic empiricism is necessary for the truth of positivism, and given that genetic empiricism is false, it follows that if, as he insists, he is no idealist, then he is no positivist either.

Of course, it does not follow from the rejection of genetic empiricism that the opposite view that all of our beliefs arise immediately or eventually from reason is true. Nietzsche is at least as critical of genetic rationalism as he is of genetic empiricism. Many passages could again be cited, but one of the most incisive and funny is also in *Gay Science* 372, immediately after what is quoted immediately above. The philosophers who engage in rationalist ways of thinking – he here names Spinoza – are 'concealed vampire[s]...who in the end [are] left with, and leave, mere bones, mere clatter. I mean categories, formulas, *words* (for, forgive me, what was left of Spinoza, *amorintellectualis dei* (intellectual love of God), is mere clatter and no more than that: What is *amor*, what *deus*, if there is not a drop of blood in them?' (GS 372). It is pretty clear that Nietzsche is trying to find some ground that allows him to reject both empiricism and rationalism, both materialism and idealism.

Another argument, one that is occasionally wrapped up with the interpretation of *Beyond Good and Evil* 15, may also be defused here. According to *Beyond Good and Evil* 15, phenomenalism is false because if it were true, then our sense organs would be the causal result of our perceptual experience, whereas physiology shows to the contrary that perceptual experience is the causal result of our sense organs. But now, suppose one tries to conjoin this rejection of phenomenalism with genetic empiricism. If, as genetic empiricism has it, all of our beliefs are generated either immediately or eventually from our sensory experience, then all of our beliefs about the physiological functions and organizational structures of our sensory organs are themselves generated from our sensory experience and there is no evidence for or against any physiological claim except that which is so formed. If so, then the claims of physiology are no more about mind-independent functions and organizational structures than are first-person reports on the qualitative feel of sexual orgasm. Despite what we may think, then, physiology provides no *evidence* that the sensory organs are causally implicated in the generation of perceptual experience. Assertions from physiologists to the contrary, their alleged evidence for inferring that phenomenalism is false instead warrants only the conclusion that phenomenalism is true. In short, so long as genetic empiricism is true, phenomenalism turns out also to be true.

Nietzsche recognizes that this argument is tempting and that it fails. He tries to defuse it in the latter part of *Beyond Good and Evil* 15. Recall:

> What? And others even say that the external world is the work of our organs? But then our body, as a part of this external world, would be the work of our organs! But then our organs themselves would be – the work of our organs! It seems to me that this is a complete *reductio ad absurdum*, assuming that the concept of a causa sui is something fundamentally absurd. Consequently, the external world is *not* the work of our organs–?

The structure of this passage is clear. If phenomenalism is true, then the external world is the product of our sense organs. If so, then our sense organs – since they are external to our mind – are also products of our sense organs. But claiming that our sense organs are products of our sense organs entails that our sense organs are causes of themselves. However, that is absurd. Hence phenomenalism is false even if genetic empiricism is true (as Hussain 2004a and Hussain 2004b notes). To think otherwise is to jump on the slippery slope that slides from epistemological premises to an ontological conclusion. Nietzsche repeatedly warns against stepping foot on these slippery slopes and he typically stays away from them.[20]

Nietzsche also rejects or is ambivalent about the other planks of positivism as well. He nowhere claims that *all* of our beliefs are justified immediately or even eventually by sensory experience, so he rejects the warrant foundationalism typically found in positivist epistemology. Consider TI '"Reason" in Philosophy' 3:

> We possess scientific knowledge today to precisely the extent that we have decided to *accept* the evidence of the senses – to the extent that we have learned to sharpen them and arm them to think them through to their conclusions. The rest is abortion and not-yet-science: which is to say metaphysics, theology, psychology, epistemology. *Or* science of formulae, sign-systems: such as logic and that applied logic, mathematics.

Here, he acknowledges two kinds of knowledge – that justified at least in part by appeal to perceptual experience and that justified because it is formally justified. This is a point reduced to a single sentence elsewhere in the *Nachlass*: 'All human knowledge is either experience or mathematics'(KSA 12 7[4] = WP 530). Of course, it must also be noted that he rejects the warrant foundationalism typically found in rationalist epistemology as well, such as is found in Descartes' equally foundationalist reliance on clear and distinct ideas. He calls reliance on clarity and distinctness a 'crude confusion' KSA 12 9[91] = WP 533) and, while he acknowledges that Descartes should be praised for conceding 'authority to reason alone' (BGE 191), he also castigates Descartes for forgetting that 'reason is merely an instrument' (BGE 191) and cannot for that reason be a foundation.

Likewise, although Nietzsche argues that religious and certain philosophical claims are demonstrably false because sensory experience plays no role of any kind in determining their truth, it does not follow that the truth of all propositions must be determined solely by sensory experience, as is required for the alethic claim of positivist epistemology. Even a passage such as *Beyond Good and Evil* 134, in which he claims that 'all credibility, all good conscience, all evidence of truth come first [*erst*] from the senses,' is consistent with evidence of truth coming sometimes from sources other than the senses. Note also that *erst* is ambiguous between first in *time*, first in *rank*, and *only*. Kaufmann's translation has it as 'only,' which is easily the most restrictive translation. Both 'first in time' and 'first in rank' are more permissive: 'first in time' makes the genetic claim that evidence for a proposition's truth must come first from the senses even if subsequently it can come from other sources, and 'first in rank' makes the evaluative claim that evidence for a proposition's truth must come above all else or primarily from the senses, even if it can also come from other sources. Only the most restrictive sense entails that the only kind of evidence for a proposition's truth is sensory evidence.

Much less is Nietzsche a semantic empiricist, for semantic empiricism is consistent with verificationism about meaning and Nietzsche's views are inconsistent with verificationism about meaning. For instance, his account of the meaning of general philosophical concept words such as 'substance' and 'causality' explicitly rejects the possibility that sensory experience has a role in determining their meaning. Instead, he argues that it is only shared linguistic structures and interrelationships between such philosophical concepts that together provide the meanings of general concept words:

> That individual philosophical ideas are not anything capricious or autonomously evolving, but grow up connected to and related to each other; that, however suddenly and arbitrarily they seem to appear in the history of thinking, they nevertheless belong just as much to a system as do all the members of the fauna of a continent – is

betrayed in the end also by the fact that the most diverse philosophers keep filling in a definite fundamental scheme of *possible* philos-
ophies. Under an invisible spell, they always revolve once more in
the same orbit; however independent of each other they may feel
themselves with their critical or systematic wills, something within
them leads them, something impels them in a definite order, one
after the other – to wit, the innate systemic structure and relationship
of their concepts. Their thinking is, in fact, far less a discovery than a
recognition, a remembering, a return and a homecoming to a remote,
primordial, and inclusive household of the soul, out of which those
concepts grew originally. Philosophizing is to this extent a kind of
atavism of the highest order.

The strange family resemblance of all Indian, Greek, and German
philosophizing is explained easily enough. Where there is affinity
of languages, it cannot fail, owing to the common philosophy of
grammar – I mean thanks to the unconscious domination and guid-
ance by similar grammatical functions – that everything is prepared
at the outset for a similar development and sequence of philosophical
systems; just as the way seems barred against certain other possibilities of interpreting the world. It is highly probable that philosophers
within the domain of the Ural-Altaic languages (where the concept of
the subject is least developed) look otherwise "into the world," and
will be found on paths of thought different from those of than Indo-
Germanic peoples and the Muslims; the spell of certain grammatical functions is ultimately also the spell of *physiological* judgments
of valuations and racial conditions. – So much by way of rejecting
Locke's superficiality regarding the origin of ideas. (*BGE* 20)

Of course, it does not follow from rejecting semantic empiricism for
general terms and abstract concept words that sensory experience plays
no role in determining the meaning of other words, perhaps even some
other concept words. But that is not on point: semantic empiricism
is contentious only if it applies to *all* terms and concept words. That
Nietzsche rejects semantic empiricism, for some, is sufficient for the
general claim to be falsified. It is another, very interesting, topic to determine what class of words and concepts he thinks semantic empiricism
is true of, if it is true of any class. He nowhere tries to find an answer to
this.

Finally, Nietzsche is not an ontological empiricist either. True, he
suggests in a *Nachlass* note that the 'opposite of the phenomenal world is
not "the true world" but the formless, unformulatable world of the chaos

of sensations' (KSA 12 9[106] = WP 569). And, in another *Nachlass* note, he claims that the idea 'that things possess a constitution in themselves quite apart from interpretation and subjectivity, is *a quite idle hypothesis*; it presupposes that *interpretation and subjectivity* are *not* essential, that a thing freed from all relationships would still be a thing' (KSA 11 36[23] = WP 560). But even this passage (and others like it – e.g., KSA 13 14[152] = WP 515; KSA 13 11[134] = WP 559; KSA 12 10[138] = WP 639) is careful not to restrict interpretation and subjectivity to our *human* interpretation and subjectivity, as would be required were ontological empiricism true. And the preponderance of textual evidence implies that his considered view is not that the world is comprised of our sensations, but that the world is comprised of complexes of force or power quanta, each of which, down to its simplest constituent elements, has its own perspective on the rest. The clearest expression of this view is, of course, the famous *Will to Power* 1067 (KSA 11 38[12]), wherein Nietzsche enthuses about the world being a 'monster of force,' a 'play of forces and waves of forces, at the same time one and many, increasing here and at the same time decreasing there; a sea of forces flowing and rushing together, eternally changing, eternally flooding back....' Here, Nietzsche offers up perhaps his most notorious ontological reduction – *everything* is reducible to forces and complexes of them.

Nietzsche sometimes conjoins this dynamicist ontological view with a rejection of the physics of his day (see e.g., KSA 11 36[34] = WP 618; KSA 13, 14[79] = WP 634, 635). And he sometimes couples the perspectivism implicit in this dynamicist ontology with a rejection of physics. One incisive expression of such skepticism about physics coupled with his perspectivist alternative is this *Nachlass* note from his last productive year:

> Physicists believe in a "true world" in their own fashion: a firm systematization of atoms in necessary motion, the same for all beings – so for them the "apparent world" is reduced to the side of universal and universally necessary being which is accessible to every being in its own way (accessible and also already adapted – made "subjective"). But they are in error. The atom they posit is inferred according to the logic of the perspectivism of consciousness – and is therefore itself a subjective fiction. This world picture that they sketch differs in no essential way from the subjective world picture: it is only construed with more extended senses, but with *our* senses nonetheless – And in any case they left something out of the constellation without knowing it: precisely this necessary

perspectivism by virtue of which every center of force – and not only man – construes all the rest of the world from its own viewpoint, i.e., measures, feels, forms, according to its own force – They forgot to include this perspective-setting force in "true being" – in school: the subject. They think this is "evolved," added later; but even the chemist needs it: it is being specific, definitely acting and reacting thus and thus, as may be the case.

Perspectivism is only a complex form of specificity. My idea is that every specific body strives to become master over all space and to extend its force (– its will to power:) and to thrust back all that resists its extension. But it continually encounters similar efforts on the part of other bodies and ends by coming to an arrangement ('union') with those of them that are sufficiently related to it: thus they then conspire together for power. And the process goes on –. (KSA 13 14[186] = WP 636)

As can be seen from these passages, Nietzsche is far from being an obedient fan of 19th century mechanistic physics. And it may also be inferred that he is far from being an obedient fan of any other science that assumes that physics provides the fundamental scientific ontology with which all other sciences must at least be consistent. (As can also be seen by consulting the dates of these passages, his criticism of physics remains more or less constant throughout the four-year period from 1885 through the end of 1888.)

For these reasons, Nietzsche thinks that physics is 'only an interpretation and exegesis of the world (to suit us, if I may say so!) and *not* a world-explanation' (BGE 14). Physics is not a world *explanation* because, first, as argued in section I, many of its theories presuppose materialism and mechanism, both of which quantify over empty domains. It can also be inferred that physics is not a world explanation because, second, its theories systematically neglect to include something that must be included, *viz.*, the perspectivism by which *every* center of force – organic and inorganic, simple and complex, atomic and molecular, molecular and cellular, cellular and systemic – interprets the rest of the world from its own viewpoint. It is difficult to see how any kind of empiricism, and hence, any kind of positivism, can agree with these extraordinary claims, as he himself notes: while positivism assumes there are facts, he claims instead that 'facts are precisely what there are not, there are only interpretations' (KSA 12 7[60] = WP 481). Hence, to the extent that positivism entails rejecting claims to which Nietzsche is committed, to that extent too must his views diverge from positivism.

We conclude that Nietzsche is not a positivist in any but a perverse sense of the term. However, if his views about perception, affect, cognition, and science are not instances of positivism and we wish nevertheless to affirm that they do fall comfortably under the umbrella of naturalism, then exactly what are his views? And are his views internally consistent with one another? To answer these questions, deeper investigation into Nietzsche's views on physiology in general, on perception and affection, on cognition and consciousness, and on subjectivity and agency is necessary.

2
Embodiedness, Embeddedness, Teleology

Nietzsche was more than a dilettante about scientific knowledge of the human body and its functioning. A barometer of his interest in physiology is the frequency of the words 'physiology' and 'physiological' in his work. Where there is one reference to physiology in *Human, All-too-Human*, there are twelve in *Daybreak*, six in *Gay Science*, sixteen in *Beyond Good and Evil*, thirty-three in *Genealogy of Morals*, twenty-six in *Twilight of the Idols*, thirteen in *Antichrist*, seventeen in *Ecce Homo*, and hundreds more in the notebooks from 1880–1888 (Brown 2004). Nietzsche's fascination with physiology can also be gauged by the books lining his bookshelves. He owned more than three dozen books and professional texts on physiology, medicine, and health, most of them purchased after 1875. If annotations are an accurate guide, he appears to have read many of these books cover-to-cover and some of them more than once (Brobjer 2004; Moore 2004). Moreover, Nietzsche himself acknowledges that physiology accounted for much of his reading after 1880. He wrote in *Ecce Homo* that by about 1880, 'a truly burning thirst took hold of me: henceforth I really pursued nothing more than physiology, medicine, and natural sciences' (EH 'Human' 3).

Nietzsche's interest in human physiology is thus of some importance to his intellectual biography. But it is of even more importance for his philosophical psychology. Although what results from all of his reading is rarely explicit in the published work or expressed with anything approaching scientific style, he is quite serious about the impact of physiology on human psychology in general and moral psychology in particular. He advises us, for example, to analyze moral degeneration as '[in]separable from the physiological; it is a mere symptom-complex of the latter; one is necessarily bad, just as one is necessarily sick' (KSA 13 14[113]); he claims that the honesty of Buddhism is a direct result of

41

the Buddha being a 'profound physiologist' (EH "Wise" 6); and he ridicules 'Christian interpreters of the body' for ascribing moral and religious significance to every outcome of 'the stomach, the intestines, the beating of the heart, the nerves, the bile, the semen' (D 86). Indeed, both religious and philosophical moralities are the direct result of 'concealed misunderstandings of the physical constitution' (GS Preface 2), and the entire edifice of Christianity is premised on 'ancient physiological errors' (KSA 9 11[173]), 'physiological confusions' (KSA 13 14[168]), and 'physiological contradiction[s]' (KSA 12 8[3]).

Had we but known more about physiology when religion initially appeared, all of the spiritualizing of poor health, malnourishment, and weakness as sin and moral wickedness might never have occurred, and millions of people would have been spared the pointless suffering that comes in the wake of religious interpretations of what are, in the end, merely physiological conditions. Likewise, when knowledge of physiology becomes widespread, the moral acid that has eaten away our psychological health for the last 2000 years will be neutralized, replaced by a 'physiology of morality' (KSA 11 27[14]) that deflates the illusion that moral qualities are gifts of reason or some god. Of course, the transition from old to new will not be easy, since the new physio-psychologists will themselves be products of the acid to which their physiological knowledge is the neutralizing antidote. The first few generations of Nietzsche's physio-psychologists will inevitably have to 'contend with unconscious resistance in the heart' (BGE 23), for they themselves will be the internal battleground on which the inherited view – that morality and physio-psychology are separate domains, each with its own methods and predictions – contends with the alternative and deflationary physio-psychological description of the conditions that initially prompted morality.

As our understanding of human physiology improves, we learn a number of valuable lessons, the most important of which is that the mind and the body are not separate kinds at all – one spiritual, one physical. As he puts it in a *Nachlass* note:

> The body and physiology the starting point: why? – We gain the correct idea of the nature of our subject-unity, namely as regents at the head of a communality, also of the dependence of these regents upon the ruled and of an order of rank and division of labor as the conditions that make possible the whole and its parts The most important thing, however, is: that we understand that the ruler and his subjects are of the same kind, all feeling, willing, thinking – and

that wherever we see or divine movement in a body, we learn to conclude that there is a subjective, invisible life appertaining to it. (KSA 11 40[21] = WP 492)

But even if this is the most important thing physiological knowledge gives us, it is far from the only thing. We also discover that all of the body's organs – from the intestines to the brain/mind – are related to one another in complex networks of causal interaction. Third, we find that at every level of physiological description – from the cellular level through to the level of tissues and organs and finally to the systemic level – there is an ongoing struggle for dominance. Fourth and fifth, we learn that nourishment is every bit as needed for the brain/mind as it is for the rest of the bodily organs and systems and that the goal of nourishment is the expansion of the organism's life and power. Finally, we discover that physiological accounts of perception underwrite rejecting some standard philosophical positions, chief among them representationalism, idealism, and realism. These are the topics of this and the next chapter.

I Physiology

If physiology is the scientific study of the functioning of living organisms and their constituent parts, then Nietzsche has only a passing interest in physiology. His curiosity is piqued neither by studies of the mouse limbic system nor by studies of the biochemistry of synaptic neurotransmitters. His mind is attracted instead towards certain general features of human physiology – gleaned in no small part from reading physiology texts by Wilhelm Roux and Wilhelm Rolph – that support his naturalizing philosophical projects. Among the features of these authors' work most congenial to Nietzsche's projects is their emphasis on the functional characterization of bodily organs and systems, the ever-changing interplay between parts of an organism, and the dynamic structure of a functioning body. Less frequently noted but equally significant is that both Roux and Rolph recognize that relations between organism and surrounding environment are dynamic and complex. Nietzsche takes this physiological work as support for his will to power hypothesis; indeed, it is possible that he developed the will to power hypothesis as a result of reading them. Yet, even if his knowledge of Lange and Boscovich, both of whom also discuss force and power, suggests instead that it was not Roux and Rolph alone who led him to the idea, it is indisputable that their work confirmed for Nietzsche that will to power applies at the level of scientific biology, human physiology, and human psychology.

Nietzsche is only occasionally forthcoming in his published work about the ontological, causal, and methodological continuity from physics through to psychology, but in at least one place, *Beyond Good and Evil* 36, he sheds this reticence. Here, Nietzsche moves from moral and psychological levels through biological levels and all the way down to physical levels of explanation, arguing that a 'conscience of method' suggests that a single form of causality might be applicable at every level of explanation. Suppose, he says, that we assume only our passions, desires, and affects as categories of causes. Given those categories, do we have everything required for biological and physical (mechanistic or material) causality? His surprising answer is 'yes.' Everything, from the noblest passion to the exchange of mitochondria across cell walls, is a symptom or ramified development of 'a kind of instinctive life in which all organic functions are still synthetically intertwined along with subject-regulation, assimilation, nourishment, excretion, and metabolism' (BGE 36). This generalization about every form of causality at the biological level underwrites his rejection of teleological causality, final causality, formal causality, and all of the other variant species of causality fancied by metaphysical and religious salespeople. Contrary to a variety of kinds of causation, we should instead consolidate *every* form of causality into one:

> The question is in the end whether we really recognize the will as efficient, whether we believe in the causality of the will: if we do – and at bottom our faith in this is nothing less than our faith in causality itself – then we have to make the experiment of positing the causality of the will hypothetically as the only one. "Will," of course, can affect only "will" – and not "matter" (not "nerves," e.g.). In short one has to risk the hypothesis whether will does not affect will wherever "effects" are recognized – and whether all mechanical occurrences are not, insofar as a force is active in them, will force, effects of the will. (BGE 36)

He concludes with a statement of the doctrine of the will to power:

> Suppose, finally, we succeeded in explaining our entire instinctive life as the development and ramification of one basic form of the will – namely, of the will to power, as my proposition has it; suppose all organic functions could be traced back to this will to power and

one could also find in it the solution of the problem of procreation and nourishment – it is one problem – then one would have gained the right to determine all efficient force univocally as – will to power. The world viewed from inside, the world defined and determined according to its 'intelligible character' – it would be "will to power" and nothing else. (BGE 36)

It is difficult to interpret this passage as anything other than a straightforward reduction of all forms of causality to will to power.[1] It will be interpreted thusly herein.

Whether reducing all forms of causality to will to power is plausible outside of organic domains is a source of long-standing disagreement among Nietzsche scholars.[2] But that dispute can be side stepped here because our interests do not intersect with unpacking causality in physics and inorganic chemistry or with delimiting fundamental ontological categories. It is not pertinent to our concerns, for example, that inorganic entities are identical to bundles of power quanta or that molecular inorganic chemical bonds are best analyzed as power struggles. Our interests lie instead in the organic domain and specifically on a part of that domain, namely us humans, our physiology and our psychology. And here it cannot be denied that Nietzsche appears to be convinced that the will to power hypothesis applies if it applies anywhere. He suggests repeatedly that physiological and psychological causality are best understood in terms of will to power. What this proposal amounts to is discussed in Chapter 6. Here, it suffices to note that applications of his proposed reduction beyond human physiology and psychology may be ignored unless they are needed to turn challenges presented to the paradigmatic applications in human physiology and psychology. So long as such challenges are met without recurring to more fundamental levels, we may safely leave them to the side. Of course, if it turns out that even the paradigmatic examples of human physiology and human psychology are domains in which the reduction is not successful, then neither will less-than-paradigmatic extensions be successful. In that case, Nietzsche's will to power proposal fails.

Just what does Nietzsche think the explanatory categories of physiology and psychology are? His answer, as will be seen, is that they are the same for both physiology and psychology: drives and affects. So, if the proposed reduction of physiological and psychological causation to will to power is to be compelling, then drives and affects must be kinds of entities that support the reduction. To begin analysis of this argument, the influence of Roux and Rolph on Nietzsche's thinking must be better understood.

Wilhelm Roux was a student of the evolutionist Ernst Haeckel and is now acknowledged to be the father of experimental embryology because of his fundamental contributions to our understanding of epigenetic embryo development and organization. In 1881, he wrote *The Battle of the Parts of the Organism*. Here, Roux argues that physiology has as its domain self-organizing dynamic systems whose components at every level of size and every order of complexity – from molecules to cells to tissues to organs – are processing stimuli and struggling for sustenance and space. Components that enhance the organism's adaptation to the external environment tend to survive the intra-organismic battle; those that do not so function do not last. Since each such part is a component whose particular function is partially determined by the overall functioning of the organism of which it is a part, transitory equilibria are likely to develop and dissolve over and over in service of the organism's larger projects. Further, since the organism and its component parts are themselves embedded in an environment that also constantly undergoes change, whatever internal equilibria emerge are continuously subjected to ongoing external perturbation and disruption. Organisms flourish in a changing environment only when they are self-regulating and self-governing, that is, only when comprised of intra-individual processes and systems that continuously adjust their internal milieu to other such intra-individual processes and systems and to the external environment. For only then can an individual control the external environment (further details about Roux's dynamic physiology and similarities between Roux and Nietzsche may be found in Salaquarda 1978; Müller-Lauter 1978; Moore 2002).

Nietzsche frequently deploys an idiosyncratically phrased version of Roux's dynamicist physiology. Consider KSA 11 37[4], from 1885:

what is more astonishing is the *body*: there is no end to one's admiration for how the human *body* has become possible; how such a prodigious alliance of living beings, each dependent and subservient and yet in a certain sense also commanding and acting out of its own will, can live, grow, and for a while prevail, as a whole – and we can see this does *not* occur due to consciousness! For this "miracle of miracles", consciousness is just a "tool" and nothing more – a tool in the same sense that the stomach is a tool. The magnificent binding together of the most diverse life, the ordering and arrangement of the higher and lower activities, the thousand-fold obedience which is not blind, even less mechanical, but a selecting, shrewd, considerate, even resistant obedience – measured by intellectual standards, this whole phenomenon 'body' is as superior to our consciousness, our 'mind', our conscious thinking, feeling, willing, as algebra is to the times tables.

Granted, Nietzsche's physiological account of the human body is stated in language not typically found in scientific textbooks, but it is consonant with thinking that the body is a hierarchically structured, self-organized, self-regulating, non-linear dynamic organism.

Among other things, Nietzsche agrees with Roux that (a) organisms are *dynamic* and *self-organizing* complexes; (b) these self-organizing complexes or systems are *hierarchically structured* so that some constituent elements command while others obey; and (c) these hierarchically structured self-organizing systems are *self-regulating* and engage in *self-originating* motion and behavior. An *organized system* is a set of entities structured to realize a function or maintain a particular configuration. A *self-organized system* is a set of entities structured to realize a function or maintain a particular configuration and whose structure is not imposed by an external cause. Organization in general and self-organization in particular are *global* properties of groups of entities rather than *local* properties of each of those entities. Some self-organized systems are static; others are dynamic. A *dynamic* self-organized system is a self-organized system whose configuration or function is in constant motion or is constantly changing.[3] A *linear* dynamic system is one whose causal outcomes are roughly proportional to causal inputs; a *non-linear* dynamic system is one whose causal outcomes are disproportional to causal inputs.[4] Non-linear processes are the result of positive and/or negative feedback loops. A *feedback loop* occurs when the results of some node in a causal process feed back into an earlier node of that very causal process. A feedback loop is *positive* when what feeds back augments or amplifies the causal process; a feedback loop is *negative* when what feeds back limits or cancels the causal process. Positive feedback engenders instability; negative feedback engenders stability. The conjunction of positive and negative feedback loops comprise *regulation*.

These concepts from non-linear dynamics, familiar to us now, were introduced in the 19th century. Nietzsche, primarily through the knowledge he gained by reading Lange and Roux, grabs hold of them and does not let go. One additional feature of such views, not widely discussed then but which Nietzsche probably understood in an imprecise way, is that entities and processes locked into feedback and feedforward causal loops become causally entwined with each other. Causal relations between two (or more) systems (entities, processes, states, etc.) are, as suggested above, non-linear whenever positive and negative feedfor-ward and feedback loops characterize the causal relations between them. Such systems are *non-linear systems*. Two (or more) non-linear systems are *causally coupled* whenever causal relations between them are non-linear. Non-linear systems that are causally coupled with one another are *causally dependent* upon each other (Prinz 2009). Hence, individual physiological systems and events, whether linear or non-linear, can be constituents of larger non-linear causal systems and can be caus-ally coupled with other constituent systems of that larger non-linear causal system. Finally, we may introduce the notion of constitutive coupling. One system is *constitutively dependent* on another when the one is constitutively coupled with the other. Systems are *constitutively coupled* whenever the resulting conjoint system is non-decomposable (see Bechtel 1998, 2009; Bechtel & Richardson 1993; Strevens 2005). A system is *constitutively decomposable* when it is composed of constituents whose causal powers are *not* a 1–1 function of the causal powers of the other constituents, where a 1–1 function from one system to another is a mapping from the one to the other such that no element of the one maps to more than one element of the other. A system is constitutively *nondecomposable* whenever it is composed of constituents whose causal powers *are* a 1–1 function on the causal powers of the other constituents. Constitutive coupling is a stronger relation than causal coupling, for constitutive coupling, unlike causal coupling, entails that no elements of constitutively coupled systems can be implicated in a causal explana-tion of some behavior independently of one another.

A pair of examples makes the relevant point. A physical system is constitutively decomposable as to its spatial extension, since the spatial extension of any distinct constituent spatial part of the system can be fixed independently of fixing the spatial extension of any other distinct constituent spatial part of the system. So, the causal powers of the spatial extension of a physical system are a simple aggregation of the causal powers of the spatially extended parts composing the physical system. The situation is otherwise with a constitutively non-decompos-able system. Examples of constitutively non-decomposable systems are a single day in your life, the flow of a river, hurricanes, tornadoes, fire, photosynthesis, and explosions. Each of these systems is composed of constituent elements whose causal powers vary as a 1–1 function of the other constituents.

With these concepts from non-linear dynamics on hand, Nietzsche's physiological views are better understood. He argues, first, that all physi-ological structures, even the most primitive such as molecules and cells, dynamically self-organize into hierarchically structured systems and, second, that they self-regulate with hierarchically ordered feedback and feedforward loops. Molecules self-organize into functioning cells, cells organize into more complex processes and tissues, and processes and tissues self-organize into even more complex organs and systems. These organic processes incessantly develop 'greater complexity, sharp differentiation ... by virtue of which dominant, shaping, commanding forces continually extend the bounds of their power and continually simplify within these bounds' (KSA 12 7[9] = WP 644). On this score, Nietzsche makes no distinction between animals and plants: 'To understand what life is, what kind of striving and tension life is, the formula must be applicable to trees and plants as well as to animals. ... All expanding, incorporating, growing is a striving against what resists. ... What do the trees in a jungle fight each other for? For "happiness"? – For power...' (KSA 13 11[111] = WP 704).

Nietzsche extends the dynamic and self-organizational view to human physiology. Again with Roux, he thinks of human physiology in dynamic and hierarchical terms. The body is an 'aristocracy' of struggles between different 'cells and tissues,' systems and organs, a structured self-regulatory and self-governing community characterized by a pervasive 'division of labor' between its internal parts such that 'the higher type is possible only through the subjugation of the lower until it becomes a function' (KSA 12 2[76] = WP 660). This set of command and obedience relations is a kind of causal coupling. The emphasis on hierarchical causal coupling found in such passages is already found in Roux's physiology and is likely one of the aspects that Nietzsche found most attractive about his work. Nietzsche concurs with Roux that command and obedience are at the core of *every* level of physiological description: '...there must be commanding (and obeying) all over again right down to the smallest units, and only when then command is dissected into a vast number of tiny sub-commands can the movement take place, which commences *with the last and smallest* obeying structure' (KSA 11 27[19]). Hence, causal coupling between systems occurs at every level of physiology.

Not only does this command and obedience structure characterize every level of physiological description, it also provides the organization necessary for self-regulation. Nietzsche's commitment to physiological self-regulation and self-governance cannot be overestimated: it is the basis of his understanding of what makes both a non-social organism such as a tree flourish in its environment and a social organism such as a human flourish in its environment. Typically, Nietzsche talks of the organism rather than its constituent systems, processes, and organs, although what he says about the former applies equally to the latter. For example, he notes that 'the creature most capable of *regulating* itself, *disciplining* itself, judging – with the greatest excitability and even greater self-control – always survives' (KSA 11 25[427]). The point extends to sub-organismic levels as well, since the 'individual itself is a struggle between parts (for food, space, etc.): its evolution [is] tied to the victory or predominance of individual parts, to an atrophy, a "becoming an organ" of other parts' (KSA 11 36[29] = WP 646). In short, the body comprising a person, as much as the person thus comprised, is a battleground of causally coupled competition between self-regulating systems, tissues, and organs, each playing a role in satisfying physiological functions that are themselves self-regulating and competing with other such functions.

Given that the growth of the organism occurs embedded in an environment that is itself subject to ongoing changes, static organismic and sub-organismic self-regulation would quickly result in death. Rather, the internal environment changes incessantly: 'the center of gravity is something changeable; the continual *generation* of cells, etc. produces a continual change in the number of these beings' (KSA 11 34[123]). Additionally, the elements that comprise a system of command and obedience are such that all of them are reciprocally dependent on one another in massively complex feedforward and feedback loops. As noted already, 'we gain the correct idea of the nature of our subject-unity, namely as regents at the head of a communality, also of the dependence of these regents upon the ruled and of an order of rank and division of labor as the conditions that make possible the whole and its parts' (KSA 11 40[21] = WP 492). This mutual dependence of commanding elements on the obeying elements and of the obeying elements on the commanding elements is typically expressed in overtly aggressive language: 'the hierarchy establishes itself through the *victory* of the stronger and the *indispensability* of the weaker for the stronger and of the stronger for the weaker...' (KSA 11 25[430]). Again: '*Ruling* is enduring the counter-weight of the weaker force, therefore a kind of *continuation* of the struggle. *Obeying* is likewise a *struggle*: so much force as remains for resisting' (KSA 11 26[276]). But the ongoing dynamic of commanding and obeying demands that the commanding elements 'provide for those which obey everything they need to preserve themselves.... [O]therwise, they could not serve and obey one another' (KSA 11 26[276]). Indeed, 'in more delicate cases, the roles must temporarily switch so that what otherwise commands must, this once, obey' (KSA 11 26[276]).

Such mutual dependence suggests that, at least on occasion, Nietzsche toys with the idea that some systems are not only causally coupled but constitutively coupled as well. After all, mutual dependence can lead to non-decomposability, which is sufficient for constitutive dependence of two or more systems on one another. By these entrenched systems of commanding and obeying, together with occasional role-reversals to prevent dominant elements from ruining the organism, physiological self-regulation and self-governance is achieved.

Even those cognitive abilities we think of as uniquely human and noble – our rationality, logic, and consciousness – are part of this non-linear self-regulative regime. For example,

> The 'apparatus of nerves and brain' is *not* constructed this subtly and "divinely" so as to bring forth thinking, feeling, willing at all. It seems to me, instead that precisely this thinking, feeling, willing does not require an "apparatus" but that the so-called apparatus, and it alone, is the thing that counts. (KSA 11 37[4])

It is, as this passage claims, the apparatus of nerves and brain that is important and not the conscious thinking, feeling, and willing that boils out of that apparatus. The apparatus of the central nervous system is comprised of complex systems interacting with each other, each system in turn comprised of tissues and organs interacting with one another, each kind of tissue and each organ in turn comprised of cells interacting with one another. Nietzsche holds, consistent with contemporary embodied neuroscience, that the central nervous system and its brain is a 'centralizing apparatus' (KSA 11 27[19]). Again:

> consciousness is just a "tool" and nothing more – a tool in the same sense that the stomach is a tool. The magnificent binding together of the most diverse life, the ordering and arrangement of the higher and lower activities, the thousand-fold obedience which is not blind, even less mechanical, but a selecting, shrewd, considerate, even resistant obedience – measured by intellectual standards, this whole phenomenon "body" is as superior to our consciousness, our "mind", our conscious thinking, feeling, willing, as algebra is to the times tables. (KSA 11 37[4])

Indeed, the 'whole of *conscious* life, the mind including the soul, including the heart, including goodness, including virtue...' works in the service 'of the *enhancement of life*' (KSA 13 11[183]).

Characterizing the central nervous system as a complex dynamic system of interacting component processes in the service of enhancing life is so compelling for Nietzsche that he suggests that we rehabilitate the old philosophical term 'soul' in its terms. The central nervous system can be understood as one of the most enduring systems in the human body, one of the 'arrangements' or 'conspiracies' (KSA 13 14[186] = WP 636) that the human organism develops to monitor and control the welter of informational input from the external environment and the internal milieu. We can think of the soul as 'subjective multiplicity' or 'as social structure of the drives and affects' (BGE 12). On this reconfiguration, the term 'soul' can again denote, but it refers in this dynamic view to something natural rather than something abstract and transcendental. However, understanding this reconfigured naturalized soul is even more daunting than understanding the wispy feather tossed around by religion, for comprehending the soul as a social structure of drives and affects requires nothing less than a full account of our human form of life and the role of consciousness in that life, as noted in *Beyond Good and Evil* 12:

> When the *new* physiologist puts an end to the superstitions which have so far flourished with almost tropical luxuriance around the idea of the soul, he practically exiles himself into a new desert and a new suspicion – it is possible that the older psychologists had a merrier and more comfortable time of it; eventually, however, he finds that precisely thereby he also condemns himself to *invention* – and – who knows? – perhaps to discovery.

Given a better understanding of human physiology, then, we will have to re-invent our conception of ourselves, the nature of our subjectivity, and the nature of our unity or identity at and over time. We return to these issues in Chapter 6's discussion of Nietzsche's views on willing and the self.

Rolph's thoughts about the nature of life and about the role of self-preservation add two other dimensions to Nietzsche's physiological tendencies. Rolph wrote but one book, *Biologische Probleme*. In it, he argues that the struggle for existence is not the primary mechanism for evolutionary development and that the instinct for self-preservation does not exist. He counters with an alternative mechanism for development, according to which organisms seek to expand themselves and their influence on the world, even to the point of jeopardizing their own existence, by assimilating and appropriating whatever they find. But, again, not only organisms are described in this manner: every level of biological explanation, from the cellular upwards, is likewise characterized by an insatiable drive to appropriate and assimilate, and incorporate.

Nietzsche read Rolph's book in 1884, and thereafter his *Nachlass* notes are peppered with concepts and arguments similar to those found in Rolph. For example, he concurs with Rolph on the importance of assimilation and appropriation, going so far as to claim that 'insatiable' appropriation and will to power are equivalent (KSA 12 2[76] = WP 660). Having marked the equivalence, every passage that discusses will to power is equivalent to that passage in which 'will to power' is replaced with 'assimilation and appropriation.' So, for example, Nietzsche has it that:

> Life… strives after a maximal feeling of power; essentially a striving for more power; striving is nothing other than striving for power; the basic and innermost thing is still this will. (KSA 13 14[82] = WP 689)

This view is elaborated in another note:

> The will to power can manifest itself only against resistances; there-fore it seeks that which resists it – this is the primeval tendency of the protozoa when it extends pseudopodia and feels about. Appropriation and assimilation [*Einverleibung*] are above all a desire to overwhelm, a forming, shaping and reshaping, until at length that which has been overwhelmed has entirely gone over into the power domain of the aggressor and has increased the same. – If this incorporation is not successful, then the form probably falls to pieces; and the duality appears as a consequence of the will to power: in order not to let go what has been conquered, the will to power divides itself into two wills (in some cases without completely surrendering the connection between its two parts). (KSA 12 9[5] = WP 656)

Here, Nietzsche's indebtedness to Rolph *and* Roux is apparent, for he deploys Rolph's emphasis on assimilation and appropriation as princi-ples for explaining organic functioning and Roux's emphasis on their violent nature. In addition, it also displays one of Nietzsche's worst tendencies – reifying will to power as a supra-individual force with its own unique and describable behavior (for criticism of this tendency, see Moore 2002).

Nietzsche also agrees with Rolph, although typically with qualifica-tions, that self-preservation is not found in every organism. Occasionally,

Nietzsche's view is indistinguishable from Rolph's: he affirms at one point that 'life, as the form of being most familiar to us, is specifically a will to the accumulation of force; all the processes of life depend on this: nothing wants to preserve itself, everything is to be added and accumulated' (KSA 13 14[82] = WP 689). Frequently, however, he suggests a slightly different, weaker, claim:

> Physiologists should think again before positing the "instinct of preservation" as the cardinal drive in an organic creature. A living thing wants above all to *discharge* its force: "preservation" is only a consequence of this. (KSA 12 2[63] = WP 650)

What is true of all living organisms is, of course, true of humans, as *Gay Science* 349 makes clear:

> The wish to preserve oneself is the symptom of a condition of distress, of a limitation of the really fundamental instinct of life which aims at the expansion of power and, wishing for that, frequently risks and even sacrifices self-preservation... in nature it is not conditions of distress that are dominant but overflow and squandering, even to the point of absurdity. The struggle for existence is only an exception, a temporary restriction of the will to life. The great and small struggle always revolves around superiority, around growth and expansion, around power – in accordance with the will to power which is the will of life.

These passages are inconsistent with Rolph's view that there simply is no self-preservation instinct. Nietzsche allows instead that there is an instinct of self-preservation, but it is, he thinks, a symptom of distress and weakness rather than of health and strength. It is only when an organism is exhausted and weak that its concerns turn to self-preservation: 'the exhausted want rest, relaxation, peace, calm' (KSA 13 14[174] = WP 703) so that they might recover. The healthy and strong, on the other hand, often ignore what is best for self-preservation. They 'want victory, opponents overcome, the overflow of the feeling of power across wider domains than hitherto' (KSA 13 14[174] = WP 703). Indeed, 'all healthy functions of the organism have this need – and the whole organism is such a complex of systems struggling for an increase of the feeling of power' (KSA 13 14[174] = WP 703).[5]

Power expansion through appropriation and assimilation explains both sub-organismic processes, such as the physiological division of labor and the functioning of organs and tissues, and organismic physiological processes, such as nutrition and reproduction. At sub-organic levels, the behavior of cells, tissues, and organs is explained as regimens of outward expansion and appropriation: '"procreation," the crumbling that results when the ruling cells are incapable of organizing that which has been appropriated' (KSA 12 2[76] = WP 660). The behavior of simple organisms, such as protozoa, is likewise explained in terms of assimilation and appropriation:

> One cannot ascribe the most basic and primeval activities of protoplasm to a will to self-preservation, for it takes into itself absurdly more than would be required to preserve it; and, above all, it does not thereby "preserve itself," it falls apart – The drive that rules here has to explain precisely this absence of desire for self-preservation ... (KSA 13 11[121] = WP 651)

Similarly, at the level of organismic processes, nourishment is understood best as 'a consequence of the insatiable appropriation, of the will to power' (KSA 12 2[76] = WP 660). Asexual reproduction too is explained in these terms as a 'derivation; originally: where one will is not enough to organize everything that's been appropriated, a *counter-will* comes into force which does the releasing, a new organizational center, after a struggle with the original will' (KSA 12 5[64]). Even sexual reproduction is explained thusly: '... procreation is the real achievement of the individual and consequently his highest interest, his highest expression of power' (KSA 12 7[9] = WP 680).

Nietzsche is fitfully aware that relentless assimilation and appropriation risks self-destruction. Where a system's assimilation and appropriation reach beyond its capacity to self-organize and self-regulate, disorganization ensues, with self-destruction or division being the only way forward. Nietzsche describes this process in a handful of *Nachlass* notes written between 1885 and 1887. In one, he claims that 'the greater the impulse towards variety, differentiation, inner decay, the more force is present' and, correlatively, that 'the greater the impulse toward unity, the more firmly may one conclude that weakness is present' (KSA 11 36[21] = WP 655). Variety and differentiation are hallmarks of power because appropriation and assimilation are 'above all a desire to overwhelm, a forming, shaping and reshaping' (KSA 12 9[151] = WP 656). A system engages in this forming–shaping–reshaping behavior 'until at length that which has been overwhelmed has entirely gone over into the power domain of the aggressor' (KSA 12 9[151] = WP 656). On occasion, however, incorporation of the weaker by and into the stronger fails: 'where one will is not enough to organize the entire appropriated material, a *counter-will* comes into force which does the releasing; a new organizational center, after a struggle with the original will' (KSA 12 5[64] = WP 657). In this way, 'the form probably falls to pieces; and *duality* appears as a consequence of the will to power' (KSA 12 9[151] = WP 656). Although it is not entirely clear at what level of explanation – sub-organismic or organismic – these claims are made, it is clear that they are of a piece and consistent with Nietzsche's claims elsewhere that the best expression of the will to power in humans is to live an experimental life. It appears, then, that at every level of description appropriation, assimilation, and incorporation – power – are risky, even to the point of self-destruction.

II   The end of teleology

On Nietzsche's account, human physiology is best characterized as a dynamic causal coupling between various non-linear systems and subsystems that comprise an individual organism. Of course, the organism thus comprised is, in turn, dynamically coupled with its surrounding environment. As will be argued in greater detail in Chapter 3, the best interpretation of his view is that while organisms are causally coupled with the surrounding environment, they are not constitutively coupled with the environment. That is to say, the organism–environment system is not a constitutively non-decomposable complex. Here, it is pertinent to note that a dynamicist physiology provides Nietzsche with the concepts he needs to argue that many, if not all, of the teleological elements found in much of then-contemporary philosophy, biology and physiology are superfluous and can therefore be jettisoned easily.

Attacks on teleological thinking are scattered throughout Nietzsche's work. His primary targets in his attacks are what he calls 'superfluous teleological principles' (BGE 13; KSA 12 2[63] = WP 650). What makes a teleological principle superfluous is that some other teleological principle or some other non-teleological principle explains everything that the superfluous one does without being objectionable in the way it is. And what makes a teleological principle objectionable is that it introduces goals that organisms try to achieve as a way to explain its behavior when no goals are needed to explain the organism's behavior. Nietzsche's skepticism about goals (*Zeile*) is rooted in a general suspicion of purposes and ends (both 'end' and 'purpose' are English translations of *Zwecke*), all of which, he thinks, presuppose conscious thought, either in the form of a conscious agent bestowing a purpose on something that otherwise would lack it or as something reflectively entertained by a conscious agent.

Certain understandings of goals and purposes do, it is true, entail attributing them to organisms as a conscious mental representation, the entertainment of which comprises the initial event of a long causal chain of mental, physiological, and overt behavior processes whose final state satisfies the goal entertained. So, if biological functions are understood as goals, and if we articulate goals as conscious mental representations, it will turn out that any and all biological functions entail conscious mental representation. The entirety of nature, down to the simplest fungi, then becomes a domain of organisms capable of consciously entertaining goals and organizing their behavior to satisfy them. That looks like vitalism, the thesis that there is a unique something in virtue of which all living organisms have the property of life. Indeed, it looks like a pan-psychist kind of vitalism, the thesis that the unique something in virtue of which all living organisms are living is something conscious.

Vitalism was widespread in the science and philosophy of Nietzsche's day and it must be admitted that he falls victim to it more than once. Rolph explicitly affirmed a pan-psychist vitalism, and Nietzsche on occasion falls right in line with him. For example, he allows that 'There must be an *amount of consciousness* and will in every complex organic being' (KSA 11 25[401]), that '*self-consciousness itself* is already present in the cell' (KSA 11 26[36]), and that 'that which is commonly attributed to the *mind [Geiste] seems to me to constitute the essence of the organic:* and in the highest functions of the mind I find only a sublime kind of organic function (assimilation, selection, secretion, etc.)' (KSA 11 25[356]).

Even if these pan-psychist pronouncements are dismissed as non-representative exceptions, Nietzsche really struggles to eliminate goals of the objectionable kinds from statements of his physiological and psychological views. In the end, his attempts to do so are not entirely successful.[6] A quick survey confirms the worry. Consider: 'All "purposes" (*Zwecke*), "goals" (*Zeile*'), "meanings" (*Sinne*), are only modes of expression and metamorphoses of one will that is inherent in all events: the will to power. To have purposes, aims, intentions, willing in general, is the same thing as willing to be stronger, willing to grow – and, in addition, willing the means to this' (KSA 13 11[96] = WP 675). Again:

"Attraction" and "repulsion" in a purely mechanistic sense are complete fictions: a word. We cannot think of an attraction divorced from an intention. – The will to take possession of a thing or to defend oneself against it and repel it – that, we "understand" that would be an interpretation of which we could make use.

In short: the psychological necessity for a belief in causality lies in the inconceivability of an event divorced from intent; by which naturally nothing is said concerning truth or untruth (the justification of such a belief)! The belief in *causae* falls with the belief in *tele* ... (KSA 12 2[83] = WP 627)

Nietzsche's claim here is remarkably ambitious: *all* causation – even something as fundamental as mechanical attraction and repulsion – entails an intention (*Absicht*), and, in virtue of that entailment, *all* causation presupposes ends or goals. Another *Nachlass* note likewise affirms that, as the concept of causation has been developed in science, it has become apparent (at least to Nietzsche) that 'the *causa finalis* is the *causa efficiens*' (KSA 11 34[53]).

Nietzsche sometimes folds the ineliminability of goals as found in an analysis of causation into his proposals about the will to power, as here, where the equivalence of mechanical force and will to power is affirmed: 'The victorious concept of "force," by means of which our physicists have created God and the world, still needs to be completed: an inner world must be ascribed to it, which I designate as "will to power," i.e. as an insatiable desire to manifest power; or as the employment and exercise of power, as a creative drive, etc.' (KSA 11 36[31] = WP 619). Nietzsche is explicit that, 'in the case of an animal, it is possible to trace all its drives to the will to power; likewise, all the functions of organic life to this one source' (KSA 11 36[31] = WP 619). Elsewhere he affirms that causation and will to power are the same:

Critique of the concept: cause. – From a psychological point of view the concept "cause" is our feeling of power resulting from the so-called act of will – our concept "effect" the superstition that this feeling of power is the motive power itself –

A condition that accompanies an event and is itself an effect of the event is projected as the "sufficient reason" for the event; – the relation of tensions in our feeling of power (pleasure as the feeling of power), of a resistance overcome – are they illusions? –

If we translate the concept "cause" back to the only sphere known to us, from which we have derived it, we cannot imagine any change that does not involve a will to power. We do not know how to explain a change except as the encroachment of one power upon another power.

The will to accumulate force is special to the phenomena of life, to nourishment, procreation, inheritance – to society, state, custom, authority. Should we not be permitted to assume this will as a motive cause in chemistry, too? – and in the cosmic order?

Not merely conservation of energy, but maximal economy in use, so the only reality is the will to grow stronger of every center of force – not self-preservation, but the will to appropriate, dominate, increase, grow stronger. (KSA 13 14 [81,82] = WP 689)

In each of these passages, Nietzsche identifies assimilation, appropriation (i.e., power) as goals that are aimed at, either by sub-organismic drives or by the organisms that have those drives, or by life itself. To the extent that the activity of aiming cannot occur without mentally entertaining a goal, to that extent does Nietzsche commit himself to a problematic kind of goal.

However, such passages co-exist with others that are more skeptical about mentally entertained goals being constitutive elements of the natural world. In these passages, he is clearly aware that pan-psychist temptations have to be avoided. The following passage reveals a deep ambivalence about any explanation of organic phenomena that relies on psychological principles:

Neither of the two explanations of organic life have yet succeeded, neither that from mechanism, *nor that from the mind* [*Geiste*]. I emphasize the *latter*. The mind is more superficial than you think. The governance of the organism occurs in such a way that the mechanical *as well as* the mental world can be invoked only *symbolically* as an explanation. (KSA 11 26[68])

On the one hand, Nietzsche acknowledges here that he emphasizes explanations of organic life that rely on mental concepts over those that rely on mechanical concepts. But he immediately qualifies his endorsement of mental explanations by allowing that the mind is superficial and that both mechanical and mental explanations are merely 'symbolic,' by which he means (as suggested in Chapter 1) that they are translational interpretations. This kind of passage makes it clear that Nietzsche is struggling to find an explanation-type that avoids the pitfalls of both mechanism and panpsychist vitalism. He appears to be uncertain about what the conceptual framework needed to achieve his desire looks like.

The root of Nietzsche's suspicions about teleological principles is that they presuppose ends or purposes, and he thinks ends and purposes are irrelevant. *Gay Science* 109, for example, bluntly rejects the existence of all purposes in nature, and *Twilight of the Idols*, 'Four Great Errors,' states that thinking there are purposes in nature is our invention (see also KSA 11 34[55]; KSA 12 10[137] = WP 707; KSA 13 11[72] = WP 708). A *Nachlass* passage describes the disenchantment of nature that follows once we recognize that 'purposiveness in the work of nature can be explained without the assumption of an ego that posits purposes' (KSA 10 24[16] = WP 676). He expands elsewhere:

> one must understand that an action is never caused by a purpose; that purpose and means are interpretations whereby certain points in an event are emphasized and selected at the expense of other points, which, indeed, form the majority; that every single time something is done with a purpose in view, something fundamentally different and other occurs; that every purposive action is like the supposed purposiveness of the heat the sun gives off: the enormously greater part is squandered; a part hardly worth considering serves a "purpose," has "meaning". (KSA 12 7[1] = WP 666)

He even goes so far as to deny that purposes play any role in explanations of not only non-human action, but also of human action:

> why could a "purpose" not be an epiphenomenon in the series of changes in the activating forces that bring about the purposive action – a pale image sketched in consciousness beforehand that serves to orient us concerning events, even as a symptom of events, not as their cause? – But with this we have criticized the will itself: is it not an illusion to take for a cause that which rises to consciousness as an act of will? Are not all phenomena of consciousness merely terminal phenomena, final links in a chain, but apparently conditioning one another in their succession on one level of consciousness? (KSA 12 7[1] = WP 666)

Such thoughts are not isolated. And, as discussed in Chapter 6, the argument broached here is one of the foundations for Nietzsche's criticism of the will.

Nietzsche's hostility towards purposes sits uncomfortably with the doctrine of the will to power. Indeed, his ambivalence is so severe that in some passages he affirms both that the will to power exists and that the will is altogether unneeded. For example, in a *Nachlass* note, he affirms both that the way that we process the raw material of sensation into conscious perception is guided by a 'will to overpower, assimilate, consume' and that the will is a 'superfluous assumption' (KSA 11 34[55]). In such passages, Nietzsche appears both to affirm that willing, striving, and aiming towards some purpose is the foundation of all species of causation and that all striving and aiming towards some purpose is epiphenomenal, that is, caused but without causal consequence. Yet, if the former, then every instance of striving is an instance of causation, and if the latter, then no instance of striving is an instance of causation. It is hard to imagine a more manifest pair of contraries.

III Embodiment, embeddedness, and naturalizing teleology

At this juncture, a naturalized analysis of ends/goals may be offered to help ease Nietzsche out of the tangle he is caught up in.[7] The first step in this analysis is to replace the consciousness-inducing 'end,' 'purpose,' and 'goal' with 'function.' So, for example, instead of saying that the goal of the processes that circuit through the kidney is to clean the blood, the recommendation would be to say instead that the function of the processes that circuit through the kidney is to clean the blood. Replacing 'end' or 'goal' with 'function' neatly scrubs teleological explanations of intentionalist elements, and once the recommendation is implemented, having a mental representation of a goal towards which an organism aims its behavior is no longer a required element of a teleological explanation. In fact, teleological explanations in biology can be reconfigured wholesale as functional explanations. In general, then, biological explanations become functional explanations, where a functional explanation of some property F is one that explains an organism's O having F as O's tendency or disposition to acquire or produce F because F enhances O's fitness and has been selected for in the past.[8] So, take a particular organism O (say a person), and a particular property F (say the property of having a kidney): we may say that a person's having a kidney is explained as a disposition to acquire a kidney because having a kidney enhances that person's fitness and has been selected for in the past. Similarly, the kidney's function of being part of blood cleaning system is explained as its disposition to acquire blood cleaning as one of the results of its processing, and that particular result enhancing the fitness of an organism with it, and that fitness being selected for.

In a little greater detail: of all of the causal results that ancestral kidneys may have produced, only some became sedimented in the lineage of organisms with kidneys: those that enhanced the organism's fitness. It is only because a system of blood cleaning that contained kidneys allowed the host organism to survive to reproductive age that kidneys survived at all, and the features of kidneys that best accomplished blood cleaning became entrenched properties of kidneys because their host organism was disproportionately fit when compared to an organism with kidneys that did not accomplish blood cleaning as effectively. Thus do the apparent but superfluous design elements appear in evolutionary explanations: since we are the inheritors of a phylogenetic success story, we project onto the current function of systems and organs that they were once designed to perform that function. In a sense, of course, the appearance of design is correct: certain behaviors and processes of systems and organisms have been selected for over the course of evolutionary time by the differential reproductive rates of certain organisms over others. But in another sense, the appearance of design is illusory: those behaviors and processes are not the causal result of implementing a plan or blueprint.

For all of his disapproving bluster against Darwin, Nietzsche saw clearly, and appreciated, that evolutionary explanations have a corrosive effect on the pretensions to design that philosophers in particular are disposed to discover. If true, evolutionary explanations warrant replacing all explanations that refer to goals, ends, and purposes with explanations that refer only to the deflationary processes of organismic reproductive success, some of which organisms have certain properties and some of which lack them. Of course, these phenotypic explanations must in turn be explained as the result of some genotypic processes that have cross-generational inheritance as a result. On this score, Nietzsche, with rare exceptions, concurs entirely with evolutionary theory, even if his concurrence is supplemented by what appears to be an unfortunate Lamarckism. He repeatedly utilizes evolutionary thinking and a version of the distinctions just introduced in his debunking arguments against philosophers' inflationary analyses of natural and psychological phenomena. It is hard to overstate just how pervasive evolutionary argument types are in his mature work (Kaufmann 1978, Schacht 1983, and Smith 1986 all grasp their importance). Take some phenomenon of interest to philosophers – the nature of thought, logic, knowledge, truth, or mathematics, the activities of perception, categorization or conceptualization, the metaphysical categories of modality, substance, the ego, the real world, identity, or causation, the feelings of pleasure and pain, the nature of morality and moral psychology, and of religion and religious psychology – and one can find in Nietzsche's mature work arguments that berate others for thinking that they must be understood as the result of unique and noble human faculties, or as presupposing unique and mysterious domains, or as entailing unique and transcendental causal processes. In their place, Nietzsche offers one deflationary and vaguely evolutionary explanation after another, all of them focusing on our mistaken commitment to understanding these phenomena in philosophical terms and all of them re-directing our attention to the role these commitments play in preserving individuals and the species *Homo sapiens*.

A sampling of passages suffices to illustrate how fond Nietzsche is of this argument type. Here's what he says, for example, about *perception*: 'All our organs of knowledge and our senses are developed only with regard to conditions of preservation and growth' (KSA 12 9[38] = WP 507). Likewise: 'the sum of perceptions the becoming-conscious of which was useful and essential to us and to the entire organic process – therefore not all perceptions in general (e.g., not the electric); this means: we have senses for only a selection of perceptions – those with which we have to concern ourselves in order to preserve ourselves' (KSA 12 2[95] = WP 505). Again, he famously claims that *truth* is a kind of existence condition: 'Truth is the kind of error without which a certain species of life could not live. The value for life is ultimately decisive' (KSA 11 34[253] = WP 493). Concerning *knowledge*, he is equally deflationary. Perhaps the most infamous passage is this one, from *Beyond Good and Evil*:

> The falseness of a judgment is for us not necessarily an objection to a judgment; in this respect our new language may sound strangest. The question is to what extent it is life-promoting, life-preserving, species-preserving, perhaps even species-cultivating. And we are fundamentally inclined to claim that the falsest judgments (which include the synthetic judgments a priori) are the most indispensable for us; that without accepting the fictions of logic, without measuring reality against the purely invented world of the unconditional and self-identical, without a constant falsification of the world by means of numbers, man could not live – that renouncing false judgments would mean renouncing life and a denial of life. To recognize untruth as a condition of life – that certainly means resisting accustomed value feelings in a dangerous way; and a philosophy that risks

this would by that token alone place itself beyond good and evil. (BGE 4)

Again:

> Of the multifariousness of knowledge. To trace one's own relation-ship to many other things (or the relationship of kind) – how should that be "knowledge" of other things! The way of knowing and of knowledge is itself already part of the conditions of existence; so that the conclusion that there could be no other kind of intellect (for us) than that which preserves us is precipitate: this actual condition of existence is perhaps only accidental and perhaps in no way necessary. Our apparatus for acquiring knowledge is not designed for "knowl-edge". (KSA 11 26[127] = WP 496; see also KSA 11 36[19] = WP 494)

Rather, the human knowledge apparatus 'is to be regarded in a strict and narrow anthropocentric and biological sense. ... The utility of preserva-tion ... stands as the motive behind the development of the organs of knowledge' (KSA 13 14[122] = WP 480). Even our most abstract accom-plishments, such as *logic*, the *law of identity*, and the *law of non-contradic-tion* are brought under the evolutionary umbrella:

> *Origin of the logical.*– How did logic come into existence in man's head? Certainly out of illogic, whose realm originally must have been immense. Innumerable beings who made inferences in a way different from ours perished; for all that, their way might have been truer. Those, for example, who did not know how to find often enough what is "equal" as regards both nourishment and hostile animals – those, in other words, who subsumed things too slowly and cautiously – were favored with a lesser probability of survival than those who guessed immediately upon encountering similar instances that they must be equal ...

> The course of logical ideas and inferences in our brain today corre-sponds to a process and a struggle among impulses that are, taken singly, very illogical and unjust. We generally experience only the result of this struggle because this primeval mechanism now runs its course so quickly and is so well concealed. (GS 111; see also BGE 3)

Indeed, our entire *cognitive apparatus* is best explained by evolution: 'To what extent even our intellect is a consequence of conditions of exist-ence – : we would not have it if we did not need to have it, and we would not have it as it is if we did not need to have it as it is, if we could live otherwise' (KSA 11 26[137] = WP 498).[9]

If our cognitive/affective apparatus is subject to deflationist evolutionary explanations, then what historically have been taken to be fundamental metaphysical categories are subject not only to reductive evolutionary explanations but also on occasion to elimination altogether. In these cases – causality, the categories in general, logic, substance, and the real world – Nietzsche urges that their necessity for us is no guarantee of their applicability or truth and is indeed reason to think that they are fictions. For example, consider what Nietzsche has to say about *causality*: 'The most strongly believed a priori "truths" are for me – provisional assumptions; e.g., the law of causality, a very well acquired habit of belief, so much a part of us that not to believe in it would destroy the race' (KSA 11 26[12] = WP 497). Concerning Kant's *categories of pure reason* and the law of non-contradiction, he is equally dismissive: 'The categories are "truths" only in the sense that they are conditions of life for us: as Euclidean space is a conditional "truth." The subjective compulsion not to contradict here is a biological compulsion: the instinct for the utility of inferring as we do infer is part of us, we almost *are* this instinct' (KSA 13 14[152] = WP 515. Likewise, the real world is only a projected existence condition for humans: 'because we have to be stable in our beliefs if we are to prosper, we have made the "real" world a world not of change and becoming, but one of being' (KSA 12 9[38] = WP 507). The category of *substance* is similarly explained: 'In order that the concept of substance could originate – which is indispensable for logic although in the strictest sense nothing real corresponds to it – it was likewise necessary that for a long time one did not see nor perceive the changes in things...' (GS 111). The structure of the argument-type across the various instances of it is more or less the same. From a premise that *a priori* reason is a condition of existence or preservation for humans and a premise that the products of *a priori* reason are either fictitious or are unlikely to be true or cannot be assumed to be true, Nietzsche infers that products of *a priori* reason are either fictitious or are unlikely to be true or cannot be assumed to be true.

When stated thusly, Nietzsche's argument is not at all persuasive. In particular, the premise affirming that if a category is a product of *a priori* reason, then it is either fictitious, unlikely to be true, or cannot be assumed to be true stands out as gross overstatement. Even if it is allowed that a category cannot simply be assumed if it is a product of *a priori* reason, thinking that such products are either unlikely to be true or fictitious appears to be much too strong. Indeed, contrary to what

Nietzsche claims, it is every bit as plausible to argue that since preservation or existence are better served by accurate representations than by inaccurate ones, it is less likely that preservation or existence conditions are fictions than not and less likely that they are false than not. This contrary view, a kind of scientific realism, suggests that the best scientific theories are the most likely to help us survive precisely because they are true. Nietzsche mistakenly assumes that the utility of the categories of reason and of logic implies that they are fictitious frameworks or calculi that are uninstantiated and uninstantiable. There is no reason to think that this assumption is correct. At best, all that is supported is that a category's utility is no guarantee of its truth. The claims that a category's utility renders it unlikely to be true and that a category's utility renders it a fiction are both unwarranted.[10]

A similarly guarded assessment of Nietzsche's understanding of certain explanatory categories of evolutionary theory is warranted. Even if he does not use the terms 'adaptation,' 'co-opted by-product,' and 'co-opted adaptation' themselves, Nietzsche appears to recognize distinctions between them and he sometimes uses the distinctions as a wedge to pry apart the aspects of Darwin's thinking with which he agrees from those with which he disagrees. Unfortunately, Nietzsche's apparent Lamarckism undermines some of this criticism.

Phenotypic differences are observable physical differences across individuals in a species and *phenotypes* are observable physical properties of individuals. In order for phenotypic differences to be subject to evolutionary explanation, they must subject to the evolutionary processes of genetic drift, random mutation, or natural selection. Phenotypes that enhance an organism's chances of surviving to mating age are *survival phenotypes* and phenotypes that enhance an organism's chances of mating are *competitive phenotypes*. Survival and competitive phenotypes together compose the class of *adaptive phenotypes* and are selected for. Phenotypes that either inhibit an organism's chances of surviving to mating age or of mating itself are *maladaptive phenotypes* and selected against. Phenotypes that neither enhance nor inhibit survival and mating are *neutral phenotypes* and are neither selected for nor selected against.

In order for phenotypic differences to be subject to natural selection, they must have a genetic basis, for even if what natural selection acts upon is the genotype as phenotypically implemented by an organism in an environment, what is inherited from parent to offspring is a particular genetic code. But of all phenotypes, only a subset of them is genetically coded for and inheritable. Such inherited adaptive phenotypes are *adaptations*. Inherited maladaptive phenotypes are *maladaptations*, and inherited phenotypes that are neither adaptations nor maladaptations are *nonadaptations*. Human adaptations include bipedalism, opposable thumbs, noses, and skin pigmentation. Nonadaptations include wisdom teeth, male nipples, little toes, chins, navels, and baldness. Maladaptations include sleep apnea, Huntington's chorea, hemophilia, and, perhaps, color blindness.

Even if a phenotype is adaptive, directly inferring that it is an adaptation is fallacious, for evolutionary theory has nothing to say about noninheritable adaptive phenotypes. Since they are epigenetic, they are epiphenomenal from an evolutionary perspective. If one person climbs mountains and loses his life before reproducing and another climbs mountains and does not lose her life before reproducing, the first person has a maladaptive phenotype but does not for all that have a maladaptation. Similarly, it is well known that one consequence of better nutrition over the last one hundred years is that average human height has increased quite dramatically. Yet even if greater height is adaptive, it does not follow that increased height due to improved nutrition is an adaptation, for improved nutritional practices are not inherited.

Some inherited phenotypes are currently adaptive and have always served the same adaptive function. These are *fixed adaptations*. Some currently adaptive inherited phenotypes served no adaptive function at the time they emerged and were neutral by-products of another adaptation. Such phenotypes are *spandrels* or *co-opted by-products*.[11] An example of a co-opted by-product is the ability to read. It is currently adaptive, but the brain's evolutionary changes were already set when reading was invented, so whatever they were adaptive for they were not adaptive for reading. Again, some currently adaptive inherited phenotypes served a distinct adaptive function at the time they emerged and were a distinct adaptation. Such re-applied adaptations are *co-opted adaptations*. Feathers are a paradigmatic co-opted adaptation, originally an adaptation to aid thermal regulation and only later an adaptation for flying. Together, co-opted by-products and co-opted adaptations comprise the class of *exaptations*. (A third class may be mentioned. This class is inherited phenotypes that, while currently nonadaptative or maladaptative, were once adaptations. Our taste for fats and sweets is an example. When fatty and sweet food was scarce, eating sweets and fats was adaptive, but now that fatty and sweet food is plentiful, our taste for them is maladaptive.)

On occasion, Nietzsche displays an astute understanding of the difficulties attached to assigning an adaptive function to a phenotype and of the differences between fixed adaptations, co-opted by-products and co-opted adaptations. In *On the Genealogy of Morals*, essay II, section 12, for example, Nietzsche argues that the social practice of punishment has no single function and that trying to distil from its current functions some original function is plagued with indeterminacy. But, philosopher that he is, he establishes this point with a completely general argument: 'The cause of the origin of a thing and its eventual utility, its actual employment and place in a system of purposes, lie worlds apart; whatever exists, having somehow come into being, is again and again reinterpreted to new ends, taken over, transformed, and redirected by some power superior to it...' (GM II 12). Original function, if there was one, simply cannot be inferred from current function: 'However well one has understood the *utility* of a physiological organ, ... this means nothing regarding its origin.... [O]ne has always believed that to understand this demonstrable purpose, the utility of a thing... was also to understand the reason why it originated – the eye being made for seeing, the hand being made for grasping' (GM II 12). On the contrary, 'the entire history of a "thing," an organ, a custom can in this way be a continuous sign-chain of ever new interpretations and adaptations' (GM II 12).

Of course, Nietzsche thinks that evolutionary theory is incomplete because it is fundamentally reactive rather than active and emphasizes the impact of the external environment on the organism to the detrimental negligence of the organism's inner world, which is epigenetically engaged as the organism pursues its existence. Darwinian evolutionary theory 'would rather be reconciled even to the absolute fortuitousness, even the mechanistic senselessness of all events than to the theory that in all events a *will to power* is operating' (GM II 12). He calls this preference a 'democratic idiosyncrasy' and claims that it has 'taken charge of all physiology and theory of life – to the detriment of life, as goes without saying, since it has robbed it of a fundamental concept, that of *activity*' (GM II 12). Given the direction of causal influence in the view, evolutionary theory's fundamental reactivity is inevitable:

one places instead 'adaptation' in the foreground, that is to say, an activity of the second rank, a mere reactivity; indeed, life itself has been defined as a more and more efficient adaptation to external conditions (Herbert Spencer). Thus the essence of life, its *will to power*, is ignored; one overlooks the essential priority of the spontaneous, aggressive, expansive, form-giving forces that give new interpretations and directions. (GM II 12)

This passage states one of Nietzsche's central disagreements with Darwinian evolutionary theory: it makes organisms and their sub-organismic systems and processes nothing more than vehicles of 'mere reactivity' to the external environment; it thereby neglects the 'essence of life,' namely, an organism's aggressive, assimilative, and form-giving energies, which reshape the external environment as surely as it shapes them.

Nietzsche's understanding of Darwinian evolutionary theory is in many ways a caricature, and in some ways simply mistaken.[12] However, his insights that systems can have variable functions and that some adaptations are exaptations are both significant. For they suggest to him that organisms are not merely passive vehicles for reproduction of particular genetic codes, but are instead active, albeit complicated, agents in biological, social, and cultural environments. His supplement to Darwin's views – the will to power hypothesis – is, if nothing else, a recommendation that organisms and their embedding environments are causally coupled – that is, that organism and environment are causally dependent upon one another. But typically he rejects the more controversial view that organism and environment are constitutively coupled on that grounds that both organism and environment have causal powers that do not continuously vary as a function of one another. Hence, an organism's internal milieu *must* be included in any explanation of its behavior. The will to power hypothesis is for him a speculative empirical hypothesis that something is at work within an organism as it tailors itself to, and imposes itself on, its biological, social, and even cultural environments. He summarizes this point succinctly: 'life is not the adaptation of inner circumstances to outer ones, but will to power, which, working from within, incorporates and subdues more and more of that which is "outside"' (KSA 12 7[9] = WP 681).

It has sometimes been alleged that Nietzsche's hostility to Darwinian thinking cannot be disentangled from a commitment to Lamarckian modes of evolutionary explanation.[13] For our purposes, only one of the facets of Lamarck's multifaceted view is relevant. That facet is Lamarck's claim that phenotypes acquired within a generation can be bestowed upon subsequent generations. The standard example is a giraffe's long neck, which, Lamarck supposed, is initially acquired from constantly stretching to reach leaves. Having lengthened a little, that phenotype is bestowed upon offspring, which offspring repeat the process, thus lengthening giraffe necks over multiple generations. It is easy to ridicule Lamarckian inheritance because we now know that the inheritance mechanism by which evolution works is an organism's genetic code and not its epigenetically acquired, phenotypic behavior. Still, it is helpful to remember that when Nietzsche was writing, Mendel's discoveries about genetic inheritance mechanisms were almost completely unknown beyond the readers of the obscure journal in which his results were published in 1866. Although Lamarck's views were put into eclipse by *The Origin of Species*, even Darwin reserved a minor place in his evolutionary theories for inheritance of acquired adaptations (see Darwin [1859](2003), where he calls it inheritance by use and disuse).[14]

The benefits of Lamarckian inheritance for Nietzsche's views are apparent. Were Lamarck correct, then Nietzsche would have a respectable biological mechanism for will to power to exploit as its implementation mechanism. Since, if Lamarck were correct, the distinction between, on the one hand, epigenetic adaptive and exaptive phenotypes and, on the other, genetic adaptations and exaptations, would not entail the epiphenomenality of either adaptive phenotypes or exaptive phenotypes, will to power and all of its historical twists and turns could be added to evolutionary explanations as a needed supplement to Darwinian explanations, especially of the psychological milieu of individual organisms. But more is likely on Nietzsche's agenda: if Lamarck were correct, will to power could also be inserted as the needed supplement for explaining the phenotypic behavior of all of an organism's constitutive processes, tissues, and systems. Consider this passage:

> Greater complexity, sharp differentiation, the contiguity of developed organs and functions with the disappearance of the intermediate members – if that is perfection, then there is a will to power in the organic process by virtue of which dominant, shaping, commanding forces continually extend the bounds of their power and continually simplify within these bound: the imperative grows. (KSA 12 78[9] = WP 644)

Were Lamarckism true, then passages such as this one would be provided with a naturalistic realization mechanism. So, it can easily appear that Nietzsche's will to power implies the truth of Lamarckian evolution and that if the latter is mistaken, then so must the former be mistaken.

However, the explanatory purchase of will to power as a psychological category does not require that Lamarck be correct. So long as some *other* realizing or implementing mechanism can be exploited by will to power, Lamarckian mechanisms are superfluous. If so, then their non-existence need not doom will to power as an explanatory category. And this is so even if Nietzsche himself thinks that Lamarckian inheritance mechanisms are required – all that would follow from his so thinking is that he is wrong that they are required, not that they are required. Of course, it is a separate question whether Nietzsche *is* mistaken. The textual evidence is less than convincing on either side of the question. To begin with, in the works published or prepared for publication by Nietzsche, Lamarck is mentioned by name but rarely. Moreover, even the passages that look the most Lamarckian do not actually require the inheritance of acquired phenotypic behaviors. Consider one of the most obvious examples:

> A species comes to be, a type becomes fixed and strong, through the long fight with essentially constant unfavorable conditions. Conversely, we know from the experience of breeders that species accorded superabundant nourishment and quite generally extra protection and care soon tend most strongly toward variations of the type and become rich in marvels and monstrosities (including monstrous vices).

> Now look for once at an aristocratic commonwealth – say, an ancient Greek polis, or Venice – as an arrangement, whether voluntary or involuntary, for breeding: human beings are together there who are dependent on themselves and want their species to prevail, most often because they have to prevail or run the terrible risk of being exterminated. ... Manifold experience teaches them to which qualities above all they owe the fact that, despite all gods and men, they are still there, that they have always triumphed; these qualities they call virtues, these virtues alone they cultivate. They do this with hardness, indeed they want hardness; every aristocratic morality is intolerant – in the education of youth, in their arrangements for women, in their marriage customs, in the relations of old and young, in their penal laws (which take into account deviants only) – they consider intolerance itself a virtue, calling it "justice."

> In this way a type with few but very strong traits, a species of severe, warlike, prudently taciturn men, close-mouthed and closely linked (and as such possessed of the subtlest feeling for the charms and nuances of association), is fixed beyond the changing generations; the continual fight against ever constant unfavorable conditions is, as mentioned previously, the cause that fixes and hardens a type. (BGE 262)

This passage has everything someone looking for Lamarckian inheritance could hope to find: talk of acquired epigenetic phenotypic behaviors *and* talk about breeding individuals with those phenotypes. Yet it does not in the least entail Lamarckian inheritance of acquired epigenetic phenotypic behaviors. Everything said here is consistent with there being genetic inheritance of non-acquired, non-epigenetic behaviors and there being no Lamarckian inheritance of any acquired and epigenetic behaviors.[15] Certainly, breeding between particular men and particular women with particular non-acquired and non-epigenetic phenotypes will produce offspring with a greater likelihood to possess such genetically coded phenotypes. But Nietzsche recognizes that breeding particular individuals with each other to encourage increased genotypic phenotype expression will not, on its own, be successful for creating an aristocratic class: as he notes, breeding must be supplemented with particular kinds of education, particular social arrangements for relations between men and women, particular kinds of penal codes to enforce and reinforce social behavior (and one might add, any number of other epigenetic means available in a society). These are social and cultural mechanisms for the transmission of social and cultural – that is, epigenetic – phenotypes, not Lamarckian inheritance mechanisms. We therefore conclude that Nietzsche's commitment to will to power as a psychological explanatory category can be defended without commitment to Lamarckian inheritance mechanisms.

3
Perception, Perspectivism, Falsification

Nietzsche claims that all conscious experience, whether perceptual or interoceptive, affective or cognitive, is constrained by ineliminable limits imposed by the finite reach of our sensory organs and by the nature of subconscious cortical processing that precedes conscious experience. Characterizing these limits is the topic of Section I. That all conscious experience is limited suggests to him that the contents of even basic kinds of conscious experience, such as sensory perception and interoception, are perspectival. Perspectivism is not a single thesis but a set of claims, some of them having to do with causal or genetic issues, some of them having to do with justificatory issues, some of them having to do with issues surrounding truth. In Section II, we show that the causal genetic doctrine of perspectivism is grounded in, but not exhausted by, his reflections on perception and interoception. In addition to genetic perspectivism he also offers an epistemological version of perspectivism, according to which all knowledge claims, whether about basic kinds of conscious experience, reflection, or sophisticated abstract thought, are perspectival. And on the basis of these epistemological claims he argues that the philosophical ambition of achieving unbiased, objectively true beliefs is in vain. In Section III, we argue that one of his most infamous claims, viz., that all of our conscious experience is false, is not entailed by genetic perspectivism. However, even if not entailed, the falsification view is not far away from genetic perspectivism, and only two additional premises are needed to infer falsification from it.

I Perception and interoception

In order to understand Nietzsche's claims about perceptual experience, a distinction between the sensory and cortical processes that result in perceptual experience and the perceptual experience fashioned by those processes is necessary. This distinction is comfortably and typically marked in contemporary neuroscience and philosophy of perception by saying that sensory and neurophysiological processes that begin with transduction of environmental information and route through the central nervous system into cortex are not conscious and that the products of those processes are conscious. Unfortunately, 'consciousness' is one of those awful words whose reference varies across authors and whose extension therefore expands and contracts as those authors' philosophical commitments demand. Nietzsche's own use of *'Bewuttstein'* is no exception. To avoid confusion, we therefore begin by marking restrictions that will be used to help us understand what Nietzsche claims about sensory perception and interoception, both of which he considers conscious in at least one sense of the term. More complex species of consciousness are discussed in Chapter 5.

We restrict the domain of consciousness to transitive conscious psychological states as enjoyed by persons, where a *transitive conscious psychological state* is a personal or sub-personal psychological state that has some content, has some qualitative or affective character, and is widely available for subsequent reasoning, emotional response, and control of action. Views of consciousness that take it to be a free-floating supra-personal field, or the fundamental and perhaps only ontological category, or a socio-political construct, are thus excluded as too outlandish for consideration. Besides, consciousness is strange enough without considering these more esoteric claims.

Restricting consciousness to transitive consciousness prevents the present discussion from going down some dark rabbit holes. Still, an entire cluster of processes, states, and events (unless otherwise necessary, we gather all three categories together under the terminological umbrella of 'state' to avoid unnecessary prolixity) still remains. To help identify the appropriate members of this cluster, consider certain states that one might be tempted to call conscious but that really should not be so counted. For instance, no kind of consciousness is the same as *arousal*. Arousal is a neurochemical state of the central nervous system when the system is activated to a sufficiently high level that responses to stimuli occur. An individual who is not aroused is either asleep or in a stupor (a deeply unresponsive state interrupted only by applying repeated and forceful stimuli) or a coma (a deeply unresponsive state that continues uninterrupted despite repeated and forceful stimuli).[1] Nor is any kind of consciousness the same as *tonic alertness*. Tonic alertness is a higher level of neurochemical activity than arousal but a level that yet contains no specific content. Arousal and tonic alertness together underwrite the sustenance of a coherent line of conscious experience, thought or action, rather than being that line of conscious experience, thought or action itself (Filley 2001, 2002). Tonic alertness is, thus, intermediate between arousal and any form of consciousness. If a metaphor may be permitted, tonic alertness is like a television that is on and displaying a blue screen, whereas consciousness is like a television that is on and displaying a stream of images.

The most basic conscious states (at least the most basic *typical* conscious states) are those that have *content, qualitative* (or *phenomenal* or *affective*) character, and are such that their content is immediately *accessible* for subsequent reasoning, emotional response, and control of action. These three properties are properties of some psychological states and are, we shall assume, the three properties in virtue of which psychological states are conscious in the most fundamental sense.[2] We call such states *basic* conscious states. Psychological states without these three properties are not conscious in even this basic sense. The ongoing sequence of basic conscious states comprises the occurrent process of being physiologically awake, psychologically aware, and in possession of a stream of perceptual, interoceptive, cognitive and affective experiences. A simple example of a basic conscious state is listening to a Mozart piano concerto. It has content, that is, the Mozart piano concerto, and qualitative character, that is, the way that the piano sonata sounds, and it is widely accessible for subsequent response.

Psychological states that are not basically conscious are *non-conscious* states. Non-conscious states are either unconscious, subconscious, or preconscious. A psychological state is *unconscious* whenever it can be, but occurrently is not, a basic conscious state, that is, whenever it occurrently lacks content, is not widely accessible, and lacks qualitative character or affect. An example might be the dispositional belief one has that if 2 is multiplied by 1, the result is 2 – this disposition is not occurrently conscious but could become so. A psychological state is *subconscious* whenever it occurrently is not and moreover cannot be a basic conscious state. An example might be the state that a particular region of cortex is in whenever one types the letter 'x' on a keyboard – this state, no matter the circumstances, is beyond the reach of awareness. The contrast between unconscious and subconscious states is thus between psychological states that can be but don't happen to be basically conscious and those that are not, because they cannot be, basically conscious. We will also say on occasion that states are *preconscious* states whenever they are subconscious states that occur upstream in the causal order from basic conscious perception, interoception, affection, and cognition – that is, preconscious states are causally subsequent to exteroceptive or interoceptive transduction yet causally precedent to basic conscious experience. On this way of thinking of the matter, basic conscious perception, interoception, affection and cognition are causally downstream from the preconscious processes that produce them.

The distinction between exteroception, interoception, and proprioception introduced above is widespread in contemporary neuroscience and philosophy of mind. *Exteroception* is conscious perception of the extra-organismic milieu; *interoception* is conscious perception of the intra-organismic milieu; and *proprioception* is the conscious sense of one's spatio-temporal embeddedness in the extra-organismic milieu. Exteroception is thus conscious perception through the sensory modalities of tasting, touching, hearing, seeing, and smelling; interoception is conscious perception through the modalities of hunger, thirst, air hunger, micturition, pain, and so forth; and proprioception is conscious perception through one's sense of balance in space and one's feeling of temporal flow. In what follows, we will avoid using the term 'exteroception' as much as possible because it is clunky and will instead use 'sensory perception' and 'perceptual experience' and variations on them. We will also collapse the distinction between interoception and proprioception, bundling proprioceptive phenomena together with interoceptive phenomena under the term 'interoception.'

As noted, some psychological states occur downstream from transduction and upstream from basic conscious experience. These states are the states of sub-cortical and cortical processes that occur either subsequent to information transduction at the sensory organs or subsequent to being propagated within the organism and yet are still prior to basic conscious experience. Basic conscious experience (or, as we will also say, basic consciousness) is thus the terminal product of a set of preconscious processes. Of course, basic conscious states can in turn be nodes in larger networks of states, processes, and events, for basic conscious states can themselves become the target of more complex forms of psychological activity, such as reflection, monitoring, self-awareness and other higher-order states. In this chapter, the focus is on Nietzsche's claims about what happens to produce basic consciousness, that is, what he considers to be the physiology and psychology of basic consciousness. In Chapter 5, attention will turn to other kinds of conscious states, the reflective and reflexive conscious states that Nietzsche criticizes as marginal shadow entities and sometimes as entirely epiphenomenal.

Gay Science 354 provides as good a starting point as any into Nietzsche's views on sensory perception. In this passage, a form of consciousness that he labels 'animal consciousness' is identified, described, and immediately aligned with sensory perception:

> This is the essence of phenomenalism and perspectivism as *I* understand them: Owing to the nature of *animal consciousness*, the world of which we can become conscious is only a surface- and sign-world, a world that is made common and meaner; whatever becomes conscious *becomes* by the same token low, think relatively stupid, general, sign, herd signal; all becoming conscious involves a great and thorough corruption, falsification, reduction to superficialities, and generalization.

One interesting aspect of this passage is of course what is *not* discussed, *viz.*, the world outside animal consciousness. This is the world that is not a surface- and sign-world, a world that has not been made common, mean, low, stupid, and general, a world that is neither corrupted, falsified, nor reduced to superficiality. This space outside of sensory perception and interoception exercises Nietzsche's ontological curiosity frequently, especially in the *Nachlass*, but, for better or worse, this region of his thought lies beyond our scope. Our concern is instead with the dynamic relations between the extra-organismic world and the organism with perceptual and interoceptual experience and with the dynamic intra-organismic processes that result in perceptual and interoceptive experience.

As suggested, the domain of basic consciousness is a set of content-bearing, qualitatively/affectively loaded, and accessible perceptual and interoceptive states. It is not going too far out on a limb to claim that basic consciousness and animal consciousness are co-extensive, and in what follows, the two terms will be assumed to be interchangeable. When discussing this basic kind of conscious experience, Nietzsche addresses all of the following, each of which will be analyzed in due course:

1. *sensory perceptual* processes such as audition, vision, gustation, touch, and olfaction that provide information about the extra-organismic environment;
2. *interoceptive* processes such as thirst, hunger, pain, balance, air hunger (and others) that provide information about the intra-organismic environment;
3. *affective* processes such as fear, disgust, love, depression (and others) that are built up out of exteroceptive and interoceptive processes; and

4. *cognitive* processes such as attention, alertness, executive functions, reasoning, control, metacognition (and others) that operate on, organize, and direct, output from the other three kinds of process.

In this chapter, attention is directed towards sensory perceptual and interoceptive processes; in the next chapter, affects and drives are analyzed; and in subsequent chapters, cognitive processes are analyzed.

Nietzsche really does not have much to say about sensory perception that is detailed. Consistent with his general disinterest in specific findings of physiological science, his concerns with sensory perception lie less in the details of sensory physiology and more in using the embodied and embedded nature of sensory perception as a means of criticizing long-standing mistakes about perception made by philosophers. Vague as they may be, his descriptions of preconscious sensory and cortical processes are similar, at least at a general level and even in a few particular ways, to certain then-current physiological accounts.[3] As will also be argued, contemporary neuroscience of sensory perception agrees not only with his speculative explanations but also with his contention that these processes underwrite the more complex species of consciousness found in humans.

Nietzsche thinks correctly that sensory perception is crucial for, even if it does not exhaust, what is needed for understanding our kind of embodied and embedded existence: it provides information about the extra-organismic environment but does not inform us about the intra-organismic milieu (interoception does that). He therefore finds it unbelievable that philosophers from Plato to Descartes doubt sensory perception's overall reliability or disparage it in their attempts to promote the superiority of reason. He sums up the arguments of such philosophers as follows:

> These senses, *which are so immoral as well*, it is they which deceive us about the *real* world. Moral: escape from sense-deception, from becoming, from history, from falsehood – history is nothing but belief in the senses, belief in falsehood. Moral: denial of all that believes in the senses, of all the rest of mankind: all of that is mere "people". Be a philosopher, be a mummy, represent monotono-theism by a gravedigger-mimicry! (TI '"Reason" in Philosophy' 1)

Nietzsche intends to reverse the philosophers' dismissive judgments. He famously claims that the senses 'do not lie at all' (TI '"Reason" in Philosophy' 2) and that 'all credibility, all good conscience, all evidence of truth comes first from the senses' (BGE 134). In addition, he also extols particular kinds of sensory perception. For example, he thinks the nose is 'the most delicate tool we have at our command: it can detect minimal differences in movement which even the spectroscope cannot detect' (TI '"Reason" in Philosophy' 3). And when it comes to hearing, his deep reverence for the wonders of music is coupled with a deep ambivalence about spoken language, which in comparison is '...shameless; words dilute and brutalize; words depersonalize; words make the uncommon common' (KSA 12 10[60] = WP 810).

Although the senses are defended against what most philosophers have to say about them, Nietzsche is elsewhere of a notably unsettled mind about their role in our psychological and epistemological economies. For example, on occasion he warns against what he calls the 'prejudice of the senses' (KSA 12 9[73] = WP 581; see also KSA 12 9[97] = WP 516 and KSA 13 14[9] = WP 635), and he castigates the educated middle classes for 'their lack of modesty and the comfortable insolence of their eyes and hands with which they touch, lick, and finger everything' (BGE 263). Moreover, he is convinced that even if the senses don't lie, 'what we *make* of their evidence' introduces 'a lie into it' (TI '"Reason" in Philosophy' 2). Among the lies we introduce into sensory perception are those of unity, materiality, substance, and duration (TI '"Reason" in Philosophy' 2). Finally, as argued in Chapter 1, he rejects epistemological empiricism, the view that in the tradition of philosophy anyway has historically placed the greatest emphasis on the role of sensory perception in knowledge justification. Although he affirms a kind of genetic empiricism as a regulative principle about how in general we are best advised to go about acquiring reliable knowledge, he rejects empiricism as an epistemological principle about the warrant of beliefs. These nuances must be respected.

In the most general terms, Nietzsche holds that sensory perception begins with a manifold of inputs transduced at the sensory organs into a form compatible for preconscious processing, which information streams forward and culminates in conscious perceptual experience. Variants on the following are relatively easy to locate:

That which becomes conscious is involved in causal relations which are entirely withheld from us – the sequence of thoughts, feelings, ideas in consciousness does not signify that this sequence is a causal sequence; but apparently it is so, to the highest degree. Upon this *appearance* we have founded our whole idea of spirit, reason, logic, etc. (– none of these exist: they are fictitious syntheses and unities), and projected these into things and behind things! (KSA 13 11[145] = WP 524)

Here it is apparent that whatever we become even basically conscious of floats on top of a set of causal relations that are preconscious. Again:

> *Belief in the senses*. Is a fundamental fact of our intellect, which receives from the senses the raw material that it *interprets*. This way of treating the raw material offered by the senses is, considered *morally*, *not* guided by an intention to truth but as if by a will to overpower, assimilate, consume. (KSA 11 34[55])

And again:

> Without the transformation of the world into figures and rhythms there would be nothing "the same" for us, thus nothing recurrent, and thus no possibility of experiencing and appropriating, of *feeding*. In all perception, i.e, in the most original appropriation, what is essentially happening is an action, or more precisely: an imposition of shapes upon things – only the superficial talk of "impressions." In this way, man comes to know his force as a resisting and even more as a determining force – rejecting, selecting, shaping to fit, slotting into his schemata. There is something active about our taking in a stimulus in the first place and taking it on as *that particular* stimulus. It is in the nature of this activity not only to posit shapes, rhythms and successions of shapes, but also to appraise the formation it has created with an eye to incorporation or rejection. Thus arises our world, our whole world: and no supposed "true reality," no "in-themselves of things" corresponds to this whole world which we have created, belonging to us alone. Rather it is itself our only reality, and "knowledge" thus considered proves to be only a *means of feeding*. But we are beings who are difficult to feed and have everywhere enemies and, as it were, indigestibles – that is what has made human knowledge *refined*, and ultimately so proud of its refinement that it doesn't want to hear that it is not a goal but a means, or even a tool of the stomach – if not itself a kind of stomach! – . (KSA 11 38[10])

According to these passages, even perceptual experience is interpreted transduced sensory information upon which is imposed certain features. Moreover, as the latter passage in particular makes clear, sensory perception is a kind of active assimilation or incorporation of the external world. If even sensory perception is a kind of feeding, then it folds neatly into Nietzsche's general view, discussed in Chapter 2, that all physiological processes are a kind of appropriation.

Since sensory perception is a kind of appropriation, the biological and other needs of the individual help determine what is sensed, what is perceived, and how what is sensed is perceived. We call this intra-organismic activity *scaffolding*. Scaffolding is the result of preconscious cortical processing, the occurrence of which Nietzsche assumes in any number of passages, states in a few, and nowhere more directly identifies than in a *Nachlass* note from 1885: 'Sense-perception happens without our awareness: whatever we become conscious of is a perception that has already been processed' (KSA 11 34[30]). Nietzsche uses a number of verbs to describe this preconscious processing: 'falsify' and 'retouch' (BGE 230); 'process' (KSA 11 34[30]); 'interpret,' 'simplify,' and 'schematize' (KSA 13 11[113] = WP 477; KSA 11 34[55]); 'arrange' (KSA 13 11[113] = WP 477, KSA 12 9[106] = WP 569); 'assimilate' (KSA 11 40[15]); 'translate' (GS 354); 'measure' (D 117, KSA 12 5[36] = WP 563), among others. These colorful descriptions of sub- and preconscious processes are more than examples of Nietzsche's delight in provocative language. They are expressions of his view that temporally prior to the basic conscious end-products of perception, preconscious cortical processes are already injected with biological, cognitive and affective structures and organizing elements.

It may be noted, and will be assumed henceforth, that Nietzsche thinks that what is true for sensory perception is true also for interoception, namely, that, as with sensory perception of the extra-organismic world, so too experiences of our intra-organismic states and of ourselves are the result of substantial pre-conscious processes: 'the actual process of inner "perception," the causal connection between thoughts, feelings, desires, between subject and object, are absolutely hidden from us' (KSA 13 11 [113] = WP 477). When experiencing interoceptive phenomena, we are little better than 'the deaf-and-dumb, who divine the words they do not hear through movements of the lips' (KSA 13 14[144, 145] = WP 523). Since we lack 'any sensitive organs for this inner world,' we take 'a thousand-fold complexity as a unity' and 'we introduce causation where any reason for motion and change remains invisible to us' (KSA 13 14[144, 145] = WP 523). But thinking that the 'sequence of thoughts and feelings' provided by basic conscious interoceptive experience maps to what is going on preconsciously is 'completely unbelievable' (KSA 13 14[144, 145] = WP 523).

Passages such as these make it clear that Nietzsche is convinced that no less than with perceptual experience, the conscious end-products of preconscious interoceptive processes are routinely and mistakenly assumed to be simple and transparent first causes rather than nodes in larger causal networks that contain a significant amount of preconscious scaffolding. Indeed, if anything, the tendency to misidentify causal sequences is even more pronounced in the case of interoception than it is in sensory perception, for unlike sensory perception, where a long skeptical tradition uses the existence of illusions, mirages and bent sticks in the water to underscore the cognitive distance between subject and object, an equally long philosophical tradition, exemplified by Descartes, assumes that interoception and introspective reports are transparent, immediate, and certain (i.e., indubitable, infallible, and incorrigible). These matters are investigated in greater detail in Chapters 5 and 6.

Returning again to sensory perception, Nietzsche's view is that the scaffolding interposed between transduction and conscious perception is bound up with human need. At the ontogenetic level of individuals, he asserts that all of the 'sense activities that support reason' engage in 'simplification, coarsening, emphasizing, and elaborating' (KSA 12 9[144]= WP 521) and that 'everything of which we become conscious is arranged [zurechtgemacht], simplified, schematized, interpreted through and through' (KSA 13 11[113] = WP 477). The simplification, coarsening, emphasizing and elaborating are compelled by 'our needs,' which make 'our senses so precise that the "same apparent world" always reappears and has thus acquired the semblance of reality' (KSA 12 9[144] = WP 521). These individual ontogenetic needs are in turn the consequence of deep-seated phylogenetic survival conditions for the species: 'the *utility of preservation* – not some abstract-theoretical need not to be deceived – stands as the motive behind the development of the organs of knowledge – they develop in such a way that their observations suffice for our preservation' (KSA 13 14[122] = WP 480).

Here too in explaining the preconscious cortical processes that produce basic conscious experience out of the information generated by sensory transduction, Nietzsche contends that our ongoing survival and preservation provide both the boundaries and the contours of their functioning. As a consequence of this phylogenetic set of constraints on perception, states of sensory perception and interoception, that is, basic conscious states, are selective rather than catholic:

Our perceptions, as we understand them: i.e, the sum of all those perceptions the becoming-conscious of which was useful and essential and to the entire organic process – therefore not all perceptions in general (e.g., not the electric); this means: we have senses for only a selection of perceptions – those with which we have to concern ourselves in order to preserve ourselves. *Consciousness is present only to the extent that consciousness is useful.* (KSA 12 2[95] = WP 505)

Nietzsche immediately infers from the selectivity of sensory perception that it is evaluatively saturated as well:

> It cannot be doubted that *all sense perceptions are permeated with value judgments* (useful and harmful – consequently, pleasant or unpleasant). Each individual colour is also for us an expression of value (although we seldom admit it, or do so only after a protracted impression of exclusively the same colour; e.g. a prisoner in prison, or a lunatic). Thus insects also react differently to different colours: e.g., ants. (KSA 12 2[95] = WP 505)

Let us forgive the homuncularism present in this passage as a slip of the pen – it cannot really be that sensory perceptions are capable of value *judgments*.[4] What Nietzsche is after can be stated less provocatively as follows: the selectivity of sensory perception is the result of a long process of evolutionary development that favors one kind of sensory and perceptual apparatus over another. If that is his point, he is undoubtedly correct: every known species has its perceptual idiosyncrasies.

Occasionally, when Nietzsche is thinking carefully about the scaffolding provided to sensory perception by cortical processing, he introduces some additionally detailed contours to its behavior. In these passages, it is apparent that what the mind provides to sensory perception consists in what he calls 'logical' categories. (We will not quibble over his use of the term 'logical' even if it is more Kantian than correct.) For instance, he says that what feeds forward from sensory transduction is "arranged by the understanding, reduced to rough outlines, made similar, subsumed under related matters. Thus the fuzziness and chaos of sense impressions are, as it were, logicized" (KSA 12 9[106] = WP 569). In a note with the title 'On the *origin of logic*' he condenses the point: 'The fundamental inclination to posit as equal, to *see* things as equal, is modified, held in check, by consideration of usefulness and harmfulness, by consideration of success' (KSA 12 7[9] = WP 510; see also KSA 12 6[11] = WP 513). And, as with sensory perception in general, this pragmatic need is explained by our preservation: 'In the formation of reason, logic, the categories, it was *need* that was authoritative ... The categories are "truths" only in the sense that they are conditions of life for us' (KSA 13 14[152] = WP 515; see also KSA 12 6[11] = WP 513; KSA 13 14[105] = WP 514).

Above all, preconscious cortical processing regularizes, simplifies, orders, and equalizes because 'a world in a state of becoming could not, in a strict sense, be "comprehended" or "known"' (KSA 11 36[23] = WP 520; see also KSA 12 9[144] = WP 521). Such passages can easily suggest that Nietzsche's logical categories are layered over basic conscious experience as *ex post facto* veneers and could with cognitive effort be peeled off, revealing an unlogicized kind of experience. However, while categories are added after sensory transduction, they cannot be erased, for, very much like Kant, Nietzsche holds that our actual experience is imbued with them:

> Our subjective compulsion to believe in logic only reveals that, long before logic itself entered our consciousness, we did nothing but introduce its postulates into events: now we discover them in events – we can no longer do otherwise – and imagine that this compulsion guarantees something connected with "truth." It is we who created the "thing," the "identical thing," subject, attribute, activity, object, substance, form, after we had long pursued the process of making identical, coarse and simple. The world seems logical to us because we have made it logical. (KSA 12 5[22] = WP 521)

In a way that Nietzsche does not understand and cannot explain, thing-ness, subject, attribute, activity, object, substance, form, equality, and whatever else is constitutive of our kind of basic conscious experience, are unavoidable and built into human sensory perception and interoception, and so into every basic conscious state.[5] Even if we can imagine a world populated by beings whose sensory perception or basic conscious experience is stripped of the categorical scaffolding that our experience comes loaded with, we cannot ourselves occupy that world longer than the time consumed by the thought experiment: 'we cannot look around our own corner: it is a hopeless curiosity that wants to know what other kinds of intellects and perspectives there *might* be' (GS 374). Our preservation conditions as a species entail a particular kind of sensory perception infused by these categories. In a slogan, we are condemned to be logical; or, if that's too strong, we are condemned to a kind of basic conscious experience that is inherently logicized and rationalized: '*Rational thought is interpretation according to a scheme that we cannot throw off*' (KSA 12 5[22] = WP 522, Nietzsche's emphasis).

Contemporary neuroscience has confirmed many of Nietzsche's speculative hypotheses in rather striking, surprising, and impressive ways. For example, at the general levels that Nietzsche regularly flies at, his evolutionary leanings and his commitment to a dynamicist view have received confirmation from neuroscience. The work of Gerald Edelman (Edelman 2003), for instance, stands out for incorporating both evolutionary thought and dynamic systems theory in an embodied neurophysiological model of sensory perception. Edelman hypothesizes that organisms have an evolutionary advantage over others if they can integrate massive amounts of interoceptive and perceptual input with memory, affective valence, and cognitive planning to produce highly adaptive responses to complex environmental inputs. This *theory of neural group selection* or *neural Darwinism* models evolutionary neural selection both ontogenetically and phylogenetically.[6] Phylogenetically, the integrative features of the neural substrates of these integrative cognitive and affective capacities are indirectly selected, which is to say that natural selection acts on the neural assemblies from which such integration emerges but not on integration itself. Ontogenetically, neural development is characterized by the proliferation and subsequent pruning of cognitive and affective pathways according to these experiential benefits (Edelman 1987).[7] The process of proliferation and pruning allows the brain to strengthen certain synapses and weaken others without changing underlying neuroanatomy, a process constrained by, and in turn constraining, ongoing input from the affective systems of the brain.

A dynamic embedded approach to sensory perception is an obvious extension of a nonlinear dynamic physiology, and several authors have developed versions. Again, Edelman's work may be taken as representative. He argues that the neural physiology that provides the substrate of conscious experience is dynamic, non-linear, and self-organized. In fact, he has localized certain assemblies that comprise this set of processes and calls it the *dynamic core* of reentrant neural processing, a cycle of snychronized and self-organized reciprocal feed forward and feedback signaling between cortical regions, especially the massive bidirectional pathways between thalamus and prefrontal cortical areas that subserve integration of perceptual and motor pathways into subjectively unified and perspectivally organized conscious experience (Edelman & Tononi 2000).[8] He calls the resulting state *primary* consciousness. It is a qualitatively endowed, egocentrically perspectival, and widely accessible state of consciousness, and is pretty obviously equivalent to what we are calling basic consciousness. Again with Nietzsche, Edelman argues that we do not differ from other animals in having widely accessible, qualitatively rich and egocentrically perspectival experience. What distinguishes us is that, in addition to primary consciousness, we also have *higher-order* consciousness and *self*-consciousness, that is, states that take other psychological states as their content and do something further with it. Higher-order consciousness is characterized by additionally complex and recursive cognitive and affective processes such as reflective, reflexive consciousness, symbolically encoded thought, and affective regulation.[9] Likewise, our kind of subjectivity, while initially a result of reentrant processing carrying interoceptive and proprioceptive information about the body and its motor systems, is not exhausted by such phenomena. For, as Edelman notes echoing Nietzsche, our forms of self-consciousness arise with and are complicated by the emergence of language and the riot of recursive possibilities that only it opens.

At more specific levels too, neuroscience of perception and interoception has unfolded some of the details that Nietzsche knew had to be there. Although Nietzsche's use of *interpretation* and *retouching* and the other descriptions of preconscious processing that he employs are admittedly different from the language used by contemporary neuroscientists, many of the problems remain the same. Among them is what is now known as *perceptual binding, viz.*, identifying and describing the subconscious processes and pathways responsible for bringing disparate sensory input together into unified conscious perceptual experience. And, second, there is the *cognitive and affective penetrability of perception, viz.*, identifying and describing how far upstream in conscious and preconscious processing certain downstream processes can reach back to influence. The amount and depth of penetration are currently under investigation and results are to date unsettled. On some accounts, cognitive and affective penetration can have an impact only on particular kinds of reflective conscious beliefs, thus making completely uncognized sensory perception as a possibility. But on other accounts, certain downstream processes reach all the way back to basic conscious perceptual experience, ruling out any sort of uncognized sensory perception. Let us consider each issue in a little greater detail.

The functional description of many of the binding cortical processes remains incomplete (Singer 2001; Treisman 1996). Consider the spatial and temporal binding of conscious perceptual experience of the world. Neuroscience sees the job of the sensory-perceptual apparatus as reconstituting in unified and integrated conscious experience the world of unified and integrated stimulus objects. The spatio-temporal coherence of conscious perceptual experience is an accomplishment achieved by ongoing neural activity that processes input from the senses, which senses in turn process input from the stimulus object. An example makes things clear. Suppose you are cooking trout over a campfire one evening. The color, shape, size, and external texture of the fish are bound together to form an integrated visual experience. Volume and pitch bind together to form an auditory experience of the fish sizzling as it cooks. Odor intensity and character bind together to form an olfactory experience of the trout's aroma. Vision, sound, and odor in turn bind together to form the multimodal perceptual experience of seeing, hearing, and smelling the fish on the fire. Each of these accomplishments is a kind of perceptual *feature binding*, the process of the distinct sensory modalities feeding information forwards for increasingly sophisticated cortical processing. The information from each of the sensory modalities is bound together to form an integrated multimodal perceptual experience. Other binding processes in addition to feature binding also occur in sensory perception. *Part binding* is that facet of conscious experience that establishes spatial groupings and *temporal binding* establishes sequentiality. Finally, conscious experience is *subjectively bound* or unified as *my* experiences and not someone else's experiences.[10]

For the most part, neural pathways of the various binding processes follow a similar pattern across the sensory modalities: processing begins at the sensory organs with preconscious transduction of extra-organismic input into bio-electrochemical information. Most modality-specific information feeds forward through the thalamus and from the thalamus to various highly modular primary sensory cortices (temporal cortex for audition, occipital cortex for vision, insular cortex for gustation, and sensorimotor cortex for touch (olfaction is an exception; see below)). In these discrete cortical locations, *unimodal* sensory information is bound across various dimensions. From each of these dedicated sensory areas, bound unimodal information streams forward to *heteromodal* cortical regions in the prefrontal cortex. Within these heteromodal regions, the information from the separate unimodal regions is bound together to comprise a unified field of subjectively perspectival, unified, and qualitatively/affectively endowed conscious perceptual experience. But the story doesn't end there. This bound multimodal perceptual information feeds forward again to *supramodal* cortical locations, also in prefrontal cortex, and in these supramodal regions, it is further processed for cognitive processing, including meta-level processing such as self-awareness, reflection, and other higher-order forms of consciousness. The same general pattern characterizes both perceptual and interoceptive processes.

The neuroanatomical details of this story would have been news to Nietzsche, but given the way he thinks about the dynamic extra- and intra-organismic relations required for sensory perception and other kinds of basic conscious experience, his view predicts that the details are there to be discovered, so it is likely that the confirmation from neuroscience of their functioning would have been welcome news. A little amazingly, Nietzsche's recognition that olfaction is the most nuanced of senses shows just how keen his judgment is (either that or he made a really good guess about it), for it turns out that human olfactory perception is unique across the sensory modalities and unique along the parameters Nietzsche emphasizes. Almost all olfactory information projects from the olfactory bulb to the primary olfactory cortex with no thalamic interposition. Pathways from the primary olfactory region project to the associative cortex in the temporal lobe, which in turn projects to the hippocampus, a crucial area for memory implantation and consolidation. A phylogenetically young and distinct pathway, present only in primates and humans, routes from the olfactory region to the thalamus and then to particular prefrontal areas, in which secondary olfactory processing occurs. From these regions, bidirectional pathways project to other heteromodal associative areas in prefrontal and parietal cortex, hippocampus, amygdala, and other subcortical regions. Particular qualitative features of olfactory perception and affective/emotional and memory responses to odors correlate with extraordinary specificity to dedicated orbitofrontal pathways in prefrontal cortex. Odor's sensory discreteness, which Nietzsche readily acknowledges, is one reason why particular odors are so easily coded for in long-term memory and so often associated with specific memories and emotions.

Contemporary neuroscience also agrees with Nietzsche that causally upstream psychological states may be penetrated by causally downstream cognitive and affective processing. Cognitive penetration of upstream pathways has been confirmed at least for vision (see e.g., Delk & Fillenbaum 1965; Raftapoulos 2005; MacPherson 2012 is a good discussion). In these cases, feedforward and feedback loops within visual cortices are infiltrated by downstream cognitive and affective pathways feeding back into them. The interesting question for neuroscientists and philosophers of perception and mind is increasingly not whether such penetration occurs but how far back into the pre-conscious processes conscious processes can reach.[11] Here there is considerable disagreement, with some authors (Pylyshyn 1999; Raftapoulous 2009) arguing that there is a point beyond which penetration does not reach; others (MacPherson 2012) arguing that there may be no such point. Pretty clearly, identifying the point beyond which penetration is supposed (or not) to go is crucial. If the candidate stage penetrated by downstream cognitive and affective processes is a reflective *belief*, then the plausibility of its being cognitively penetrated is certain; if it is a basically conscious *perceptual experience*, the plausibility of it being penetrated is probably different, varying as a function of one's comfort level with unconceptualized perceptual experience; if the stage is a pre-conscious *cortical state* that is some node in the neural work-up of basic perceptual experience, the plausibility of cognitive penetration is probably lower; and if it is a pre-conscious and *pre-cortical* state somewhere at some node in the neural pathways streaming from sensory transduction forward to the thalamus, the plausibility of cognitive penetration is still lower.

Were Nietzsche to unequivocally identify the point to which penetration is supposed to extend, further assessment of the plausibility of these various claims would be in order. But here matters are inconclusive. Some passages suggest that he thinks it is only reflective beliefs that are penetrated by other beliefs, affects, and drives. For instance, in a *Nachlass* note from the end of 1886 entitled 'To What Extent Interpretations of the World are Symptoms of a Ruling Drive' (KSA 12 7[3] = WP 677), Nietzsche presents the hypothesis that entire sets of beliefs are a function of complex drives (he identifies the artistic drive, the scientific drive, the religious drive, and the moral drive), each with its own goals and purposes and through which every belief filters, resulting in a particular set of beliefs consistent with one drive but not the others. Such a view is hardly contentious, for it amounts to the claim that what we believe can change depending on other beliefs, on particular affects, and on particular drives.

However, some passages suggest instead that not only beliefs but also basically conscious states of perceptual experience are cognitively and affectively loaded. Recall: 'It cannot be doubted that *all sense perceptions are permeated with value judgments* (useful and harmful – consequently pleasant or unpleasant). Each individual colour is also for us an expression of value... Thus insects also react differently to different colours...' (KSA 12 2[95] = WP 505; see also KSA 12 5[36] = WP 563; KSA 12 6[14] = WP 565; KSA 12 9[38] = WP 507; KSA 12 9[144] = WP 521). Here, a more controversial claim is entertained, namely that even the most basic kinds of basic perceptual experience are infiltrated by those evaluative assessments provided by the conditions of continued survival and sedimented into the preconscious scaffolding of experience discussed above.

Two comments may be made about this suggestion. First, the transduction activity of the sensory organs is left untouched by this claim, thus making this kind of scaffolding consistent with Nietzsche's claim in *Twilight of the Idols* that 'the senses...do not lie at all' (TI '"Reason" in Philosophy' 2). Second, it is not really accurate to characterize this kind of preconscious scaffolding as a kind of penetration by conscious down-stream processes. For the scaffolding of sensory transduction information accomplished by preconscious cortical processing occurs prior to any state of perceptual experience. It is more accurate to say, as argued above, that cognitive, affective, and evaluative scaffolding is the cortical realization of genetically inherited evolutionary advantages and that every state of basic conscious perceptual experience already has built into it significant evaluative and logical scaffolding. Scaffolding has, on this view, become so sedimented over evolutionary time in the physiology of *Homo sapiens sapiens* that its penetration of sensory information feeding forward from the sense organs is constitutive of all perceptual experi-ence. This is a quite extraordinary claim, substantially more provoca-tive than most penetration claims, and it implies that our perceptual experience is causally coupled with the extra-organismic world. For the biological needs served by the dynamic processes of perceptual experi-ence *presuppose* causal intercourse with the environment in which the organism is embedded. One direct consequence is that 'the opposition of subject and object' can be left 'to the epistemologists who have become entangled in the snares of grammar' (GS 354).

Finally, one can also find occasional passages that suggest that penetra-tion extends at least into the domain of pre-conscious and pre-cortical sensory states: 'every creature different from us senses different quali-ties and consequently lives in a different world from that in which we live' (KSA 12 6[14] = WP 565). However, attributing to Nietzsche the claim that affective/cognitive penetration or scaffolding extends even to the transduction activity of different kinds of sensory organs assumes that 'senses' here refers to pre-cortical electro-chemical activity and not to basically conscious perceptual experience that eventuates from such activity. If so, then sensory organs themselves embody evolutionarily established evaluations and affects. If, on the other hand, this assump-tion is false, then this passage suggests instead the view discussed in the previous paragraph.

So, we may say that while it might be tempting to attribute to Nietzsche the view that basic kinds of conscious states such as perception and inte-roception are not perspectival even if more complex kinds of conscious states are perspectival, the arguments of this section demonstrate that this view cannot be correct. Even primary kinds of conscious experience are already scaffolded, and that this is so forms the basis of genetic and epistemological perspectivism.

II Perspectivism

The preconscious arranging, simplifying, translating, and interpreting discussed in the previous section provides the requisite groundwork for two of Nietzsche's most famous claims. The first is the *perspectivism thesis*, *viz.*, the claim that all basic conscious experiences (i.e., sensory perception, interoception, and non-reflective cognition) are indexed to spatio-temporal, affective, and evaluative loci. It is tempting to align perspectivism entirely with perceptual experience – in particular, visual experience – and, on the basis of that alignment, to make various criticisms of it. Perspectivism as interpreted here is broader in scope and entails that some of these criticisms are misplaced. The second claim is the *falsification thesis*, *viz.*, the claim that all sensory perception, interoception, and cognition falsify. Some interpreters are so horrified at the prospect that the falsification thesis might be true that they go to considerable dialectical lengths to avoid having to attribute the view to him.[12] The interpretation defended here is more sanguine: a fairly benign version of the falsification thesis is defensible and may be attributed to Nietzsche. Unfortunately, this benign version is not the version that he appears on all counts to endorse.

From *Daybreak*, published in 1881, through to *Anti-Christ*, published in 1888, Nietzsche affirms a robust form of perspectivism. Textual evidence confirms his ongoing commitment to perspectivism through at least 1887. It suffices to note *Gay Science* 374, from that year:

How far the perspective character of existence extends or indeed whether existence has any other character than this; whether existence without interpretation, without 'sense,' does not became 'nonsense'; whether, on the other hand, all existence is not essentially actively engaged in interpretation – that cannot be decided even by the most industrious and most scrupulously conscientious analysis and self-examination of the intellect; for in the course of this analysis the human intellect cannot avoid seeing itself in its own perspectives, and only in these. We cannot look around our own corner: it is a hopeless curiosity that wants to know what other kinds of intellects and perspectives there might be; for example, whether some beings might be able to experience time backward, or alternately forward and backward (which would involve another direction of life and another concept of cause and effect). But I should think that today we are at least far from the ridiculous immodesty that would be involved in decreeing from our corner that perspectives are permitted only from this corner. Rather has the world become 'infinite' for us all over again, inasmuch as we cannot reject the possibility that it may include infinite interpretations.

This passage is one of the clearest statements of perspectivism to be found in Nietzsche's entire corpus, and it is from the next to last year of his productive career. Moreover, it is far from being the only such late passage. Interested readers may confirm for themselves that he continued to rely on perspectivism until he stopped writing.[13] The conclusion must be that he remains a perspectivist until the end.

Perspectivism is the conjunction of a psychological genetic claim about how we acquire beliefs and two epistemological claims, the first about the justification of beliefs so acquired, and the second about their truth. Our interest lies primarily in the genetic claim, which amounts to the thesis that the processes of belief formation are always indexed to perceptual, interoceptive, interpretive, and evaluative loci. But let us also introduce epistemological perspectivism. Epistemological perspectivism affirms, first, that the justification of beliefs indexically formed is itself likewise indexed and, second, that the truth of indexically formed beliefs is also indexed. So, parallel to our characterization of empiricism in Chapter 1, we may say that perspectivism as a psychological thesis is *genetic perspectivism*; that perspectivism about justification is *warrant perspectivism*; and that perspectivism about truth is *alethic perspectivism*. We may also say that the conjunction of warrant perspectivism and alethic perspectivism comprise *epistemological perspectivism*.[14] In the next section, it will be shown that epistemological perspectivism plus another premise or two imply the falsification thesis. Here, consider genetic perspectivism.

Daybreak 117 is a clearly worded statement of genetic perspectivism. Even though Nietzsche does not identify the view by name, he articulates various constituent elements of perspectivism and provides brief support for them. He also draws three inferences from perspectivism thus understood: first, all pretensions to absolute or objective knowledge are mistaken; second, the "real" world is forever beyond us; and, third, everything we believe is false:

My eyes, however strong or weak they may be, can see only a certain distance, and it is within the space encompassed by this distance that I live and move, the line of this horizon constitutes my immediate fate, in great things and small, from which I cannot escape. Around every being there is described a similar concentric circle, which has a mid-point and is peculiar to him. Our ears enclose us within a comparable circle, and so does our sense of touch. Now, it is by these horizons, within which each of us encloses his senses as if behind prison walls, that we *measure* the world, we say that this is near and that far, this is big and that small, this is hard and that soft: this measuring we call sensation – and it is all of it an error! According to the average quantity of experiences and excitations possible to us at any particular point of time one measures one's life as being short or long, poor or rich, full or empty: and according to the average human life one measures that of all other creatures – all of it an error! If our eyes were a hundredfold sharper, man would appear to us tremendously tall; it is possible, indeed, to imagine organs by virtue of which he would be felt as immeasurable. On the other hand, organs could be so constituted that whole solar systems were viewed contracted and packed together like a single cell: and to beings of an opposite constitution a cell of the human body could present itself, in motion, construction and harmony, as a solar system. The habits of our senses have woven us into lies and deception of sensation: these again are the basis of all our judgments and "knowledge" – there is absolutely no escape, no backway or bypath into the *real world*! We sit within our net, we spiders, and whatever we may catch in it, we can catch nothing at all except that which allows itself to be caught in precisely *our* net.

Given that sensory perception is inherently perspectival, and given that sensory perception is a kind of basic conscious experience, it follows immediately that even basic conscious experience is already perspectival.

Despite the apparent spatio-temporal and perceptual – in particular, visual, auditory, and tactile – characterization given of perspectivism in the above passage, Nietzsche elsewhere makes it clear that the grounds of perspectivism do not lie only in sensory features of experience. First, he argues that perspectivity is characteristic not only of all forms of organic life outfitted with sensory organs, but also of all forms of organic life that do not come so equipped: 'The same equalizing and ordering force that rules in the idioplasma, rules also in the incorporation of the outer world: our sense perceptions are already the result of this assimiliation and equalization in regard to all the past in us' (KSA 12 2[92] = WP 500). Since idioplasma have perspectival experience and since they lack sensory organs, it follows directly that not all aspects of perspectivism are introduced through sensory perception.

Second, even for organic forms equipped with sensory perception, perspectivity is at least as firmly grounded on the affective and evaluative character of conscious experience as it is on the contents of sensory perception. A famous passage from *Genealogy of Morals* makes the point:

> But precisely because we seek knowledge, let us not be ungrateful to such resolute reversals of accustomed perspectives and valuations ... to *want* to see differently, is no small discipline and preparation of the intellect for its future "objectivity" – the latter understood not as 'contemplation without interest' (which is a nonsensical absurdity), but as the ability *to control* one's Pro and con and to dispose of them, so that one knows how to employ a *variety* of perspectives and affective interpretations in the service of knowledge.... There is *only* a perspective seeing, *only* a perspective "knowing"; and the *more* affects we allow to speak about one thing, the *more* eyes, different eyes, we can use to observe one thing, the more complete will our "concept" of this thing, our "objectivity," be. (GM III12)

Here, Nietzsche expands the elements of a perspective well beyond those supplied by sensory perception: he says the more *affects* we allow to speak about a thing, the more complete will our concept of a thing be. It bears emphasis that Nietzsche's use of 'affect' is incredibly broad and includes not only affective states such as emotions, moods, and drives, but also the qualitative character of sensory perception – for example, the taste of a kiss, the sound of thunder, the way granite feels, the way the ocean smells, the hue of glacial ice – and interoception – for example, the feeling of orgasm, the stabbing pangs of hunger, the headaches that accompany dehydration. He even speculates that there is a 'tiny amount of emotion to which the "word" gives rise, as we contemplate similar images for which *one* word exists' (KSA 11 25[168] = WP 506), thus extending the reach of affect and qualitative character into all linguistically structured thought. All of the various qualitative and affective characters that typical basic conscious states come loaded with thus contributes to the perspectivity of basic consciousness:

> all our sensations of value (i.e., simply our sensations) adhere precisely to qualities, i.e., to our perspective 'truths' which belong to us alone and can by no means be "known"! ... [T]o demand that our human interpretations and values should be universal and perhaps constitutive values is one of the hereditary madnesses of human pride. (KSA 12 6[14] = WP 565)

In short, then, it is the content of basic conscious experience in its various perceptual modalities, *plus* the qualitative character nature of the various kinds of conscious states, *plus* emotion, evaluation, moods, and drives all working together that provide us with the perspectives found in the most basic conscious experience. As he puts it: 'It is our needs that interpret the world; our drives and their For and Against. Every drive is a kind of lust to rule; each one has its perspective that it would like to compel all the other drives to accept as a norm' (KSA 12 7[60] = WP 481; we discuss evaluative affects again in Chapter 4).

Without these affective and qualitative aspects, perspectivism cannot really get off the ground, for it is only qualitative and affective character that contributes to basic conscious experience its interest-and evaluative-relativity. Even if Nietzsche is not particularly forthcoming about how this contribution occurs (i.e., he does not say nearly enough about the mechanisms by which they operate), it is clear, as suggested above, that he thinks that even sensory perception is imbued with evaluative content. Lacking a description of any mechanism, we may suggest on Nietzsche's behalf that the affective/qualitative character of basic conscious experience *discloses* and thus *enables* its evaluativity. That even basic conscious experience is permeated with evaluative character is, of course, a crucial element of perspectivism, and so, not surprisingly given his reliance on evolutionary thinking, he thinks that evaluative character is implied by biological need: 'The apparent world, i.e., a world viewed according to values; ordered, selected according to values, i.e., in this case according to the viewpoint of utility in regard to the preservation and enhancement of the power of a certain species of animal. The perspective therefore decides the character of the "appearance"!' (KSA 13 14[184] = WP 567). Again:

> ... the origin of our apparent "knowledge" is ... to be sought solely in older evaluations which have become so much part of us that they belong to our basic constitution. ...
>
> The world seen, felt, interpreted as thus and thus so that organic life may preserve itself in this perspective of interpretation. Man is not only a single individual but one particular line of the total living organic world. That he endures proves that a species of interpretation (even though accretions are still being added) has also endured, that the system of interpretation has not changed. "Adaptation." (KSA 12 7[2] = WP 678)

Perspectives are, thus, also evaluative interpretations, phylogenetically implanted codes or blueprints for particular kinds of appropriation and assimilation rather than others. But they are more than individual evaluative interpretations that are phylogenetically encoded. For perspectives operate not only over individuals but classes of individuals, and provide not only phylogenetically implanted codes but those inherited from social and cultural structures.

As may be gathered, Nietzsche's perspectivism is seriously at odds with any epistemological claim that stresses the role of disinterested reason in belief acquisition and knowledge justification and that hold that beliefs infused by perspectival interests are *ispo facto* degraded and cannot be knowledge. For Nietzsche, reason is never unbiased, and it is laughable to think that there are *any* instances of disinterested knowledge: 'trust in reason and its categories, in dialectic, therefore the valuation of logic, proves only their usefulness for life, proved by experience...' (KSA 12 9[38] = WP 507; see also KSA 12 9[89] = WP 517; KSA 12 9[97] = WP 516; KSA 12 9[144] = WP 521; KSA 13 14[152] = WP 515). Expecting neutral reason to generate knowledge is a 'demand that we should think of an eye that is completely unthinkable, an eye turned in no particular direction, in which the active and interpreting forces, through which alone seeing becomes seeing *something*, are supposed to be lacking' (GM III 12). On Nietzsche's perspectivist alternative, it is the activity of multiplying perceptual, cognitive, and affective responses to the world, refining them, cultivating them, comparing one to others, discarding some while highlighting others depending on context, and being able to 'control one's Pros and con' (GM III 12) that are constitutive of knowledge acquisition, for the variety of perceptual, cognitive, and affective responses to the world maps to the variety of perspectives active in belief acquisition and justification. Nietzsche condenses the argument neatly: 'In so far as the word "knowledge" has any meaning, the world is knowable; but it is *interpretable* otherwise, it has no meaning behind it, but countless meanings. – "Perspectivism."' (KSA 12 7[60] = WP 481).[15]

Genetic perspectivism is as close as Nietzsche ever gets to empiricism. However, while genetic perspectivism, like genetic empiricism, accepts that the extra-organismic world provides information to organisms, it rejects the genetic empiricist claim that the intra-organismic processes add nothing to the information transduced at the sensory organs. To the contrary, as has been argued, cortical processing adds at least the logical categories to every bit of sensory information.

III The falsification thesis

Nietzsche sometimes says that our knowledge, our beliefs, even our perceptual and interoceptive experience are false and that the world is a fiction comprised of fictitious entities standing in fictitious relations. For instance, subject, substance, and reason are fictions (KSA 12 9 89 = WP 517), as are form, species, law, idea, and purpose (KSA 12 9 144 = WP 521). So too are the axioms of logic (such as self-identity), synchronically and diachronically identical things (KSA 12 9[97] = WP 516), all of the categories and Euclidean space (KSA 13 14[152] = WP 515), the ego and subject (KSA KSA 12 2[91] = WP 518; KSA 12 7[55] = WP 519 among others), and the real and apparent world (KSA 12 9[38] = WP 507; KSA 12 2[108] = WP 616; TI 'Real World,' among others). All of these concepts are, he thinks, the result of one fundamental erroneous assumption: that there are synchronically and diachronically 'identical cases' (KSA 11 40[13] = WP 512). As he notes, 'this condition must first be treated fictitiously as fulfilled. That is: the will to logical truth can be carried through only after a fundamental *falsification* of all events is assumed' (KSA 11 40[13] = WP 512). His claims here are not that particular beliefs or particular kinds of beliefs or even that particular kinds of perceptual or interoceptive reports are false; his claim is that *all* beliefs and *all* perceptual and interoceptive reports are false as a corporate body. That he takes this claim seriously has seemed to some to be a good reason not to take him seriously as a philosopher. Even to those who do take him seriously, this facet of his thought is an irritant and a prompt for some unusual interpretations. We argue here that a version of the falsification thesis is reasonable and that its appearance to the contrary can be defused. But we also argue that this benign version of the falsification thesis is not the version to which Nietzsche appears to commit himself.

A couple of points may be made before discussing falsification in greater detail. The first is that the falsification thesis is an epistemological claim and not a genetic or psychological claim. The falsification thesis has to do not with how the contents of basic conscious experience are generated but with whether the contents so generated are true or false. As an epistemological claim, the falsification thesis is thus a development out of alethic perspectivism. Alethic perspectivism asserts that the truth or falsity of a proposition, or the truth or falsity of some content-bearing basic conscious experience, is indexed to a perspective. The falsification thesis is likewise a claim about truth: Nietzsche appears to think that the ineliminable perspectival indexicality of even basic conscious experience implies that the contents of all of our basic conscious experience – and, indeed, all of our beliefs, reflective or not, reflexive or not – are false.

Second, at least as Nietzsche thinks about these matters, the falsification thesis is true only if perspectivism is. That is just to say that if perspectivism is incorrect, then so is the falsification thesis. Since perspectivism is for Nietzsche a necessary condition for the falsification thesis, any passage that affirms the falsification thesis entails perspectivism. But the converse need not be true: it is consistent to affirm perspectivism and reject the falsification thesis. For it may be that perspectivism is in itself not sufficient for the falsification thesis and that what is in addition required to derive the falsification thesis from perspectivism is indefensible. Nietzsche himself does not take advantage of the logical gap between the two – he affirms both perspectivism and falsification and thinks that perspectivism is not only necessary but also sufficient for falsification. But he could have affirmed perspectivism and declined to affirm falsification. As now argued, had he realized that the former was not sufficient for the latter, he might have taken the time to defend the additional premise.

Genetic perspectivism is the claim that the formation of all basic conscious experience (perceptual, interoceptive, cognitive) is indexed to spatio-temporal, affective, and evaluative loci. In the previous section, we unpacked the indexicality of perceptual and interoceptive experience by noting Nietzsche's commitment to the existence of preconscious processing that scaffolds transduced sensory input into basic perceptual experience and scaffolds interoceptive information into basic interoceptive experience. Some significant amount of this preconscious scaffolding is inherited from our phylogenetic past, that is, the mechanisms by which preconscious scaffolding works are the causal results of a long evolutionary path for members of the species, and the survival benefits of particular mechanisms has yielded these rather than any others. Finally, Nietzsche hypothesizes that preconscious scaffolding works by infusing transduced sensory input and interoceptive information with what he calls 'logical' categories: synchronic and diachronic identity, thingness, the philosophical subject, the categories of attribute, activity, object, substance, form (KSA 12 5[22] = WP 521) and certain affective and evaluative dimensions. Without these categorical, affective, and evaluative dimensions, our peculiarly human kind of basic conscious experience would not be the basic conscious experience peculiar to us.

Suppose this characterization of genetic perspectivism is granted. Various epistemological assessments of the scaffolding constitutive of perspectivism may be made, and these differing assessments reveal the additional premise required to infer the falsification thesis from the genetic perspectivism thesis. Nietzsche focuses consistently on the scaffolding's phylogenetic entrenchment. That the occurrent presence of preconscious scaffolding is the result of a phylogenetic path stretching back millions of years implies the strong probability that it is generally reliable. Since individuals lacking reliable scaffolding are less likely to survive (either to reproduce or rear offspring) than those so outfitted, the relative frequency of individuals so outfitted has predictably increased over time. However, reliability is a comparative measure, and from the greater reliability of one over another it cannot be inferred that the one is true while the other is false. After all, plenty of reliable beliefs have turned out to be, or can or will turn out to be, false.

Moreover, we cannot escape our own perspective. Yet doing so is, Nietzsche thinks, required to achieve the epistemic independence necessary to say that the contents of even our basic conscious states are true or false. He states this directly in *Beyond Good and Evil*:

> The falseness of a judgment is for us not necessarily an objection to a judgment; in this respect our new language may sound strangest. The question is to what extent it is life-promoting, life-preserving, species-preserving, perhaps even species-cultivating. And we are fundamentally inclined to claim that the falsest judgments (which include the synthetic judgments a priori) are the most indispensable for us; that without accepting the fictions of logic, without measuring reality against the purely invented world of the unconditional and self-identical, without a constant falsification of the world by means of numbers, man could not live – that renouncing false judgments would mean renouncing life and a denial of life. (BGE 4)

Again:

> The most strongly believed a priori "truths" are for me – provisional assumptions; e.g., the law of causality, a very well acquired habit of belief, so much a part of us that not to believe in it would destroy the race. But are they for that reason truths? What a conclusion! As if the preservation of man were a proof of truth! (KSA 11 26[12] = WP 497)

The scaffolding that our basic conscious experience comes loaded with prevents us from satisfying one of the necessary conditions for attributing truth or falsity to the contents of basic conscious experience. If all of basic conscious experience is scaffolded by life- and species-preserving and cultivating preconscious processing, and if that scaffolding can never be detached from even the most basic conscious experiences, then it is just hubris to think that it is possible to describe a kind of experience or a world without it. But that hubris is just what is required to assert that the contents of basic conscious experience (and, as will be seen in

Chapter 5, the contents of reflective conscious experience) are true or false.

The point can again be made by focusing instead on the epistemological gap between the scaffolding's reliability and whether the contents of basic conscious experience that result when it attaches to transduced sensory and interoceptive information are true. A negative judgment here yields the assessment that they are not true. The argument for this negative conclusion is as follows. First, our basic conscious experience does not and cannot occur without preconscious scaffolding. Second, the only assessment we can make of this scaffolding is to say that it is reliable. Third, if the only assessment we can make of this scaffolding is to say that it is reliable, then we cannot know whether that reliability is a function of the way the world is or is a function of our needs. Fourth, if we cannot know whether that reliability is a function of the way the world is or is instead a function of our needs, then we cannot know that the content of any basic conscious experience is true. So, we cannot know that the content of any basic experience is true. In brief, not only *do* we not know that the content of any basic conscious experience is true, we *cannot* know that the content of any basic conscious experience is true.

The dialectic of this second, more direct, argument should be familiar from Chapter 1. However, as was noted there, a particular kind of slippage in the argument has to be guarded against, and Nietzsche, it has to be said, does not succeed in avoiding it. Even if we do not and cannot know that basic conscious experience is true, it does not follow that we do know and can know that basic conscious experience is false. Inferring the latter from the former involves the same kind of fallacy as that discussed earlier concerning our knowledge of the real world. There, it was noted that even if knowing that the real world does not exist entails not knowing that the real world exists, not knowing that the real world exists does not entail knowing that the real world does not exist. Recall:

$$K(\neg R) \to \neg K(R)$$

is true, but:

$$\neg K(R) \to K(\neg R)$$

is false. Similarly, from 'It is necessary that we know that not-*p*,' that is:

$$\Box K \neg p$$

we may infer 'It is not possible that we know that-p,' that is:

¬◊K*p*

So, the following is true:

(1) □K¬*p* → ¬◊K*p*

However, the converse is not true. That is:

(2) ¬◊K*p* → □K¬*p*

is not true. That is, even if we cannot know that-*p*, it does not follow that we must know that-not-*p*. After all, our cognitive limitations may prevent us from knowing either *p* or from knowing not-*p*, in which case '¬◊K*p*' is true and '□K¬*p*' is false.[16] And if perspectivism is correct, then (1) is what we should *expect* Nietzsche to say, for (1) amounts to no more than the acknowledgment of the ineliminable indexicality of all justification.

Nietzsche does, indeed, say things that should be expected. Consider, for example, the following *Nachlass* note:

> The intellect cannot criticize itself, simply because it cannot be compared with other species of intellect and because its capacity to know would be revealed only in the presence of "true reality," i.e., because in order to criticize the intellect we should have to be a higher being with 'absolute knowledge.' This presupposes that, distinct from every perspective kind of outlook or sensual-spiritual appropriation, something exists, an "in-itself." – But the psychological derivation of the belief in things forbids us to speak of "things-in-themselves". (KSA 12 5[11] = WP 473)

Here, Nietzsche identifies what he calls 'absolute knowledge' with a perspectiveless perspective. He then uses the impossibility of our ever occupying that perspectiveless perspective as sufficient for rejecting any criticism of our intellect. However, he also sometimes says things that are not what we might expect from perspectivism, and, worse, some of the things he says appear on all accounts to commit the just-described fallacy or some variant on it.

Given the indexicality of knowledge, it should not be a surprise that Nietzsche explicitly affirms '¬◊K*p*,' (the consequent of (1) and the antecedent of (2)). Furthermore, perspectivism is consistent with (1): *if* we must know that not-*p*, *then* we cannot know that-*p*. But perspectivism is consistent with (1) only because (1) is trivially true. Its antecedent, '□K¬*p*,' is false: if perspectivism is affirmed, then we cannot know either that-*p or* that-not-*p*. For *knowing* that-*p* or not-*p* entails that *p* is believed, is justified, and is true. But even if *p* is true, the preconscious scaffolding we come equipped with rules out occupying the perspectiveless perspective necessary to assert it. Worse, the falsification thesis requires (2), not (1), and perspectivism cannot support (2) because the preconscious scaffolding constitutive of the perspectivity of basic conscious experience entails that we admit that it is 'a hopeless curiosity that wants to know what other kinds of intellects and perspectives there might be' (GS 374). We cannot occupy any perspective other than our own, and so we cannot land in any possible world other than the one we actually occupy. Put briefly: the cognitive limitations imposed by the preconscious scaffolding of basic conscious experience (and in virtue of which (2) is false) imply that we can never access, and therefore never occupy, a perspective other than the one constituted in part by that scaffolding. But since the only perspective from which we can assess the truth or falsity of the content of basic conscious experience is an inaccessible perspective we cannot occupy, we cannot assert the truth or falsity of any content-bearing basic conscious experience.

The trials of epistemological perspectivism and the falsification thesis to the side, Nietzsche's views on the emergence of perceptual experience and interoception in humans are largely defensible and anticipate contemporary dynamic neuroscientific views of perception. In the next chapter, we turn to the category of entity that Nietzsche nominates as the primary fundamental explanatory category of psychological explanations: the drive.

4
Drive, Affect, Thought

Nietzsche's dismemberment of the philosophical subject – the self – is well known. He argues repeatedly that Descartes, Leibniz, Kant, and others use tendentious philosophical arguments to establish the existence of a bogus subject-substance that is distinct from the body and unified in virtue of being a conscious subject of thought and agent of action. Nietzsche counters that such a subject-substance does not exist and that the reasons provided by philosophers for thinking that it must exist are uniformly unsound. His alternative views about the subject emphasize its ephemerality and infiltration by the surrounding natural and social environments. On his alternative, the subject is a collection of drives organized as a dynamic system of nutrition and expansion – nutrition conceived not simply as an organic category but one that includes also culturally enriched affective dimensions and intellectual ambitions, and expansion conceived not simply as an organic category of increasing one's spread of influence in the world but as one that includes also inward-directed discipline and mastery of drives.

In this chapter, we analyze the Nietzschean category of drives. In Section I, drives are introduced as an explanatory category. Despite Nietzsche's more-than-occasional descriptions of them as homunculi, those descriptions may be submitted to deflationary analysis, the result being that drives are better understood as complex physio-psychological dispositions. But, as Section II shows, drives are structured dispositional states and contain as constituent elements certain internal, and, in some cases intrinsic, states that have affective character, representational content, and causal efficacy. Relations between Nietzsche's views and contemporary affective neuroscience and Hull's disequilibrium reduction theory of drives are introduced. In Section III, the affective and cognitive aspects of drives are discussed in greater detail.

I Drives

A lengthy rehearsal of Nietzsche's criticism of the philosophical subject is unneeded.[1] He thinks that the subject is not, as other philosophers have claimed, a conscious thing from which properties hang like ornaments from a tree.[2] Instead, the subject is a complex bundle of unconscious, subconscious and conscious sensory and interoceptive experiences, actions, drives, impulses, and what is thought, wanted, needed, and done. The subject is a multiplicity (BGE 12), or a communality (KSA 11 40[21] = WP 492), or an aristocracy (KSA 11 40[42] = WP 490), or a social structure (BGE 12) of such phenomena.

Since Nietzsche's conception of the subject is as an organized communality, we should expect that views incompatible with this conception are rejected, and indeed he urges that views of the subject that make of it an ego or an 'I' or a kind of thing are wrong. He has nothing but scorn for *that* kind of subject:

> [O]ne must also, first of all, give the finishing stroke to that ... calamitous atomism which Christianity has taught best and longest, the *soul atomism*. Let it be permitted to designate by this expression the belief which regards the soul as something indestructible, eternal, indivisible, as a monad, as an *atomon*: this belief ought to be expelled from science! (BGE 12)

> ... a thought comes when "it" wishes, and not when "I" wish, so that it is a falsification of the facts of the case to say that the subject "I" is the condition of the predicate "think." *It* thinks; but that this "it" is precisely the famous old "ego" is, to put it mildly, only a supposition, an assertion, and assuredly not an "immediate certainty." After all, one has even gone too far with this "it thinks" – even the "it" contains an *interpretation* of the process, and does not belong to the process itself. One infers here according to the grammatical habit: "Thinking is an activity; every activity requires an agent; consequently – ". (BGE 17)

While BGE 12 is not much more than a series of linked assertions, BGE 17 discusses a particular argument form that Nietzsche thinks lies at the core of rationalist arguments for the soul as a simple substance (see also KSA 12 10[158] = WP 484; KSA 12 7[63] = WP 487; KSA 12 9[98] = WP 488; KSA 11 35[35]). The argument moves from the claims that there is thinking, that thinking is an activity, and that all activities entail an agent, to the conclusion that thinking entails an agent of thought, viz., the subject. Nietzsche rejects the premise that all activities entail an agent, arguing to the contrary that the claimed entailment is instead an interpretation, informed by a grammatical habit, of the thinking process: 'I take the *I itself to be a construction of thinking*...a *regulative fiction* with the help of which a kind of constancy and thus "knowability" is inserted' (KSA 11 35[35], Nietzsche's emphasis). Since this is a claim that Nietzsche asserts a number of times, it bears some emphasis.

It might be thought that Nietzsche is simply rehearsing Humean and Kantian arguments against the claim that the subject's existence can be established with *a priori* argument. Nietzsche is, admittedly, impressed by Hume's arguments against the subject and with Kant's clever use of Hume to underwrite his own claims on behalf of the transcendental subject.[3] However, while Nietzsche concurs with Kant's criticisms in the *Critique of Pure Reason* that rationalist arguments claiming to establish the existence of a subject-substance about which we can have empirical knowledge are uniformly unsound, he rejects the way that Kant tries then to squeeze a transcendental subject out of the logical requirements for thought:

> ...formerly...one said, "I" is the condition, "think" is the predicate and the conditioned – thinking is an activity to which thought *must* supply a subject as cause. Then one tried with admirable perseverance and cunning to get out of this net – and asked whether the opposite might not be the case: "think" the condition, "I" the conditioned; "I" in that case only a synthesis which is *made* by thinking. At bottom, *Kant* wanted to prove that, starting from the subject the subject could not be proved – nor could the object: the possibility of a *merely apparent existence* of the subject, "the soul" in other words, may not always have remained strange to him – that thought which as Vedanta philosophy existed once before on this earth and exercised tremendous power. (BGE 54)

This passage summarizes Nietzsche's concurrence with Kant's criticism of Descartes and other rationalist philosophers, his admiration for Kant's own dialectical cleverness, and his eventual rejection of Kant's arguments for the philosophical subject of thought. Nietzsche concurs with Kant that it is a mistake to think we can establish the existence of the philosophical subject on the basis of the alleged necessity of an agent that causes thought; doing so would only fall into the trap that Kant sets, which demonstrates why, starting with the philosophical subject, the philosophical subject cannot be proven to exist. Likewise, and again with Kant, Nietzsche thinks that the only possible way to establish the philosophical subject's existence is by distilling it out of the synthesis of thought. But, contrary to Kant, he argues that this too must fail, for all that can be established by starting with the phenomenon of thought is the phenomenal existence of the subject, that is, the subject as presented in and by an act of thinking.

Nor is Nietzsche a skeptic about the subject. Despite passages such as *Beyond Good and Evil* 17 and *Nachlass* notes that claim that 'It is only thinking that posits the I' (KSA 111 35[35]) or that make of the subject a fiction – 'however habituated and indispensable this fiction may now be, that in no way disproves its having been invented: something can be a condition of life and *nevertheless be false*' (KSA 11 35[35]) – Nietzsche rejects skepticism about the subject. Admittedly, the argument for the conclusion that he is a skeptic is straightforward: no subject can be empirically demonstrated or transcendentally distilled from the pre-requisites of thought; unfortunately, there are no possibilities for establishing the philosophical subject other than these possibilities; therefore, there is no subject whatsoever. Such skepticism is not Nietzsche's view. As will be argued at greater length in Chapter 6, he offers an *alternative* conception of the subject. However, the conception of the subject on whose behalf he is prepared to offer a brief is so foreign to those familiar only with the kinds of subject that bounce around the halls of philosophy that it is not or cannot be acknowledged as a possibility.

The psychological states and processes held together as a group or community are, Nietzsche claims, for the most part not conscious. In conformance with our established use (see Chapter 3), this set of psychological states and processes is the set of non-conscious states and processes. As noted, many non-conscious processes and states are entirely *sub*conscious, lying entirely beneath the threshold of awareness. Other non-conscious processes and states are *un*conscious, occurrently beneath the threshold of awareness but not necessarily so, and, in fact, on occasion rising above that threshold and becoming states that are conscious. As will be seen in Chapter 5, this distinction underlies some of Nietzsche's critical analysis of other philosophers' thinking about consciousness. It suffices to note here that the realm of reflectively conscious experience and thought, which typically lies at the core of philosophical accounts of subjectivity, is pushed far away to the periphery in Nietzsche's analysis of subjectivity and that the importance of conscious products of our sensory perceptual and interoceptive processes is minimized in his account of perception and interoception. On Nietzsche's analysis, most psychological states – perceptual states, interoceptive states such as hunger, thirst, and pain, cognitive states, emotional states, and other affective states – are not reflectively conscious even if they are basically conscious:

> we could think, feel, will, and remember, and we could also "act" in every sense of that word, and yet none of all this would have to "enter our consciousness" (as one says metaphorically)...Even now, for that matter, by far the greatest portion of our life actually takes place without this mirror effect; and this is true even of our thinking, feeling, and willing life, however offensive this may sound to older philosophers. (GS 354)

Those psychological states and processes that do rise to being reflectively conscious thus comprise only a small corner of our psyche. Moreover, as will be shown in the next chapter, reflective conscious states and processes have no causal potency of their own. Instead, they float on top of a cauldron of causally efficacious and subconscious, unconscious, and basic conscious states and processes.

All of the psychological states and processes – conscious and nonconscious alike – that get bundled together to form a self are variously identified by Nietzsche as drives (*Triebe*), affects (*Affekte*), instincts (*Instinkte*), powers (*Mächte*), forces (*Kräfte*), passions (*Leidenschaften*), feelings (*Gefühlen*), desires (*Begierden*), and thoughts (*Denken*). When discussing these states and processes in the most general ways, he typically talks about drives and affects, subsuming all of the others under these two. *Beyond Good and Evil* 12, a passage already quoted and one of his most succinct criticisms of traditional philosophical views of the subject, supplies a rough outline of the view. After criticizing the subject-as-atom view common in Christianity and philosophy, he describes his alternative:

> Between ourselves, it is not at all necessary to get rid of "the soul" at the same time, and thus to renounce one of the most ancient and venerable hypotheses – as happens frequently to clumsy naturalists who can hardly touch on "the soul" without immediately losing it. But the way is open for new versions and refinements of the soul-hypothesis; and such conceptions as "mortal soul," and "soul as subjective multiplicity," and "soul as social structure of the drives and affects," want henceforth to have citizens' rights in science. When the *new* psychologist puts an end to the superstitions which have so far flourished with almost tropical luxuriance around the

idea of the soul, he practically exiles himself into a new desert; ... he condemns himself to *invention* – and – who knows? – perhaps to discovery. (BGE 12)

Nietzsche's eagerness to find a scientific home for the soul hypothesis is clear in this passage. But his kind of soul tries to avoid both the claim that it is a non-spatial atom and the equally mistaken claim (as found in clumsy naturalism) that the soul is to be eliminated altogether. His desire to find a middle ground on this matter is a barometer of his preference to rescue the soul from metaphysical excess and from those who think that human psychology is no more interesting than that of a frog (GS 3). A human psychology that recognizes the soul as a complex structure organized around drives and affects will, he hypothesizes, provide the conceptual space needed for scientific knowledge of ourselves to progress.

Of course, whatever Nietzsche's hopes for the explanatory powers of a drive-based psychology are is one thing; whether those expectations can be fulfilled is another. Determining whether his explanatory aspirations for drives match their explanatory capacities requires unpacking the most basic levels of psychological description and explanation that Nietzsche brings to bear.

Even from the *Beyond Good and Evil* passage quoted above, it is apparent that he places a significant burden on drives and affects. The kind *drive* is one of Nietzsche's favorite explanatory categories, appearing repeatedly throughout his career, from the *Birth of Tragedy* to *Twilight of the Idols*. Astonishingly, he never tells his readers what he thinks drives or affects actually *are*, preferring instead to assume, as he so often does, the categories as primitives so that he can then deploy them in his various projects. In part, his reticence results from circumspection. He acknowledges in a note from 1876 that 'the word drive is a convenience to be used wherever regular effects in organisms are not reducible to chemical and mechanical laws' (KSA 8 23[9]). So, at a minimum, drives are dispositions to produce regular effects when those regular effects are not reducible to either chemical or mechanical law. Elsewhere, Nietzsche suggests that drives and affects are dynamic rather than substantive (see KSA 13 14[79] = WP 635; KSA 13 14[86] = WP 636). As a result, each drive, even if it can be specified as a drive to or for F (for variable F), is also constantly changing as a function of the coupled causal relations that it enters into with other drives and that other drives enter into with it. This kind of change introduces both *plasticity* in the satisfaction of a drive and *transformation* of one drive into another. Finally, all drives and affects, as primitive as they may be, and all concatenations of drives or affects, as complex as they may be, are loci of evaluation and interpretive perspective (KSA 13 14[86] = WP 636).

Beyond these generalities, little else is to be discovered in the published works to help us understand what drives and affects actually are. Lacking much of a Nietzschean analysis, we may either search Nietzsche's precursors for analyses of the categories of drive and affect or we may offer analyses ourselves, or we may do both. Others have traced the influence that certain of Nietzsche's precursors, including Rolph and Roux, had on his views about drives.[4] Unsurprisingly, Nietzsche's views are quite similar to what they have to say about drives and their goals and functions. During the mid-19th century, drives were frequently affiliated with instincts and contrasted with learned behaviors. However, the similarities between drives and instincts extend further than being counterpoints to learned behaviors, for the operation of drives, again like instincts, is sometimes entirely subconscious. Animals can have them but never consciously experience them interoceptively. Other drives make their presence known because their affective character is consciously experienced as an interoceptive event. For example, sexual arousal, hunger, thirst, and thermal imbalance all have interoceptively experienced qualitative/affective characters unique to them.

Given the intellectual context in which Nietzsche's employment of '*Trieb*' and '*Affekt*' arises and what he himself says about drives, we may hazard on his behalf that drives are, at a minimum, *dispositions*, where by 'disposition' is understood, as *KSA* 8 23[9] has it, a tendency to produce effects or results that cannot be reduced to chemistry or mechanics.[5] The primary benefit of identifying drives with dispositions is to immediately narrow the conceptual space for understanding drives by excluding the alternative on which drives are identified with *homunculi*, that is, little persons inside a big person who replicate the activities of the big person. Attributing to Nietzsche the claim that drives are homunculi, while justifiable given some of the things he says, is both a mistake and unneeded. The most damaging objection against explanations of psychological capacities that invoke homunculi is that they merely shift the locus of explanation from something big to something small without actually explaining anything. We do not, for example, explain our ability to campaign for election by populating our brain with a little political campaigner. For, what then about the little campaigner – does *it* have an even smaller campaigner in *its* brain? The reiteration of ever-smaller campaigning homunculi never stops except by fiat.[6] If homuncular regresses are to be avoided, they must be stopped at the first step by dissolving the reasons for inducing them, and for that, some other analysis – a dispositional analysis, for instance – is preferable.

It has to be acknowledged that Nietzsche is not always successful in avoiding descriptions of drives and affects that appear on all accounts to be homuncularist. Indeed, he sometimes seems to go out of his way to attribute properties to drives that only the most rabid homuncularist would dare support. Consider two representative passages:

> It is our needs that interpret the world; our drives and their For and Against. Every drive is a kind of lust to rule; each on has its perspective that it would like to compel all the other drives to accept as a norm. (KSA 12 7[60] = WP 481)

> Anyone who considers the basic drives of man to see to what extent they may have been at play just here as *inspiring* spirits (or demons or kobolds) will find that all of them have done philosophy at some time – and that every single one of them would like only to represent just *itself* as the ultimate purpose of existence and the legitimate master of all the other drives. For every drive wants to be master – and it attempts to philosophize in *that spirit*. (BGE 6)

As with other Nietzschean passages that appear to be a little loopy, three interpretive strategies may be adopted: first, we can try to dismiss such passages as non-representative and unfortunate slips of the pen; second, we may instead accept the view affirmed in such passages and try to defuse the criticism that is bound to follow; third, we may suggest a deflationary interpretation of such passages, one that tries to preserve whatever can be preserved without lapsing into loopiness.[7] In the case at hand, the view suggested in these two passages cannot be dismissed as a slip of the pen, for more than a dozen passages assuming the same view may be found scattered throughout Nietzsche's work. So that option is ruled out.

We might instead accept the homuncularism of these passages and try to disarm the inevitable criticism by suggesting that homuncularism is not so dotty after all. But this is bound to fail, for homuncularism really is preposterous: were it true, then *all* of the properties reasonably attributed to persons would also be reasonably attributed to sub-personal processes, states, and events. It's hard to see how such a view can fail to be a ludicrous instance of a fallacy of division. Even if a person consciously thinks, lusts to rule, and does philosophy, it doesn't follow that all or even some of his/her sub-personal processes, states, and events engage in these activities. At a minimum, *some* argument is required to establish the claims for the particular sub-personal processes.

Since defending homuncularism has to be ruled out, the only remaining options are deflationary in some way. On such alternatives, we try to preserve what might be valuable about Nietzsche's view on the condition that homuncularism does not re-enter through the back door. And here it may be allowed that a dispositional analysis of drives is more than deflationary enough to warrant rejecting homuncularism. After all, a disposition is nothing more than the whatever-it-is in or about an object or a person that satisfies a particular kind of sentence. If we like, we can describe a disposition in a completely general way as follows:

An object *x* (perhaps a person) has a disposition *D* to manifest behavior *B* when a certain causal backstory *C* is satisfied if and only if that object would manifest behavior *B* if it were the case that the causal backstory *C* is satisfied

On this understanding, dispositions go no deeper than a certain kind of conditional and its satisfaction by an object, person, or groups of such. Dispositions are, thus, plentiful and thoroughly insipid. It is impossible to object to them on any grounds other than their sheer number and banality. A loudspeaker's paper cone has the disposition to tear if and only if bass frequencies below certain frequencies were to go beyond a certain volume; a cottonwood tree has the disposition to shed its leaves if and only if night length were to be greater than X and night temperature lower than Y; I have the disposition to scream like a baby if and only if my tibia breaks clean in two. Examples can be multiplied virtually *ad infinituum*.

II The ontology and structure of drives

If Nietzschean drives were nothing more than dispositions as described above, we would be entitled to be disappointed. For without some internal, and perhaps sub-personal ingredient, drives so understood amount to an explanatory category so thin as to be of no interest to any kind of psychology other than the most astringent species of behaviorism. But behaviorism has long been known to be seriously incomplete as a psychological theory because it ignores the most important part of what psychology is supposed to be about, namely, what is going on inside us. So, if behaviorism is all that a dispositional analysis of drives can be consistent with, then the prospects for Nietzsche's drive psychology are likewise gloomy.

Might something be added to the bare-bones analysis of drives provided above to more felicitously capture what Nietzsche has in mind when making drives the building blocks of human psychology? The obvious addition is to include a property of the object or person that plays a role in satisfying the dispositional sentence. In many standard analyses of dispositions, the property added is an intrinsic property (Lewis 1983). The result is the following:

> An object x (perhaps a person) has a disposition D to manifest behavior B when a certain causal backstory C is satisfied if and only if x has an intrinsic property P such that, if it were the case that C, and if x were to retain P for a sufficient time, then C and P would jointly cause x to B.

An *intrinsic property* is a property that a thing has always and only in virtue of the way it is itself and not at all or ever in virtue of the way other things are – in other words, an internal and essential property. An example of an intrinsic property is shape. The contrasting type is an *extrinsic property*, that is, a property that a thing has always and at least in some part in virtue of the way other things are – in other words, a relational and non-essential property. An example of an extrinsic property is being someone's uncle.

On this way of thinking about them, drives are a kind of complex, a concatenation of certain causal conditions, an intrinsic property or state, and some resulting manifested effect. Is this Nietzsche's view? The unsatisfying answer is that he cannot make up his mind. In some passages, versions of this view appear to be precisely what he proposes, while in others he commits himself to views that are incompatible with the proposal. Consider the former. Nietzsche repeatedly writes about drives and passions in ways that appear at least to make them sub-personal and internal processes and states. For instance, every one of his genealogical investigations into the bad conscience, guilt, decadence, *ressentiment*, and melancholy presupposes that at least some drives and affects are, at a minimum, internal sub-personal states, if not also essential sub-personal states. *Genealogy of Morals* III 15 is a concise expression of this view as it applies to *ressentiment*:

> For every sufferer instinctively seeks a cause for his suffering; more exactly and agent; still more specifically, a *guilty* agent who is susceptible to suffering – in short, some living thing upon which he can, on some pretext or other, vent his affects, actually or in effigy: for the venting of his affects represents the greatest attempt on the part of the suffering to win relief, *anaesthesia* – the narcotic he cannot help

desiring to deaden the pain of any kind. This alone, I surmise, constitutes the actual physiological cause of *ressentiment*, vengefulness, and the like: a desire to *deaden pain by means of affects*.

Nietzsche paints a quite specific picture of drives and affects here. Among other things, he claims that (i) suffering is an internal and sub-personal property of the sufferer; (ii) suffering has the affective character of *ressentiment* and vengefulness; (iii) *ressentiment* and vengefulness have physiological causes; (iv) the *ressentiment* and vengefulness caused by suffering's can be deadened by venting; and (v) venting can be accomplished (or at least attempted) by displacing the pain and anger caused by suffering onto another person who is believed to be guilty for one's suffering.

The description of *ressentiment* presented in *Genealogy of Morals* III 15 contains numerous features typical of Nietzschean psychological hypotheses and explanations. As such, its commitment to drives and affects is symptomatic of his willingness to talk about internal sub-personal processes, states, and events that are causally efficacious. At least on occasion, he also suggests views that come close to affirming that some drives are comprised in part of an essential internal process, that is, an intrinsic process. Here again, for example, is *Beyond Good and Evil* 6:

> Anyone who considers the basic drives of man to see to what extent they may have been at play just here as *inspiring* spirits (or demons or kobolds) will find that all of them have done philosophy at some time – and that every single one of them would like only too well to represent just *itself* as the ultimate purpose of existence and the legitimate *master* of all the other drives.

Claiming that basic drives can do philosophy or be a master is not only outrageously homuncularist, but it also appears to presuppose that some drives are basic and characterize all humans. To the extent that such drives characterize all humans, to that extent do they begin to look essential to being a human.

For that matter, consider again *Beyond Good and Evil* 36. After announcing his methodological recommendation that we assume that 'nothing else were "given" as real except our world of desires and passions,' he adds that some desires and passions are more basic than others and that one, the will to power, is the most basic of all:

> Suppose, finally, we succeeded in explaining our entire instinctive life as the development and ramification of *one* basic form of the

will – namely, of the will to power, as *my* proposition has it; suppose all organic functions could be traced back to this will to power and one could also find in it the solution of the problem of procreation and nourishment – it is *one* problem – then one would have gained the right to determine *all* efficient force univocally as – *will to power.* The world viewed from the inside, the world defined and determined according to its "intelligible character" – it would be "will to power" and nothing else.

In this passage (and others – cf. KSA 11 36[31] = WP 619; KSA 13 14[79] = WP 635), Nietzsche's view is that at least some drives are internal, that some of these internal drives are more basic than others, and that at least one of these drives – the will to power – is not only internal but also essential to any entity. But the conjunction of being both internal and essential makes at least that drive intrinsic to whatever hosts it.

On the other hand, Nietzsche also writes as if there can be no internal processes or states of any kind, whether essential or not, and at still other times he writes as if there can be no essential processes or states of any kind, whether internal or not. Since intrinsic processes and states are both internal and essential, it would seem that if either they are not internal or they are not essential, then drives cannot be intrinsic. In a *Nachlass* note, for instance, he asks whether thinking that 'things possess a constitution in themselves quite apart from interpretation and subjectivity' is not an 'idle hypothesis' (KSA 12 9[40] = WP 560). Another note likewise suggests that there are no internal processes or states of any kind:

> [t]he world...is essentially a world of relationships; under certain conditions it has a differing aspect from every point; its being is essentially different from every point; it presses upon ever point, every point resists it – and the sum of these is in very case quite incongruent. (KSA 13 14[93] = WP 568)

If the view suggested here is correct, then all monadic properties are instead dyadic relations. But then, if there can be no monadic properties, there can be no internal properties of *any* kind, even if, as he allows here, the nature of the world is essentially relational. And if there can be no internal properties of any kind, then drives cannot be internal processes or states either. Hence, even if there are essential relations and drives are members of that set, drives cannot be intrinsic processes or states. Similarly, Nietzsche affirms on occasion that there are no

essential properties of any kind. For example, a *Nachlass* note has it that
'"Essence," the "essential nature," is something perspective and already
presupposes a multiplicity. At the bottom of it there always lies "What
is that for *me?*" (for us, for all that lives, etc.)' (KSA 12 2[149] = WP 556).
Again:

> It is *not* the case that the world is thus and thus, and living beings
> see it as it appears to them. Instead: the world consists of such
> living beings, and for each of them there is a particular little angle
> from which it measures, notices, see and does not see. There is *no*
> "essence".... (KSA 12 7[1] = WP 472)

These passages are consistent with the existence of monadic internal
properties but inconsistent with any of those internal properties being
essential. Hence, again, drives cannot be intrinsic processes or states.

Nietzsche's equivocation on these issues is instructive, for it reveals his
unsettled mind. And he is right to be uncertain about these matters, for
even if some drives and affects are internal, sub-personal, and causally
efficacious, that they are does not entail that they are *essential* to the
person who has them, and even if some drives are essential to the person
who has them, that they are does not entail that they are *internal* to the
person who has them. Some drives and affects may instead be internal
and inessential, and others may be processes that a person has at least
partially in virtue of the way other things or persons are even if they are
essential to the person with them.

Rejecting all monadic properties and making of them dyadic relations
is not representative of many of Nietzsche's claims about drives; it is
typically only when he is in a destructive metaphysical mood that he
suggests that all properties are instead relations. However, when it comes
to drives and affects, he rarely wavers from the view that they are sub-
personal internal processes and states. So, if a choice is forced between
abandoning a drive's internality and abandoning a drive's essentiality,
the weight of textual evidence suggests preserving the internality of a
drive as against the essentiality of a drive. Happily, that forced choice
can be avoided, for the *causal history* or *formation* of drives is one thing,
and the *causal consequences* of drives thus formed is another. Nietzsche
may endorse a dynamic analysis of the formation of internal processes
(and perforce of drives) without abandoning his commitment to the
place of drives and affects in our psychological economy as causally efficacious internal processes and states. Indeed, a dynamicist account is
well suited to what Nietzsche has in mind, for on such an account of

drive formation, the causal coupling of an organism with its larger environment may be accounted for without abandoning that organism's own internal milieu or the causal roles that its drives play in its interaction with that larger environment.

The resulting logical space opened up by adopting an embodied, embedded dynamicist view of drive formation allows Nietzsche to affirm that all organic processes are formed only in a larger environment in which the organism is embedded and with which the organism is causally coupled, and that the larger environment provides certain enabling conditions and constraints on their formation. But drives and affects, even if causally coupled with the larger environment, are not constitutively coupled with it. For the drives and the extra-organismic environment are decomposable: the drive/environment system is composed of constituent elements whose causal powers are not a mapping from a drive to the larger environment in which it is embedded such that every element of the drive maps only to one element of the larger environment. And the reason that drives are decomposable is that, once formed, they re-orient the organism's responses to the environment and their activity opens up new possibilities for it. Were this not so, that is, were drives constitutively coupled, then the organism's drives would be so sensitive to the larger environment that any alteration to the latter would entail an alteration to the former. And that is inconsistent with Nietzsche's claim that 'the influence of "external circumstances" is overestimated by Darwin to a ridiculous extent' (KSA 12 7 [25] = WP 647) and his belief that what is crucial is what the organism's own idiosyncratic perspectivity contributes.

The same point may be defended by noting that although the formation of an organism's drives is not possible without extra-organismic circumstances being as they are, extra-organismic circumstances neither completely determine nor become a constitutive element of what an organism does with the drives thus formed. That is, an organism is causally coupled with the external circumstances necessary for the formation of its drives, but those external circumstances never provide a sufficient condition for explaining what the organism thus equipped does with those drives. For, as he notes it: 'the essential thing in life processes is precisely the tremendous shaping, form-creating force working from within' (KSA 12 7 [25] = WP 647). In brief, 'external circumstances' are causally coupled with and necessary for the formation of our drives, but those drives' 'form-creating forces working from within' are likewise causally coupled with and necessary for the organism to survive in a larger environment. Where those form-creating forces are a good fit in the larger environment, the organism can flourish, and where those form-creating forces change the larger environment, the organism can transform both itself and the larger environment. In that way, external circumstances and internal form-creating forces are not only consistent with one another; they mutually imply one another. Expanding on these claims is reserved for Chapter 6.

The creeping essentialism sometimes thought to be lurking in Nietzsche's psychological views is thus revealed to be not as serious a threat as has been thought.[8] The issue can be stated as follows: either Nietzsche is an essentialist about all human drives and affects, about some human drives and affects, or about no human drives or affects. If the first, then he is committed to the existence of a set of drives and affects that all humans have simply in virtue of being human, and no drives or affects are excluded from this set; if the second, then he is committed to the existence of a set of drives that all humans have simply in virtue of being human, and to the existence of other sets of drives and affects that some humans have while others do not; and if the third, then he is committed to there being no set of drives and affects that all humans have simply in virtue of being human.

On a charitable interpretation, affirming that there are essential drives and affects is not particularly problematic so long as the set of them is kept restricted in number and narrowly circumscribed. Perhaps the only essential drives and affects are those we inherit as a result of our biological constitution. To make such an interpretation a plausible interpretation of Nietzsche, it must be noted that whatever our biological inheritance might be, it cannot exclude those 'form-creating forces' that Nietzsche thinks other biologists, such as Darwin, ignore. On such an interpretation, passages that claim that 'a living thing wants above all to *discharge* its force' (KSA 12 2[63] = WP 650), or that self-preservation mistakenly describes 'the most basic and primeval activities of protoplasm' (KSA 13 11[121] = WP 651), or that 'the essential thing in life processes is precisely the tremendous shaping, form-creating force working from within' (KSA 12 7[25] = WP 647), or that 'all organic functions could be traced back to this will to power' (BGE 36) may be cited in support of ascribing to Nietzsche a view that is not openly hostile to some drives and affects being essential.

Even if some drives and affects are essential, it hardly follows that all are. Beyond the drives and affects that biology might bestow upon us – for nourishment and fluids, for shelter, for sex, and for shelter, and whatever else the best science suggests – there may well be other drives that are not, strictly speaking, essential. However, while not essential, these other drives and affects may yet be conditionally essential, for there may well be drives and affects without which particular psychological types would not be the types they are. Even if those particular psychological types are not essential to being human, nothing prevents us from saying that there are essential drives and affects for those particular psychological types. This sort of view comports well with Nietzsche's fondness for typing humans as healthy or unhealthy, life-affirming or decadent, flourishing or resentful (Leiter 2002 discusses typecasting humans in greater detail).

While such an interpretation fits most of Nietzsche's claims better than any other interpretation, it does not fit them all. And it does nothing to ease residual queasiness about essentialism. But the same typology of drive-kinds drawn above using the distinction between essential and conditionally essential properties can be drawn without appeal to essential properties of any kind, and in this way, those who are nervous about the essentialist odor that 'intrinsic' exudes may be appeased. On such an interpretation, we deny that anything – biological or otherwise – entails the existence of essential human psychological properties, processes, or states. The change required to our understanding of a disposition is simple and minimal: allow that 'intrinsic' unavoidably brings with it essentialist overtones that we hope to eschew as much as possible and add another category of property – simple internal properties – to cover the majority of cases. An *internal* property is a property that an individual thing or person has, and, hence, it is a monadic property, but it is not a monadic property that all members of a class have solely in virtue of the way they are themselves. Adding internal properties to the analysis of disposition, the relevant notion of disposition can be re-formulated:

An object x (perhaps a person) has a disposition D to manifest behavior B when a certain causal backstory C is satisfied if and only if x has an internal property P_{in} or an intrinsic property P_{is} such that, if it were the case that C, and if x were to retain P_{in} or P_{is} for a sufficient time, then C and P_{in} or C and P_{is} would jointly cause x to B.

We can then understand Nietzschean drives as follows:

A person x has a drive Dr to manifest behavior B when a certain causal backstory C is satisfied if and only if x has an internal property P_{in} or an intrinsic property P_{is} such that, if it were the case that C, and if x were to retain P_{in} or P_{is} for a sufficient time, then C and P_{in} or C and P_{is} would jointly cause x to B.

Since most drives are internal but not something had only and always in virtue of the way an individual and nothing else is, most worries about essentialism may be turned.

On this charitable and largely de-essentialized version of the dynamic embodied-embedded view, most drives are monadic properties of individuals that are causally coupled with elements of the external environment in such a way that neither their formation nor their causal consequences can be specified without embedding them in an external environment. That is, a particular drive would not be the drive it is without its dynamic causal coupling with – its embeddedness in – a larger environment. Nor would it be the drive it is without its dynamic causal coupling with – its embodiment in – the organism that hosts it. This is one of the constituent claims of the dynamic embodied-embedded view of cognition and affect, and it is Nietzsche's view of drives as well.

According to the view being developed, a drive is a disposition to behave, one of whose elements is a subpersonal and internal state. But this remains a thin description, for neither the energizing nature nor any of the incentivizing qualities usually associated with drives has yet to make an appearance. Consider that there are many dispositions that are not drives. For example, all of the physiological organs and systems in a human body enter into dispositional states and yet are not, except on an unusual extension of the term, plausibly thought of as drive. The liver's function of cleaning blood is a firmly entrenched sub-personal and internal dispositional state, but it strains credulity to call that function a drive. Two key differences between the liver's dispositional function and what most people think of when they think of drives is that the internal property that is a constituent element of a drive can be, or is often, an interoceptively experienced state that has affective character and propulsive impact. One often feels drives but one cannot feel the liver functioning properly (even if improper liver functioning, i.e., jaundice, can be felt); and when one feels a drive, one will act in certain ways to realize the drive's functions. So, adding affect to the mix, we then have:

A person x has a drive Dr to manifest behavior B when a certain causal backstory C is satisfied if and only if x has an internal property P_{in} with affect A or an intrinsic property P_{is} with affect A such that, if it were the case that C, and if x were to retain P_{in} or P_{is} for a sufficient time, then C and P_{in} or P_{is} would jointly cause x to B.

Even if the internal property's affective character is a welcome addition, one might think that this description of a drive is still not sufficient, for it appears to be lacking the incentivizing, appetitive aspect of drives. But this concern is misplaced, for the incentivizing and appetitive aspect of a drive is its proper affect and not a separable component in addition to that affect. Consciously experienced drives are experienced as *effective* because their *affective* character is that of being a stimulus, an impetus, a spur (note that this does not exhaust the role of affect in Nietzsche's analysis of drives; we discuss what else a drive's affect accomplishes and what relations drives have to affects in Section III below).

Even if Nietzsche understands the efficacy of drives, contemporary philosophy of mind and affective neuroscience have both struggled to get a handle on this unique facet. Some researchers, including Jan Panksepp, have recognized the need for empirical investigation at just this point. Panksepp, like most contemporary neuropsychologists and neurophysiologists, eschews the category of drive as being too broad and too abstract for an internal intervening variable in physio-psychological explanations (the main problem is that drives do not map comfortably with brain processes (Panksepp 2005: 168)). Still, he is acutely aware that affective character, which Nietzsche attributes to drives, needs neurophysiological explanation and that, in particular, the inquisitive, appropriative, and assimilative behavior that all animal life engages in needs explanation. He nominates complexes of neurophysiological pathways and networks, called SEEKING systems, to subserve such behaviour. On Panksepp's description, SEEKING systems are neurophysiological networks that promote 'foraging/exploration/investigation/curiousity/ interest/expectancy,' that is, systems that 'lead organisms to eagerly pursue the fruits of their environment – from nuts to knowledge...'. (Panksepp 2005: 145)

These SEEKING systems can serve as candidates for the internal properties identified above as partially constitutive of a Nietzschean drive. Consider what Panksepp says about SEEKING systems' proper functioning. They:

> lead our companion creatures to set out energetically to investigate and explore their worlds, to seek available resources and make sense of the contingencies in their environments. These same systems give us the impulse to become actively engaged with the world and to extract meaning from our various circumstances. (Panksepp 2005: 145)

Again, the set of SEEKING systems is:

an incentive system because it establishe[s] an appetitive arousal basis within animals so they can seek and eventually come to anticipate the diversity of rewards the environment has to offer ... [T]he brain's intrinsic, evolutionarily derived mechanisms add a new dimension to those inputs – namely, the incentive-directed psychobehavioural "energy" of the animal. The system sensitizes animals to respond vigorously when there are predictable rewards. (Panksepp 2005: 168)

Both passages describe phenomena that are entirely congruent with Nietzsche's claims about the causal efficacy of drives. For Nietzsche too, a drive includes as a proper part an evolutionarily derived and dynamic system of affectively loaded internal states, each of which takes up perceptually provided information about the internal and external environments and adds "new dimensions" to them.

One of the new dimensions that Panskepp's SEEKING systems and Nietzschean drives add to the information provided to them by the internal and external environments is responsive plasticity. Recall the preconscious cortical activity that scaffolds and structures pre-cortical information forwarded from the sensory organs. All of that preconscious cortical activity eventuates in organized perceptual and interoceptive experience of individuated and bound objects in an egocentrically structured spatio-temporal field of conscious experience. Similarly, Nietzschean drives scaffold and structure the information presented in perceptual and interoceptive experience by subjecting them to saliency filters (we discuss some of these saliency filters in a little greater detail in Section III). But drives do something more – the salience filters they add to the contents of basic conscious experiences reveal to the organism that, depending on which drive(s) is (are) dominant at a particular time and in a particular milieu, a variety of responses is available to any given set of environmental information. If, for example, one is ruled by the artistic drive, then the content of one's basic conscious perceptual and interoceptive experience presents an opportunity to play with forms, to take 'pleasure in change, in impressing one's soul on something foreign' (KSA 12 7[3] = WP 677). If, on the other hand, one is ruled by the scientific drive, then that same content presents an opportunity to make it 'comprehensible ... practical, useful, exploitable' (KSA 12 7[3] = WP 677). And, instead, if one is ruled by the moral drive, that same content is an opportunity to impose 'irremovability, law, classification and coordination' (KSA 12 7[3] = WP 677).

These claims are generalizable to all other drives and all other combinations of drives. And Nietzsche identifies a *lot* of different drives. A (very) incomplete list includes familiar ones such as drives for sex, nourishment, fluids, survival, preservation, and homeostatic equilibrium. But he expands on these obvious drives to include drives to doubt, to negate, to collect, and to dissolve (GS 113); to laugh, lament, and curse (GS 333); for truth (KSA 12 9[60] = WP 585, KSA 12 2[91] = WP 552, KSA 13 15[52] = WP 457); to knowledge (KSA 13 14[142] = WP 423); to worship (KSA 12 2[165] = WP 253); for curiosity, dialectical investigation, and contradiction (UM III 6); for distinction (D 113); for beauty (KSA 13 14[117] = WP 800); pride, joy, health, love of the sexes, enmity and war, beautiful gestures and manners, strong will, high spirituality, discipline, gratitude to the earth and life, beneficence, transfiguration (KSA 13 14[11] = WP 1033); compassion, anger, revenge (KSA 13 15[94] = WP 929); magnanimity, heroism (KSA 12 10[128] = WP 388); decadence (KSA 13 14[137] = WP 401); to revenge (KSA 10 24[31] = WP 255); for the herd (GS 50); for weakness (GS 347); hatred, envy, covetousness, (BGE 23); enterprising spirit, foolhardiness, vengefulness, craftiness, rapacity, lust for rule (BGE 201); sentimentality, nature-idolatry, the anti-historical, the idealistic, the unreal and the revolutionary (TI "Skirmishes" 49); to appropriate and conquer (KSA 11 36[21] = WP 655, KSA 13 14[142] = WP 423); to destroy, anarchism, and nihilism (KSA 13 14[182] = WP 864); and of course power (KSA 12 1[33] = WP 720, among others). All of these are distinct drives because their characteristic functions (their aims or overall goals) are different. Suffice it to say, then, that there is considerable responsive plasticity afforded by the huge number of different drives and that there is a virtual riot of combinatorial possibilities across the numerous drives. These become constituent elements of Nietzsche's repeated affirmations that we are fantastically complicated animals.

We may also note that the responsive plasticity afforded us in virtue of our drives' variety expands well beyond the differences across drives' characteristic functions. For example, drives differ as to their generality or specificity: gender indifferent sexual arousal (Freud's polymorphous perversity) is a much more general form of the sexual drive than that found exemplified by foot fetishists or masochists. Again, drives differ as to their strength or weakness: in one person, the drive to, say, nature-idolatry may be stronger than their drive to be revolutionary, whereas in another person the converse may be the case. That is, the nature worshipper will predictably act on his nature-idolatry more regularly than on his drive to be revolutionary and will subjugate the latter to the former, either by delaying acting on the latter in favor of the former, or by re-organizing the latter so that it can find expression by realizing the former, or by avoiding opportunities for gratifying the latter, or by imposing on himself a strict schedule for the satisfaction of the latter, or by associating the latter with a painful thought, or by squelching the latter entirely (see D 109 for more disciplining techniques; we return to these matters in Chapter 6, Section III).

Drives are plastic in yet another sense as well. They are long-standing dispositions with an internal state component that is also long-standing. That the internal state is persistent over time is evidence that the drive's characteristic function is also fairly settled, even if subject to re-combination and sometimes to transformation. As others (Katsafanas 2013; Anderson 2012) have argued, this aspect of a drive licenses a distinction between the characteristic function of a drive (its aim and characteristic activity) and the object that is the occurrent opportunity for the drive's expression. For instance, a person's drive for nourishment has that as its characteristic function. But the particular object that satisfies this drive – the apple currently in hand – is distinct from that characteristic function. The drive for nourishment expresses itself in propelling the person to locate the apple, to pick it up, and to eat it. So, on this distinction, the apple is the object and occasional goal for satisfying the drive for nourishment, but the drive does not wither as a result of having been satisfied. Nietzsche makes the point with considerably more flair in two *Nachlass* notes:

> It is *not* the satisfaction of the will that causes pleasure (I want to fight this superficial theory – the absurd psychological counterfeiting of the nearest things –), but rather the will's forward thrust and again and again becoming master over that which stands in its way. The feeling of pleasure lies precisely in the dissatisfaction of the will, in the fact that the will is never satisfied unless it has opponents and resistance. – "The happy man"; a herd ideal. (KSA 13 11[75] = WP 696)

> [T]he normal dissatisfaction of our drives, e.g. hunger, the sexual drive, the drive to motion, contains in it absolutely nothing depressing; it works rather as an agitation of the feeling of life, as every rhythm of small, painful stimuli strengthens it (whatever pessimists may say). This dissatisfaction, instead of making one disgusted with life, is the great stimulus to life. (KSA 13 11[76] = WP 697)

Nietzsche's claim here about the relation between a drive's characteristic function and the occasional object that satisfies the drive at a particular time without diminishing the drive's saliency and his recognition that it is the activity spurred on by a drive's not being satisfied (rather than the drive having been satisfied by an occasional object) that is the source of pleasure are inversions of typical folk psychologies, which claim instead that drives aim at reducing disequilibrium and that pleasure occurs only on the attainment of the occasional object.

An example of the kind of view Nietzsche rejects is the drive psychology from the 1930s and 1940s as developed by Clark Hull. Hull restricted the scope of drives to simple biological and physiological needs and proposed that drives are aimed only at re-establishing *homeostatic equilibrium* (Hull 1943). For instance, the kidney regulates salt and water balance, the pancreas regulates blood sugar, and the body in general regulates its temperature to avoid becoming too hot or too cold. All are homeostatic physiological processes that maintain a prescribed equilibrium necessary for ongoing functioning. According to Hull, a human's set of overt behaviors – which, because the view was developed in the heyday of behaviorism, is coextensive with the domain of scientific psychology – is every bit as much a self-regulatory regime as internal physiological processes are: we shiver to get warm; we blink to remove particles from our eyes; we yawn when we need oxygen; we put a rain jacket to stay dry; we move close to a fire to become warm. Hull's drive theory as a theory of psychological motivation is an attempt to explain the roles of homeostasis and disequilibrium in human behavior. A drive is a physiological state of tension or arousal caused by a biological/ physiological requirement (or a need) that is in a state of disequilibrium. For instance, hunger is a drive because it is the physiological state of tension or arousal that results when the biological need for more energy is unmet. Drives induce an unpleasant affect, a feeling of tension, which throws us into movement – motivates us – so that the biological/physiological need is fulfilled and the disequilibrium reduced. This feature made Hull's theory a disequilibrium *reduction* theory: the affective quality of a drive is sufficiently unpleasant that we do what we can to reduce its saliency.

Although numerous aspects of a disequilibrium reduction view of drives overlap with Nietzsche's speculations about drives, he flatly rejects any claim that disequilibrium reduction is the end-state of all drives. One need only consult the partial list above to see how different Nietzschean drives can be and how pinched he would have found Hull's claims. And it is precisely his recognition of that extraordinary variability that suggests to Nietzsche that even basic drives, such as hunger, are poorly described as disequilibrium reducing mechanisms. For example, he claims that hunger is 'an interpretation,' a 'specialized and later form of the drive' to assimilate and appropriate (that is, the will to power), 'an expression of a division of labor in the service of a higher drive that rules over it' (KSA 13 11[121] = WP 651). It is only complex organisms that are capable of hunger, for only in complex organisms is there a 'division of labor' in which 'the will to power has learned to take other roads to its satisfaction' (KSA 13 14[174] = WP 652). Hence, only in such complex organisms is the 'need to appropriate *reduced* to hunger, to the need to replace what has been lost' (KSA 13 14[174] = WP 652).

One other point bears mention here. Nietzsche rarely denies that drives and affects are states of individuals. He also affirms that entities other than individuals, such as groups of people and even species, can have drives, affects, and evaluative structures. 'Insight: all estimation of value involves a certain perspective: that of the *maintenance* of the individual, a community, a race, a state, a church, a faith, a culture' (KSA 11 26[119] = WP 259). Indeed, an individual is not only a bundle of drives, each drive with its own drive- perspective, it is also a complex structured bundle of those drives that has its own bundle-perspective, and it is, at the same time, a bundle that is also a member of various groups – genders, ethnicities, economic classes, political groups, religions, nationalities, and all of the other groups we use to identify ourselves – each with its own group-perspective. We mention these supra-individual perspectives to forestall any misconception that Nietzsche's account of drives as sub-personal processes and states precludes supra-personal drives. It does not. All individuals are systems of drives and affects, some sub-personal, some personal, others supra-personal.[9]

III   Affect and thought

These additionally nuanced descriptions of Nietzschean drives and the relations that obtain between them make it apparent that, at least in his hands, drives are a category of significant explanatory power. For drives provide him with an explanatory psychological category that is (a) respectably naturalist; (b) intrinsically energetic, dynamic, and propulsive; (c) sufficiently combinatorial to provide extensive explanatory scope; (d) sufficiently persistent to be considered fairly stable elements in our psychological economy; and (d) sufficiently plastic to cover a wide range of psychological phenomena, from the most basic biologically informed needs of an individual to socially and culturally imbued interests. If what has been suggested so far is reasonable, it follows that our entire psychology is comprised of nothing other than dispositional drives that have internal and intrinsic states as constituents.

But this appears on all accounts to be a ham-fisted view. Thinking about a line of logical proof is not plausibly interpreted as a drive, and nor are innumerable other similar examples. Supposing sense could be made of such a claim, there seems to be little advantage in understanding human psychology as comprised entirely of drives as, compared, say, comprised entirely of beliefs and desires or connectionist networks of neurons. Moreover, although drives describe and may even explain some facets of human psychology, many other facets appear for all intents and purposes not to require description or explanation in terms of them. It appears, then, that Nietzsche's reduction of human psychology in terms of drives both overreaches to a considerable degree and misidentifies the vehicles of psychological states. Both claims are in fact true, but it nonetheless remains that far more can be captured with the category of drive than might at first appear to be the case. We focus in this section on two additional facets – affective character and semantic content – which, if drives are to be the fundamental explanatory category for psychology, Nietzsche must also accommodate.

The qualitative/affective character of drives has been mentioned repeatedly above. Some passages in the texts and some interpreters lump the two together, entailing that whatever is true of the one is true of the other. But there is good reason to distinguish them, even if it turns out that there are no drives free of affect and no affects that exist independently of some drive. We have said that drives are fairly settled dispositions that have internal component states that are also fairly settled, that they are the goads to exploration, assimilation, and appropriation (i.e., power), and that they are affectively experienced as effective, that is, they are experienced as spurs. But being affectively experienced as effective is a crude characterization of affect, for it barely scratches the surface of their complexity. Consider, to begin with, that *all* of the following affects (and others that have no doubt escaped my unsystematic sifting of passages) are discussed somewhere in Nietzsche's work:

accomplishment; affection; agitation; aggression, alarm; altruism; ambivalence; amusement; anger; angst; annoyance; anxiety; anticipation; apprehension; apathy; arrogance; astonishment; awe; benevolence; bitterness; boldness; boredom; caution; chagrin; comfort; command; compulsion; confidence; contentment; contempt; courage; coyness; coziness; cravenness; craving; curiosity; cynicism; decadence; delight; delirium; depression; derision; desire; despair; diffidence; disappointment; disdain; disgust; dismay; distrust; dizziness; dread; dumbfoundedness; eagerness; ecstasy; elation; embarrassment; empathy; emptiness; ennui; enthusiasm; envy; euphoria; exaltation; exasperation; excitement; fatigue; fear; fervor; flirtation;

fondness; forgiveness; friendship; fright; frustration; fury; generosity; giddiness; glee; gladness; glory; gluttony; gratitude; greed; grief; grumpiness; guilt; hate; happiness; hilarity; homesickness; honor; hope; horror; hostility; humiliation; humility; hysteria; impatience; indignation; infatuation; insatiability; intolerance; irritability; joy; jealousy; keenness; kindness; loathing; loneliness; longing; love; lust; magnanimity; melancholia; mercy; misery; modesty; nausea; nervousness; nihilism; nostalgia; obsession; over-fullness; panic; paranoia; patience; peevishness; perturbation; pity; pleasure; pride; queasiness; rage; regret; relaxation; relief; remorse; repentance; repulsion; repugnance; resentment; sadness; sarcasm; satiety; satisfaction; self-pity; serenity; shame; shock; shyness; sorrow; shock; strength; stress; stupefication; sublimity; subservience; suffering; sullenness; superiority; surprise; suspense; suspicion; sympathy; terror; unhappiness; voluptuousness; voracity; vulnerability; weakness; well-being; willingness; worry; zeal

Some will think that some of the listed phenomena are not really affects because they classify neither as emotions nor moods. It does not really matter: what is immediately apparent is the impressive variation in intensity, phenomenology, positive and negative valence, and degree of cognitive involvement across the listed states. Equally impressive is the fine-grainedness of some of the distinctions between these states.

Given even the abbreviated list above, it is clear that we are capable of a remarkable range of affective responses, that we have a much richer repertoire of them than any other single species that we know of, and that, as an implication of that richness, many of them are unique to us humans. What, if anything, do they share beyond being various kinds of spurs to various kinds of engagement?[10] First, affective character is, typically at least, *consciously experienced* as a particular feeling with a distinctive phenomenology. This is not to deny that unconscious affect occurs or that Nietzsche's views commit him to saying that unconscious affect does not occur. The ready availability of examples of affect that is suppressed, repressed, dissociated, dampened or displaced provides evidence of the widespread occurrence of affect that occurrently may be but need not be consciously experienced (subconscious affect is a more delicate matter left unanalyzed here). But at least in paradigmatic cases, affect is consciously experienced and, moreover, consciously experienced as attaching either to some perceptual content (feeling awe and dread at seeing El Capitan for the first time), some interoceptive content (feeling blissfully fatigued at the end of a good powder day), some object (feeling gobsmacked by the carved intricacies of a Roman sarcophagus), some person (feeling aroused by the presence of one's favorite), or, occasionally, as attaching to nothing whatsoever (feeling relaxed).

Second, affective character is *evaluatively responsive* to its object or content, and, moreover, typically responsive in characteristically positive or negative ways. Again, this is not to deny that affect can be muted or even deadened to the point of non-responsiveness. Indeed, deadening of affects and the inability to endure suffering of any kind is one of the most devastating consequences of certain decadent and ascetic regimes of self-organization (see e.g., BGE 202; KSA 13 14[99] = WP 437; GM III 16, 17). However, just as affect is consciously experienced in typical cases, so too it is evaluatively responsive to one's internal milieu or to the external natural and social environment prompting it, and usually in characteristic ways.

Disgust provides a ready and easy example. Typically, disgust is prompted by perceptual detection of insect activity, decomposing flesh, feces, urine, putrid odors, bodily secretions, viscous, oozing, festering, sticky, and slimy substances, and dirt.[11] Not surprisingly, Nietzsche adds other prompts: among others, he identifies oneself (KSA 10 24[26] = WP 29; GM III 11); bad mannered passions (KSA 12 10[181] = WP 175); nature (KSA 11 44[6] = WP 228); ancient philosophers of virtue (KSA 13 14[129] = WP 434); life itself (KSA 13 11[76] = WP 697; GM II 7, GM III 13); the failed, stunted, wasted away, and poisoned (GM I 11); and prigs, priests, and the virtuous (TI 'Morality as Anti-Nature' 6). According to contemporary cognitive psychology, disgust responses are both autonomic and behavioral, and so much alike across individuals and across cultures that an identifiable default disgust response is easily described. Autonomic responses include decreasing blood pressure and decelerating heart rate and behavioral responses include a cross-culturally shared and instantly recognized facial expression – contorted nose and mouth – sniffing, snorting, vocalizing ('eeew!' 'gross!'), withdrawal and retraction, and sometimes vomiting.

These autonomic and behavioral responses confirm, first, that affects usually have a default and distinctive phenomenology, and, second that they are typically evaluative. Disgust affect's autonomic and behavioral components are shared across individuals (indeed, across cultures) and uniformly aversive in evaluating the prompt as something to be avoided at all costs. Other affects – arousal, exaltation, exhilaration, voluptuousness, sublimity, and many others – each has its characteristic phenomenological feel and each is a favorable evaluative response to the prompt. Rather than resulting in avoidance and retraction behaviors, these affects result in inclination and partiality behaviors. Their prompts are embraced and, when they present themselves again, the prompts will again be embraced as the means of inducing the affects distinctive phenomenological feel. Anyone lucky enough not to be born into abject poverty or not to be a victim of profound neuropsychological dysfunction, disease, or illness can distinguish prompts that induce aversive evaluations and avoidance behaviors from those that induce favorable evaluations and inclining behavior.

These two features of affect are central to Nietzsche's thoughts about affect's role in our psychological economy. We have noted that all affects have distinctive default phenomenologies. Rage feels a particular way and the way it feels is not the way that suspicion feels. This feature of affect reveals that conscious experience, whether interoceptive or perceptual, is constitutively embodied. Moreover, since many affects are prompted by objects in the environment, the idiosyncratic feel of different affective responses to distinct objects also reveals that conscious experience is embedded in and causally connected with the world around us. That affects come loaded with phenomenological content directly implies that we can no more shrug off our embodied embeddedness than we can dispense with either our phylogenetic or cultural inheritance, and hence also implies that, like it or not, we cannot exempt ourselves from being actively engaged with the natural and social environment. And that affect is inherently evaluative reveals that we are active and engaged loci of conscious experience.[12]

The other property that drive states must exemplify or host if they are to be a plausible candidate for the basic psychological category is, of course, thought content. It can easily seem that a drive is not a good candidate for being the kind of state that can host thought content. After all, drives are energetic, propulsive, affective, and wildly plastic in the objects that quell (albeit briefly) their insistent demands. Thoughts, on the other hand, are rarely energetic, frequently inefficacious, often muted in their phenomenology, sometimes extraordinarily precise, and only occasionally present any demands, insistent or not. Indeed, most thoughts simply present themselves and almost immediately dissipate into the ether. It can appear, then, that assimilating thoughts to drives is a kind of category mistake and that Nietzsche's attempt to categorize all thoughts as drives must remain a non-starter.

There are at two facets that any proposed answer to this sort of challenge must exhibit. The first is the general philosophical question about how *any* natural or physical vehicle – a drive, an affect, a perceptual state, a single neuron, a neural pathway, a network of neural pathways, a network of neural pathways plus elements of the extra-cranial world, a computational program – can host thought content, especially linguistically encoded thought content. Of course, this question applies no less to Nietzsche's candidate vehicle, *viz.*, the drive, but because the challenge that this particular nominee confronts is just an instance of the challenge that *any* naturalistic account of thought content faces (whether one is a physical monist or, as Nietzsche sometimes claims to be, a force monist), a general answer is on-point and sufficient. That answer begins by suggesting that what appears to be an unanswerable demand is, in fact, subject to a plausible deflationary and naturalistic analysis. One key element in such a deflationary analysis is to distinguish the symbolic system in which thought is typically encoded and expressed from candidate relationships between such a symbolic system and the vehicle(s) proposed as the hosts for tokens of that system.

Languages are symbolic representational systems. But representation is a broad genus that includes at least three species. In general, a *representation* is a something that is asymmetrically related to another something such that (a) it is about the other thing but the other thing is not about it, and (b) it stands in for the other thing in causal chains, and (c) it can guide behavior in the other thing's place (Haugeland [1991] 1998). Thus a limping gait represents injury, but injury does not represent a limping gait; a sculpture of a horse represents a horse, but a horse does not represent a sculpture of it; the word 'horse' represents horse, but horses do not represent the word 'horse.' Since a representation stands in for another entity, it has sufficient saliency to guide or direct behavior even in the absence of additional perceptual input or in the absence of the perceptual object altogether. Following Peirce (Peirce 1976), representation is captured within the genus of *sign*, which is some perceptual stimulus pattern that carries information or stands in for something else. Within the genus there are icons, indexes, and symbols. An *icon* is a sensory representation of something, such as a painting or sculpture of something else. An *index* is a stimulus-dependent sign that correlates particular perceptual information with or points to – indexically represents or indexes – something else. A limping gait indexically represents or indexes injury; a beeping car horn indexes danger; olfactory detection of pheromones indexes sexual availability; particular kinds of vocalization index danger or contentment; a wrinkled nose and scowl index disgust. A *symbol* is a stimulus-independent sign that has a conventional significance acquired through association with other symbols. Symbols, unlike indexes, bear conventional relations to that which they represent. Thus 's' (an ink squiggle) represents or refers to a particular phoneme and 'grief' (a collection of ink squiggles) represents or refers to a particular affect only because we agree that it (the collection of ink squiggles) does so.

The word 'representation' is, unfortunately, confusion prone. It can refer either to what does the representing, to the relation between what represents and what is represented, or to what is represented by what represents. Let us try to ease this confusion by stipulating the following. First, the *representation vehicle* is the entity or event that is a relatum of a representation relation. Secondly, the *representational feature* is the vehicle's property(ies) in virtue of which it is a relatum of a representation relation. Thirdly, the other relatum of a representation relation is the *represented content*, that is, the entity or event represented by a vehicle/feature pair. Fourthly, the *representing relation* is the relation between the vehicle/feature pair and content such that the former is about the latter. In contemporary representationalist theories of thought content, the set of representation vehicles are routinely assumed to be intracranial neurons or networks of them, the representation feature is assumed to be firing rates, spiking rates, or network properties, and the represented content is assumed often to be extracranial. If some represented contents are extracranial, then many representational relations have extracranial relata and are thus not entirely intracranial. Extended mind theorists argue in addition that a representational vehicle's representational feature(s) may be extracranial as well.

Having made the requisite distinctions, a general answer to the general problem about how thought content can be hosted by something natural (or physical) is straightforward. Naturalists and, in particular, monistic naturalists such as Nietzsche, affirm that representation is a natural phenomenon, that is, that all of the elements of representation, whether iconic, indexical, or symbolic, can be subjected to naturalistic analysis. Each of the elements of representation must satisfy naturalistic standards: the representational vehicle must come from a natural domain (neurons, neural networks, drives); the representational feature must be something natural (differential synaptic firing patterns, spiking rates, emergent properties of neural networks, affective valence); the representing relation must be something natural (correlation, causation, socially conventional assignment); and the represented content must be something natural. The sticky issue turns out to be the representational feature in virtue of which a representational vehicle manages to represent. No one has been able to present a conclusive case about what the best candidate has to be. But then if the challenge to Nietzsche's drive theory that a drive cannot host thought content is this general kind of challenge, then his nominee for the representational vehicle is on no shakier ground than any other nominee: all candidates for the representational vehicle face the challenge of specifying that in virtue of which they host symbolic content. Enthusiasts for this or that proposal notwithstanding, it must be admitted that we still have only glimmers of an answer to the challenge. This is not surprising, for the challenge is, after all, a version of the hard problem of consciousness, which can be understood as the demand that the naturalist bear the burden of proof to show how something entirely natural, like a drive or a neural network, can possibly host consciousness.

Turning from the hard problem and towards particular problems that are faced by Nietzsche's candidate representational vehicle, the drive and its accompanying affect, we may note that drives are actually *better* candidate vehicles than some other candidates on the contemporary scene. They are certainly better than classical computationalist proposals that identify computational states as representational vehicle/feature pairs, for drives are non-trivially natural in a way that computational states are not. But three long-standing objections to classical computationalism have been that: (i) thinking of computational states as representational vehicles and computational properties as representational features appears to commit any view of the mind to a set of non-natural inter-lopers between conventionally-fixed language systems and whatever is going on inside the brain and its neural activity that subserves language systems; (ii) thinking of the mind as a computer implementing or real-izing symbolic software excises qualitative/affective character from the start and can provide no back door through which it might re-enter; (iii) thinking of language as a computer program immediately induces the problem of semantic meaning, as exemplified in the Chinese Room Argument.[13]

One of the virtues of nominating drives as the representational vehicles is that they avoid all three of these problems. Drives are prototypically natural elements easily incorporated into any naturalistic psychology; they are qualitatively and affectively pre-loaded; and they can be ready repositories of social convention, including semantic meanings. But perhaps the most salient difference between classical computationalist cognitive psychology and Nietzsche's drive-based cognitive psychology is that drives are dynamic. It is really quite remarkable that he antici-pates by more than a hundred years certain developments in contem-porary dynamicist models of cognition. Echoing Nietzsche's speculative claims, dynamicist models conceive of cognition as a self-organized and non-linear system of large-scale interconnected neural activities with multiple positive and negative feedback loops implemented by various neural pathways, processes, assemblies, and neuron clusters. Some dynamicists mark a sharp intra-cranial/extra-cranial distinction and restrict theoretical attention to the intra-cranial environment, but advocates of embodied cognition argue that the relevant cognitive milieu is the embodied central nervous system and all that feeds into its centralizing apparatus. Advocates of embodied and embedded cognition argue that even the intra-/extra-organismic boundary is arbitrary. Van Gelder describes this alternative in language that is more than a little reminiscent of passages to be found in Nietzsche:

> [T]he cognitive system is not just the encapsulated brain; rather since the nervous system, body, and environment are all constantly changing and simultaneously influencing each other, the true cognitive system is a single unified system embracing all three. The cognitive system does not interact with the body and the external world by means of the occasional static symbolic inputs and outputs; rather, interaction between the inner and outer is best thought of as a matter of coupling, such that both sets of processes continually influencing each other's direction of change. At the level at which mechanisms are best described, cognitive processing is not sequential and cyclic, for all aspects of the cognitive system are undergoing change all the time. Any sequential character in cognitive performance is the high-level, overall trajectory of change in a system whose rules of evolution specify not sequential change but rather simultaneous mutual coevolution. (van Gelder 1995: 373)

On this embodied-embedded dynamicist alternative, cognitive processes are for the most part non-algorithmic and non-symbolic, and, hence, not classically computationalist. They are also causally coupled through continuous and feedforward and feedback interaction with other intra-organismic processes and with the extra-organismic environment.[14]

So, it appears that we can after all load drives up with all of the properties – causal, affective, evaluative, contentful – they must have if they are going to be the basic psychological category at use in psychological explanations. Still, might Nietzsche not be overreaching just a little bit in nominating drives as the basic psychological category? Consider: when I take a break from writing, I often go outside, lean against the wall, and look at the mountains. It just so happens that I just did that. My experience consisted in the following (and this is a selective list of elements): the wall pressed against my back; the warmth of the day heated my forehead; a breeze flowed across my face; the brightness of the mountain's snow made me squint; a towhee chirped as it tramped about under a scrub oak fifteen feet to my left; my stomach grumbled a little; the hum of highway traffic was pierced by a particularly loud truck downshifting; the minty taste of chewing gum in my mouth mixed with the odor of dried oak leaves; the back of my eyeballs throbbed a little; and all the while I continued to be frustrated with my inability to solve a certain philosophical problem that was hindering my attempts to finish this chapter. Now, this stretch of experience was perceptual and qualitatively loaded (hearing the towhee's chirp, the traffic's hum, and the truck's roar; seeing the mountain and its white snow; tasting the gum; smelling the oak leaves); interoceptive and qualitatively affectively loaded (feeling my stomach grumbling, the back of my eyes throbbing, and my position in space with the wall behind me); cognitive and affectively loaded (reflecting on and being frustrated by the philosophical problem).

Yet it seems unlikely in the extreme either that the best description of all of these elements of a fragment of conscious experience lasting no more than thirty seconds will rely entirely on states, processes, and events that each reduce to drives or that the best causal explanation of these states' activities and their causal consequences will always avert exclusively to drives. Even as broadly as we have come to understand them, drives seem to be the wrong kind of state to be the reduction basis of, for instance, the auditory perception of a truck's roar. Drives are too directional, too goading, too affectively and qualitatively loaded to be the *only* fundamental psychological category (or the only physiological category, for that matter). Even if Nietzsche is allowed the almost endlessly forgiving luxury of having the term 'drive' refer to any and all "regular effects in organisms [that] are not reducible to chemical and mechanical laws" (KSA 8 23[9]), lumping every psychological phenomenon together under the term elides crucial differences between the kinds of phenomena that go into comprising a working psyche. Granted, if the set of drives is coextensive with the number of distinguishable regular effects not reducible to chemical and mechanical laws, then, by terminological fiat, every irreducible regular effect, and perforce, every psychological phenomenon, is a drive. But that is a thinner description of drives than even the most bare-boned dispositional analysis introduced above. Besides, as has been argued, Nietzsche himself is prepared to describe drives in some detail. Every additional dynamic and affective detail increases the likelihood that some kinds of psychological phenomena will strain against one of those details even if not against his dragnet definition.

If the concern that he overreaches is sound, an apology may still be entered on his behalf. Let us acknowledge that he sets off onto largely uncharted waters of psychological description and explanation equipped only with various outdated ways of thinking that he knows are hopeless and with his own speculative hypotheses and categories that, he hopes, might help us as we look for new ways of thinking about human psychological states, events and processes, and as we think about new ways to conceptualize psychological causation. Grounded in his naturalism and fueled by his trust in physiology and evolutionary explanatory models, he chooses a reasonable-looking candidate and departs. Drives and affects may not be the only constituents of our psyches, a suspicion warranted by the widespread acknowledgement that the human brain-mind is the most complex structure known to exist. Nevertheless, even if drives are not the only constituent element of this complex structure, Nietzsche's speculative explorations are far from being entirely misguided or peripheral. Moreover, he latches onto the dynamic and energetic nature of the brain-mind's perceptual, interoceptive, cognitive and affective systems, and in doing so presages many of the difficulties that contemporary thinkers, equipped with significantly more theoretical and technological resources, also face when trying to make sense of our brain-mind.

5
Reflective Consciousness, Phenomenalism, Epiphenomenalism

Nietzsche develops negative arguments against conscious subject things, against the existence of certain species of consciousness perennially popular with philosophers, and against views of consciousness that fail to acknowledge its embodiment. He also argues positively that where it is discovered, reflective consciousness exists only as a property of psychological states and then only as a property of some but not all of those states. These arguments are the topic of Section I. Nietzsche's speculative explanations imply certain contemporary views in neuroscience of consciousness and neuroscientifically informed philosophy of mind that fly under the banner of embodied and embedded cognitive neuroscience of consciousness.

On the basis of these arguments, he claims that all reflective conscious states are phenomenal. This is the topic of Section II. He also claims, more controversially, that some reflective conscious states are epiphenomenal, and he makes a plausible case for an evolutionary explanation of reflective consciousness and for the social embeddedness of certain species of higher-order conscious states. His version of the embodied and embedded view is one that takes reflective consciousness to be part of a dynamic embodied system whose behavior is in turn subject to continuing reconfiguration and recalibration as a result of its embeddedness in an external environment. These views do not, contrary to what has sometimes been claimed, undermine the causal potency of all conscious states even if they do jeopardize the causal potency of some conscious states. These claims are the topics of Section III.

I Basic and reflective consciousness

It would be silly for Nietzsche to deny that psychological states can be, and regularly are, conscious, and he rightly refrains from playing the fool. While he is prepared to allow that the number of conscious states is huge, he also insists that 'the conscious world of feelings, intentions, and valuations is a small section' (KSA 12 10[137]) of our psychological life, that 'the whole of life would be possible without, as it were, seeing itself in a mirror' (GS 354), and that consciousness is 'in the main superfluous' (GS 354). Conscious states are thus both proportionally less numerous than philosophers typically claim and may be an unnecessary surplus even where confirmed. Where he is not dismissive, Nietzsche is deflationary. Consciousness is 'the last and latest development of the organic and hence also what is most unfinished and unstrong' (GS 11), a 'kind of means' (KSA 12 10[137]) to an end that is little more than an 'idea of an idea' (KSA 11 26[49] = WP 476). This deflationary view is in stark contrast to what Nietzsche thinks most philosophers have tried to make of consciousness. Other philosophers have tried to make consciousness 'the kernel of man; what is abiding, eternal, ultimate, and most original in him' (GS 11), or 'a yardstick, as the highest value state of life' (KSA 12 10[137]), or 'the total sensorium and highest authority' (KSA 12 11[145]).

Given his ambivalence about consciousness, it is more than a little disappointing that Nietzsche rarely analyzes the terms 'conscious' and 'consciousness.' Worse, when he does discuss consciousness directly what he says is largely metaphorical. In *Ecce Homo*, he describes consciousness as a 'surface' (EH, "Why I am So Clever" 9); *Gay Science* 354 describes it as a 'net' and that to be conscious of something is a kind of 'mirror effect,' a claim made also in *Daybreak* 121 about the intellect as a whole. He also suggests at *Daybreak* 119 that consciousness is 'a more or less fantastic commentary on an unknown, perhaps unknowable, but felt text.' Together, these claims suggest that Nietzsche thinks there is something perplexing and even a little unsavory about consciousness. But what might it be that he finds puzzling and distasteful? One interpretation of these passages – the interpretation defended here – is that, typically at least, Nietzsche's target is reflective consciousness, that this kind of consciousness is reflective of and derivative on other kinds of psychological states. But then being conscious in this reflective and derivative manner is more than being awake, more than being tonically alert, and more even than having content-bearing, qualitatively loaded and accessible experiences of the kind that we have identified in Chapter 3 as basic conscious experience. What, then, is the difference between a basic conscious state and a reflective conscious state, and why does Nietzsche think that 'we could think, feel, will, and remember, ... and yet none of all this would have to "enter into our consciousness" (as one says metaphorically)' (GS 354)? To answer these questions, we turn again to *Gay Science* 354 and *Gay Science* 357, Nietzsche's most sustained discussions of consciousness outside of the *Nachlass*.

Recall basic consciousness as introduced in Chapter 3. A psychological state is basically conscious (or, is a state of basic consciousness), whenever it is content-bearing, qualitatively/affectively loaded, and widely accessible. It may be acknowledged that more complex conscious states also occur, and some of these have basic conscious states as their content. Such states are *reflective* conscious states. Reflective conscious states are also transitively structured, but when they occur, a basic conscious state is the content of another conscious state in neither an observational nor an inferential manner. An example is the thought that the peculiar brightness of the piano in a particular passage of the Mozart Piano Sonata currently being listened to is likely a function of microphone placement during the performance's recording. Some reflective conscious states are also *monitoring* states, where a monitoring conscious state is a reflective conscious state that takes another conscious state as its content and scrutinizes that state in a rationally critical manner.

Finally, some reflective conscious states are also *reflexive* or *self-conscious* states. In reflexive conscious states, the self is disclosed as a relatum of conscious states and as the owner of other conscious psychological states.[1] An example is the recognition I have of myself when I think to myself that I am listening to a Mozart Piano concerto.[2] It is typically thought that reflexive conscious states comprise a smaller set than reflective conscious states because many conscious states have basic conscious states as their content and yet do not disclose the self as the owner of that state. The distinction between reflective and reflexive conscious states is significant primarily because some versions of a contemporary theory of consciousness – the *higher-order theory of consciousness* – frequently run reflective conscious states together with reflexive conscious states. Since the higher-order theory of consciousness appears in certain ways to be similar to some of what Nietzsche says about consciousness, a brief introduction is warranted. We then return to Nietzsche's views.

Higher-order theories of consciousness claim that nothing about psychological states *per se* makes them conscious. The existence of Freudian unconscious desires and beliefs, for example, suggests to the higher-order theorist that there are plenty of unconscious psychological states. But Freudian cases are just the tip of the iceberg: postulating unconscious psychological states is ubiquitous in contemporary cognitive psychology and cognitive neuroscience, from the subconscious representations of various stages of perceptual work-up to unconscious thought, as when we 'sleep' on a problem. Such examples are fuel for the thought that something distinct from a psychological state's content – its representational properties and qualitative character – makes a psychological state conscious. So higher-order theorists partition psychological states into first-order unconscious states with content and qualitative character and higher-order conscious states that target first-order states (Rosenthal 2002). That targeting relation – whatever it is – is then the locus of consciousness, and what makes a psychological state conscious detaches from the representational and qualitatively loaded psychological state and migrates to this relation.

Higher-order theorists frequently nominate *awareness* as the relation that makes some psychological states conscious while others remain unconscious. A more precise statement of the higher-order theory may then be formulated: a person's first-order psychological state α is conscious if and only if there is a higher-order psychological state β such that β is being aware of α (Carruthers 2005; see also Rosenthal 1997, 2002). Take, for example, my hope that it will be warm and sunny tomorrow. That hope is the *conscious* hope that it will be warm and sunny tomorrow whenever the hope that it will be warm and sunny tomorrow is accompanied by the higher-order awareness of having the hope that it will be warm and sunny tomorrow. As wordy as this is, it is crucial to state the view in all of its prolixity because otherwise the higher-order view looks more benign than it is. For the higher-order theorist, my hope is and remains unconscious until there is a higher-order awareness of the hope.

The awareness relation at use in higher-order theories is typically understood be either a kind of inner perception or a kind of inner thought. Perception models conceive of awareness as an internal monitoring or perception-like state, while thought models conceive of it as an internal thought-like state. Perception theories suggest that awareness is an internal, higher-order state that scans lower-order states and the information they contain. On the occurrence of (or the disposition to have an occurrence of) such a higher-order inner scanning state, the representations provided by sensory perception and interoception become conscious. Thought theories, on the other hand, take the awareness relation to be relevantly similar to thought. Just as first-order thoughts are complexes composed of a subject, a relation such as belief, desire, or fear, and some content (which, in turn, is related to or represents that which it is about), so higher-order thoughts are complexes composed of a subject, a unique, noninferential relation of awareness, and the content believed, desired, or feared. On the occurrence of (or having a disposition for an occurrence of) such a higher-order thought, the contents provided by sensory perception and interoception again become conscious.

Perception and thought versions of the higher-order theory thus claim that a psychological state is conscious only when a distinct representation or awareness of that state occurs. In both, the subject is implicated but not yet described. A difference between members of the higher-order family of theories may be drawn at this juncture, for while all versions of the higher-order theory of consciousness model conscious states as inherently *reflective* phenomena, not all variants of the view model conscious states as inherently *reflexive* phenomena. For some, all conscious states are both inherently reflective and reflexive. On this version of the view, unconscious psychological states become conscious in virtue of being targeted by awareness: unconscious psychological states are those that the light of awareness illuminates, and in virtue of that illumination, they become reflectively conscious. And, importantly, the content of any such conscious state includes that oneself is in that state (Rosenthal 1997). So, in virtue of this self-disclosure, all conscious psychological states are also intrinsically reflexive. So, on this version of the higher-order view, reflectivity and reflexivity are a packaged property.

On another alternative, even if all conscious states are reflective, not all reflective conscious states are reflexive (Kriegel 2006, 2009; Burge [2006] 2007). These *self-representationalist* alternatives avoid commitment to the claim that a distinct representation or awareness β of a state α is necessary for α to be conscious. On these alternatives, a psychological state α is conscious whenever there is a particular way that α is represented (Kriegel 2006). As with all versions of higher-order views, self-representationalist views claim that a psychological state must be representational if it is to be conscious and that we must be aware of such states, so unlike basic conscious states of the kind we've discussed in Chapter 3, self-representationalist theories deny that a psychological state's content, accessibility, and qualitative character/affect are alone sufficient for that state being conscious. However, unlike other higher-order views that claim that conscious states are inherently reflexive, self-representationalist views deny that awareness is a distinct psychological state that discloses the self as an always-present relatum. Self-representationalist views and higher-order views are therefore united in their opposition to any view according to which consciousness is co-extensive with being contentful, accessible, and qualitatively/

affectively loaded psychological states. But self-representationalists and other higher-order views oppose one another on what must be added to a psychological state in order that it become conscious.

These nuances may seem far afield from what is required to understand Nietzsche's views of consciousness, but arguments marshaled by self-representationalists against other inherently reflexive higher-order views of consciousness are directly relevant. Whereas the higher-order view affirms that a psychological state, α, and the awareness β of α, are independent, the self-representationalist denies that independence (Kriegel 2006). The point may be put as follows: inherently reflexive higher-order views deny that the relation between α and β is constitutive, whereas self-representationalist views affirm that the relation between α and β is constitutive. This difference then underwrites a criticism of inherently reflexive views, namely, that they set the bar for being conscious too high and thus render unconscious much of our ongoing psychological life that would, were our thinking not distorted by these views, normally be thought of as conscious. It just seems false that, for every psychological state α, there must be a distinct awareness β of α in order for α to be conscious. We are reflectively aware that we are in the state we are in only intermittently (not every thought about my son Calvin snowboarding powder is accompanied by awareness of that thought, much less than that I am having the thought), and yet many such thoughts seem conscious, even if not in the way that the inherently reflexive higher-order view claims they must be. If so, inherently reflexive higher-order views are too strong because they prevent consciousness from being attributed to states that are properly labeled as such. On the other hand, for the self-representationalist, although β is necessary for α to be conscious, β and α are internally related to one another such that β is a constituent part of α (for details, see Kriegel 2006; Mulligan & Smith 1985; Van Gulick 2006). Since β is a constituent part of α, and since parts are internally related to one another, β always comes attached to α. That is, α and β form a complex.

On the basis of the model of conscious states as qualitatively loaded contentful states that are also aware, self-representationalism has the resources to avoid pervasive epiphenomenalism of consciousness. The argument is as follows. According to inherently reflexive versions of the higher-order view, awareness β is distinct from α. One consequence of the distinctness of β from α is that consciousness migrates from the representation α to β, whether it is a thought or some kind of inner perception. If so, consciousness is not an internal property of a psychological state but an external or relational property of that psychological state. But if consciousness is an external or relational property of a psychological state, then, since only internal properties are candidates for being causal powers, consciousness cannot be one of that state's causal powers. If an entity without causal powers is causally inert, it follows that consciousness is causally inert, and that entails that all conscious states are epiphenomena. If the inherently reflexive higher-order view cannot avoid epiphenomenalistic consequences, then there is an additional reason for siding with the self-representationalist and rejecting those versions.

Even if higher-order theories of consciousness are overly ambitious, not all of their ambitions need be bankrupt. In fact, higher-order theories are attractive models for reflectively and reflexively conscious states. For both reflectively conscious and reflexively conscious states are iterative in just the way that the higher-order theory claims all conscious states are. It is just that higher-order theories mischaracterize basic kinds of consciousness. As we turn now to discuss Nietzsche's views about consciousness, these points should be kept in mind.

At various places in his published work and in the *Nachlass*, Nietzsche worries about each of the issues introduced above. When he is in a debunking mood, he typically attacks the philosophical tendency to inflate the importance of reflective and reflexive conscious states. However, while reflective and reflexive conscious states may be favorite targets for criticism, his starting point in explaining human perceptual, interoceptive, cognitive, and affective experience are the states that we have called basic conscious states, *viz.*, the set of qualitatively/affectively loaded and accessible psychological states that have some content. This is the correct approach to take, since the content, access and qualitative/ affective properties of basic conscious states are logical and causal precursors of reflective and reflexive states, of monitoring states, and of other more complex species of consciousness. As such, they are not subject to the criticisms he levels against reflective and reflexive states.

As shown in Chapter 3, Nietzsche thinks, consistently with contemporary perceptual neuroscience, that sensory systems preconsciously receive a manifold of particular inputs that feed forward to our brain, where they are actively processed and worked up into basic conscious perceptual and interoceptive experience. He puts the claim as follows: the work-up of perceptual and interoceptive experience 'happens without our consciousness: whatever we become conscious of is a perception that has already been processed' (KSA 11 34[30]). He also suggests this view in more metaphorical language in a passage from *Beyond Good and Evil*:

The mind's power to appropriate the foreign stands revealed in its inclination to assimilate the new to the old, to simplify the manifold...– just as it involuntarily emphasizes certain features and lines in what is foreign, in every piece of the "external world," retouching and falsifying the whole to suit itself. Its intent in all this is to incorporate new "experiences," to file new things in old files. (BGE 230)

The general picture presented here is quite contemporary: we start with a manifold of transduced sensory inputs; we then 'retouch' and 'falsify' them by involuntarily and subconsciously processing and conceptualizing that manifold, the results of which processing are delivered as the accomplished incorporation of new experiences into old and familiar conceptual systems.

In emphasizing the subconscious work-up of sensory input into basic conscious perceptual and interoceptive experience, Nietzsche not only anticipates contemporary neuroscience, but concurs with two of his predecessors, Kant and Leibniz. Like them, a distinction between sensory input reception and scaffolding that input is common ground. All three of them agree that it is only when sensory inputs are subjected to cognitive and, for Nietzsche, affective, scaffolding that the kind of basic conscious experience with which we are all familiar obtains. Nietzsche also agrees with Kant and Leibniz on another point, that there is a distinction between the ineliminable particularity of sensory input and the generality of conscious experience. Were we to have no concept of *table*, for example, our sensory experience of *that* would be only of *that* and of nothing relevantly similar and it would not rise to the level of perceptual experience of a table.[3] Finally, all agree that the activity of the sensory organs and much of cortical processing is subconscious.

Leibniz's account of consciousness in particular provides a way of understanding at least some of what Nietzsche is on about when he makes fun of reflective consciousness. As suggested, what Nietzsche appears to have in mind most of the time when he says that a psychological state is conscious is that it is reflectively or reflexively conscious (or both), that is, it is a state in which one psychological state becomes the object of another psychological state or in which the self is revealed as the owner of psychological states, or both. Considering the former first, this view is stated clearly at *Gay Science* 354, where he claims that 'the problem of consciousness' is that 'of becoming conscious of something' (see also GS 333, 355, 357; KSA 13 11[113] = WP 477; KSA 13 14[152] = WP 478). In these passages, reflective conscious states and not more basic species of content-bearing, accessible and qualitatively/affectively loaded states are the focus. It is these reflective states that are 'merely a little corner' and a 'surplus' of what occurs in our psychological life (KSA 13 11[83]), what is 'merely an *accidens* of experience and *not* its necessary and essential attribute' (GS 357). Reflective conscious states are the only plausible candidate here, for they are the only kind of conscious state which, were they not to occur, are such that our thinking, feeling, and willing life – our basic conscious experience – could plausibly continue apace. Were Nietzsche to be discussing instead basic conscious states, he would be committing himself either to a kind of experience that has no content, that is not available for subsequent reasoning, emotional response, and control of action, or that has no qualitative/affective character, or to all three. But there is no textual evidence that Nietzsche ever claims that psychological states with any, much less all, of these properties are a mere fragment of our psychological life.

No such evidence exists because the concept of consciousness that Neitzsche is working with when he is thinking about consciousness is apperception as Leibniz understood it. *Apperception* is reflective consciousness, as can be gathered from Leibniz's own description of it: 'apperception is consciousness or reflective knowledge of this inner state itself and which is not given to all souls, or to any soul all the time' (Leibniz [1765] 1981: 637). Here, the equivalence of consciousness with reflective knowledge is explicit. So, when Nietzsche endorses what he calls Leibniz's 'incomparable insight... that consciousness is merely an *accidens* of experience (*vorstellung*) and *not* its necessary and essential attribute' (GS 357), he is referring to Leibnizian apperception, that is, to that clear and distinct intellectual reflective perception of what we are calling basic conscious exteroceptive or interoceptive states.[4] Leibniz's crucial insight is that apperception is reflective and dependent on basic conscious psychological states. While this dependency doesn't guarantee apperception's intermittency, it provides a ready explanation of it, for there is, as Leibniz and Nietzsche both claim, no reason why our ongoing experience *must* rise to the level of reflection. Much of our ongoing experience and psychological life occurs without being reflective in the way characteristic of apperception, as Leibniz calls it, or consciousness, as Nietzsche calls it, much less reflexive.

The distinction Nietzsche draws in *Gay Science* 357 between experience and consciousness drives the point home. Again: 'consciousness is merely an *accidens* of experience (*vorstellung*) and *not* its necessary and essential attribute;... in other words, what we call consciousness (*Bewusstsein*) constitutes only one state of our spiritual and psychic world (perhaps a pathological state) and *not by any means the whole of it'* (GS 357). If we take 'experience' (*vorstellung*) to refer to contentful sensory and nonsensory psychological events that are accessible and qualitatively loaded – in our terms, basic conscious states – and 'consciousness' (*Bewusstsein*) to refer to apperceptive states, or, alternatively named, reflectively conscious or higher-order states, then this passage claims straightforwardly that being reflectively conscious is an accidental property of basic conscious states and only one state among many in which they may find themselves.[5]

If, as proposed, *Gay Science* 357 marks a distinction between basic conscious states, on the one hand, and, on the other, reflective conscious states, then other passages in which Nietzsche draws related distinctions – between kinds of experience that are unproblematic because they are unreflective and kinds of experience that are problematic because they are reflective – make sense. Consider *Gay Science* 354:

> Man, like every living being, thinks continually without knowing it; the thinking that becomes *conscious* is only the smallest part of all this – the most superficial and worst part – for only this conscious thinking *takes the forms of words, which is to say signs of communication*, and this fact uncovers the origin of consciousness.

Here again, Nietzsche acknowledges that there is an unproblematic kind of thinking that not only humans but all creatures engage in and that this kind of thinking is, at least on the sense of the term that identifies conscious states with reflective knowledge states, not conscious. He further identifies the problematic kind of thinking as that kind of thinking of which we know that we are thinking. Since knowing that we think entails that we can think without knowing that we do, and since only the former is identified here as conscious, it follows that the huge swaths of our ongoing experience that has content and is accessible and is qualitatively/affectively loaded but not yet reflective is excluded from being conscious in the problematic sense of the term. In short, in this passage, Nietzsche restricts the use of 'consciousness' so that it refers only to what we are calling 'reflective consciousness.' He considers the rest of our psychological life – all of the perceptual and interoceptive experiences, all of the non-reflective thinking, all of the emotional and other affective states included in the set of basic conscious states – to fall outside the orbit of consciousness.

Nietzsche is, it must be said, a little confused in marking the distinction between conscious and unconscious states in this way. To begin with, he is not altogether consistent in the way that he describes consciousness or in his categorization of psychological states. In some passages, he marks distinctions between species of conscious experience parallel to the distinctions drawn above between basic, reflective, and reflexive conscious states. Elsewhere, he limits the set of conscious states to those identified here as reflective and reflexive conscious states, thus relegating all other kinds of experience – including what we have identified as basic conscious states – to the domain of unconscious experience. But this latter way of partitioning psychological states is wrong-headed: when 'consciousness' is used to refer only to reflectively conscious states, or, even more controversially, only to reflexively conscious states that disclose the subject as their owner, much of what is routinely and properly included in the class of conscious states ends up, as it does on the higher-order view of consciousness, being excluded from the class of conscious states simply because it is not reflective or reflexive.

One might reply that the decision to use 'consciousness' and its cognates in one way rather than another is nothing more than a decision about how to use words. If that is all that is at stake and if Nietzsche has a proprietary sense of 'consciousness' in mind, then so long as he deploys it consistently, all is well. But his use is not always consistent and all is not well. Although the distinction between unreflective and reflective states must be and is made by Nietzsche, and although the distinction between unreflective and reflective states is the basis of his ambivalence about the causal efficacy of reflective and reflexive conscious states, attributing consciousness only to reflective states is at the root of his own inconsistent categorization of psychological states. The proposed distinction – between, on the one hand, basic conscious states that are accessible and qualitatively loaded and, on the other, reflective conscious states that are about such basic conscious states and reflexive states that are reflective and that reveal the subject as their owner – is more precise without doing harm to the distinction that Nietzsche himself wields, but the proposal does so with a better set of labels. So, since the proposed labels pick out the same distinction as the distinction misleadingly labeled by Nietzsche and since they mark that distinction without rendering much of our conscious life unconscious solely in virtue of a word's extension, we will use the basic/reflective labels instead of Nietzsche's unconscious/conscious labels.

A word or two more about reflexivity may be in order. It can be tempting to argue that all reflective conscious states are *ipso facto* reflexive conscious states. It is undeniable that Rosenthal, the higher-order theory's most insistent advocate, thinks that this is the case. But a distinction must be made between pre-reflective subjective perspectivity and the reflective revelation of the subject of psychological states. Subjective perspectivity is pre-reflective, where the term *pre-reflective* refers to a conscious event or process that is not directed at itself or some other conscious event or process (Sartre [1936] 1962; Metzinger 2003; Gallagher 2005; Zahavi 2008). Contemporary philosophy of mind and philosophy of neuroscience have been particularly interested in these matters, and it can be argued that Nietzsche too is alert to the distinction.

Determining what it is to be an organism embedded in an environment with its own subjective perspective turns out to be a non-trivial matter, for subjective perspectivity is already more complex than the anodyne "geometric property" (Blanke & Metzinger 2009) of there being an embodied point of projection in experience, while also being something less complex than a property that entails either reflexivity or possession of a self-concept as a condition of instantiation (Bermúdez 1998). That all conscious experience is subjectively perspectival minimally implies that the frame of reference for conscious experience as experienced is spatio-temporally *egocentric* – a frame of reference locates entities in space and time as in relation to a particular spatial point – rather than *allocentric* – a frame of reference locates entities in space and time as in relation to one another. Conscious experience is from the perspective of the organism whose conscious experience it is. But it is something more than this geometric property, for otherwise the subjective perspectivity of experience would be no more complex than my smile being *my* smile (Sosa 2002). Since all that is required to understand why my smile is my smile is that it is caused by my facial muscles, my teeth, and my lips, subjective perspectivity would amount to no more than my conscious experience being caused by my embodied neural activity. If so, then ant and beetle experience is also subjectively perspectival, for their sensations are likewise caused by their embodied neural activity. Surely, however, this is not conclusive.

Philosophically minded neuroscientific investigators into these issues have offered the construct of a *minimal self*, which is thought of as the weakest sense of 'subject' sufficiently strong to play a role in subjectively perspectival conscious experience (Blanke & Metzinger 2009; Metzinger 2003, Welshon 2013, among others). The minimal self is intermediate between the anodyne property and other more robust forms of subjectively unified conscious experience that presuppose a reflexive subject. These more robust forms are what are implicated in subject-reflection, subject-awareness, and subject-consciousness (Metzinger 2009). The minimal self is then whatever is minimally strong enough to support a pre-reflective subjective perspective but not so strong as to require reflexive disclosure.[6] Subjective perspectivity as so characterized is the dynamic and ongoing set of processes that track 'global bodily properties' (Blanke & Metzinger 2009). Neuroimaging findings suggest that activity in upstream unimodal perceptual and interoceptive pathways provide head- and body-centered information and may well be parts of what comprises pre-reflective subjective perspectivity. They also suggest that when those unimodal assemblies feed information forward to heteromodal associative areas and transmodal associative areas in anterior insular cortex, cingulate cortex, and anterior temporoparietal cortex, the massive feedforward and feedback transformational loops thereby generated in turn help to generate the minimal self.[7]

All of this contemporary neuroscientific work on the dynamic generation of the minimal self and pre-reflective subjectivity is thoroughly consistent with Nietzsche's own thinking about the self as a natural category and all of his thinking about subjective perspectivity and the reflexively presented self in higher-order states. It almost goes without argument that Nietzsche requires pre-reflective subjective perspectivity. After all, if sense is to be made of the enormous swaths of his work that discuss animals and humans, not only the numerous passages that directly discuss humans as perspectival loci, but also all of the passages that mention or assume that we experience, feel, have drives, are engaged in thought, have hopes and desires, can be in good and bad moods, and all the rest, there must be a perspectival locus and there must be an experiencer, a feeler, a thinker. Of course, it doesn't follow that the minimal self is a simple substance or a transcendental presupposition of experience. Rather, as the neuroscientific evidence suggests, the activity of ongoing global tracking processes generates a minimal self as an emergent pre-reflective phenomenon.

Nietzsche is just as equally convinced that the reflexive subject is neither a presupposition of all conscious states (as, he thinks, Kant holds) nor an epistemological starting point (as, he thinks, Descartes holds). The reflexive subject is, instead, merely presented in conscious states, and then only in some but not all conscious states. His skepticism towards the reflexive subject as a presupposition of conscious experience and towards the reflexive subject as an epistemological given are explicit in this passage from *Beyond Good and Evil* 16:

> When I analyze the process that is expressed in the sentence, "I think," I find a whole series of daring assertions that would be difficult;

perhaps impossible, to prove; for example, that it is I who think, that there must necessarily be something that thinks, that thinking is an activity and operation on the part of a being who is thought of as a cause, that there is an "ego," and, finally, that it is already determined what is to be designated by thinking – that I know what thinking is. For if I had not already decided within myself what it is, by what standard could I determine whether that which is just happening is not perhaps "willing" or "feeling"? In short, the assertion "I think" assumes that I compare my state at the present moment with other states of myself which I know, in order to determine what it is; on account of this retrospective connection with further "knowledge," it has, at any rate, no immediate certainty for me.

Rather, 'the subject is not something given, it is something added and invented and projected behind what there is' (KSA 12 7[60] = WP 481). He goes so far as to affirm that '"The subject" is the fiction that many similar states in us are the effect of one substratum' KSA 12 10[19] = WP 485), and that belief in the ego as substance is the 'oldest "realism"' (KSA 12 7[63] = WP 487). But, as noted already in Chapter 3, 'a belief, however necessary it may be for the preservation of a species, has nothing to do with truth' (KSA 12 7[73] = WP 487). For these reasons, Nietzsche claims that whatever is presented in reflexive consciousness is phenomenal, that is indexed to a perspective: 'How could this nook-perspective of consciousness permit us to assert anything of "subject" and "object" that touched reality! –' (KSA 13 11[120] = WP 474). We return to the topic of the self in Chapter 6.

II   The phenomenality of reflective consciousness

Having marked a distinction between basic and reflective conscious states, Nietzsche's arguments that reflective conscious states are phenomenal are more clearly revealed and better situated. These arguments proceed from criticisms of a number of dubious claims made by others on behalf of reflective conscious states. Among the claims that he argues against are that: (i) reflective conscious states are capable of being an initial cause; (ii) the reports produced by reflective conscious states are known indubitably, incorrigibly, and infallibly; and (iii) there are facts about reflective conscious states. Nietzsche rejects (i) – (iii), and in so doing establishes, he thinks, the conclusion that reflective conscious states are phenomenal.

As has been argued, Nietzsche and contemporary neuroscience concur that sensory organs are transduction devices. Contemporary versions of this view have it that sensory organs take input of a certain kind – light waves, sound waves, and chemical information – and produce electro-chemical information as output, which electro-chemical information is fed forward to the brain, where, in various unimodal and heteromodal cortical pathways, it is further processed, resulting eventually in basic conscious perceptual and interoceptive states. All of this processing takes time, and neuroscientists have identified the time it takes between sensory organ input and conscious perceptual experience of the world and its inhabitants to be about 500 milliseconds. Had this discovery been made in his time, Nietzsche would probably not have been surprised, for, as already argued, he too holds that even the most basic kinds of conscious states are the result of significant preconscious cortical processing. On the basis of this view, he argues that the sequencing of reflectively conscious states routinely assumed by others in the philosophical tradition must be mistaken.[8] And, on the basis of that claim, he argues in addition that reflective conscious states are phenomenal.

Given the welter of subconscious cortical activity that continues along with, and in the background of, all conscious states – whether basic states, reflective states, reflexive states, or other higher-order states – their contents are, Nietzsche thinks, neither translucent nor first in any kind of causal or temporal order. They are instead outputs of entire chains of sub- and preconscious processing that is opaque to us from a first-person perspective:

> The "external world" affects us: the effect is telegraphed into our brain, there arranged, given shape and traced back to its cause: then the cause is *projected,* and *only then does the fact enter our consciousness.* That is, the world of appearances *appears* to us as a cause only once "it" has exerted its effect and the effect has been processed. That is, *we are constantly reversing the order of what happens.* – While "I" see, *it* is already seeing something different. (KSA 11 34[54]))

Consistent with contemporary perceptual and interoceptive physiology, Nietzsche's view is that the sense organs transduce information from objects in the extra-organismic world and feed that information forward to the brain, where it is processed. Only after information routes through the preconscious cortical pathways is the resulting product, *viz.,* basic conscious experience, achieved. Once basic conscious experience has been generated, reflective and reflexive conscious experience are possible, for as the higher-order theorist has it, the only candidate content for a reflective conscious state to be a reflection of is another conscious state. But since from the first-person perspective all of the subconscious processing is invisible, we must instead trace the resulting product back to its cause, and this carries with it the threat of reversing the causal order. Nietzsche thinks that almost all of us some of the time, and some of us (the philosophers) almost all of the time, assume that reflective conscious states – the causal outcome or effect of cortical processing – are instead that which is first in the causal series, thus incorrectly taking an effect of a cause for a cause itself.

The mistake about causal sequencing is an instance of an error that Nietzsche thinks is endemic to any introspective understanding of our psychological lives, an error that characterizes not only our understanding of conscious perceptual experience of the extra-organismic world but also of conscious interoceptive experience of the intra-organismic world and its thoughts, desires, memories, and dreams. Indeed, these causal reversals characterize *all* introspective attempts to understand our mental life:

> *The phenomenalism of the "inner world."* Chronological inversion, so that the cause enters consciousness later than the effect.
>
> we have learned that pain is projected to a part of the body without being situated there
>
> we have learned that sense impressions naively supposed to be conditioned by the outer world are, on the contrary, conditioned by the inner world: that we are always unconscious of the real activity of the outer world...The fragment of outer world of which we are conscious is born after an effect from outside has impressed itself upon us, and is subsequently projected as its "cause" –
>
> In the phenomenalism of the "inner experience" we invert the chronological order of cause and effect.
>
> The fundamental fact of "inner experience" is that the cause is imagined after the effect has taken place...
>
> The same applies to the succession of thoughts...we look for a reason for a thought before we are even conscious of it: and the reason enters consciousness first, and then its consequence...
>
> Our entire dream life is the interpretation of complex feelings with a view to possible causes, and in such a way that we are conscious of a condition only when the supposed causal chain associated with it has entered consciousness.
>
> The whole of "inner experience" rests upon the fact that a cause is sought and imagined for a stimulation of the nerve centers – and that

only a cause thus discovered enters consciousness: this cause in no way corresponds to the real cause – it is a groping on the basis of previous "inner experiences," i.e., of memory. (KSA 13 15[90] = WP 479)

According to this passage, causal mis-sequencing and inversion expands beyond perceptual states to include pain and other interoceptive and affective states, cognitive states, dream states, and memory. In short, all of our introspectively accessed psychological life is prone to causal mis-sequencing and inversion. And, on the basis of this insight, Nietzsche concludes that the introspective inner world, every bit as much as the external world, is phenomenal.

The full extent of Nietzsche's commitment to the inner world's phenomenalism is made explicit elsewhere: '*everything* of which we become conscious is arranged, simplified, schematized, interpreted through and through' (KSA 13 11[113] = WP 477, emphasis mine). As a result, it is impossible for us to discern the actual causal sequence of the states that comprise our inner life: 'the causal connection between thoughts, feelings, desires, between subject and object, are absolutely hidden from us – and are perhaps purely imaginary' (KSA 13 11[113] = WP 477). Worse, we routinely act from the assumption that we can identify the contents of our own mind 'as if there existed "facts of consciousness"' (KSA 12 2 [204] = WP 475). Nietzsche thinks that we never encounter such facts of reflective consciousness: all reflective conscious states are instead 'subsequent and derivative intellectual phenomena' (KSA 13 11[113] = WP 477), or, as he also puts it, 'symptoms of what actually happens' (KSA 12 1[61]). The point is again generalizable to any and all psychological phenomena: '*Every thought*, every feeling, every will is *not* born of one particular drive but is a *total state*, a whole surface of the whole consciousness, and results from how the power of *all* the drives that constitute us is fixed at that moment – thus, the power of the drive that dominates just now as well as of the drives obeying or resisting it' (KSA 12 1[61]).

Since they are the final causal result of complex and subconscious dynamic processes, reflective conscious states are not deep or fundamental but 'superficial' (GS 354; KSA 12 1[20]). And, contrary to those who claim we can know the contents of our own mind immediately and incorrigibly and build our knowledge on that basis, Nietzsche holds that 'nothing is so much deception as this inner world' (KSA 13 14 [152] = WP 478; see also KSA 11 34[55]). This conclusion then serves as a premise in a larger argument that judgments which follow from assuming that reflective conscious states are simple and clearly known are instead confused and that any explanation that relies on reflective consciousness will lead to confusion about how our psychological economy is organized or of how reflective thought is causally related to action:

> Feeling, willing, thinking everywhere show only outcomes, the causes of which are entirely unknown to me: the way those outcomes succeed one another as if one succeeded *out of* its predecessor is probably just an illusion: in truth, the causes may be connected to one another in such a way that the final causes give me the *impression* of being associated, logically or psychologically. *I deny* that one intellectual [*geistiges*] or psychological [*seelisches*] phenomenon is the direct *cause* of another intellectual or psychological phenomenon – even if this seems to be so. *The true world of causes is hidden from us*: it is unutterably more complicated. The intellect and the senses are, above all, a *simplifying* apparatus. Yet our *erroneous*, miniaturized, *logicized* world of causes is the one we can live in. (KSA 11 34[46])

Here, Nietzsche claims that all intellectual phenomena – that is, the set of reflective conscious states – do not directly cause any other such phenomenon. The actual causal story is much more complicated. This claim is unpacked in greater detail in Section III.[9]

Especially for those who take for granted the praise heaped on reflective consciousness as an indubitable foundation of knowledge, Nietzsche's insistence that reflective states are the last things we should be certain about is deeply disturbing. And it is not simply knowledge about our mental states that is thereby jeopardized. Nietzsche makes it clear that all reflective perceptual states – reflexive and non-reflexive alike – are subject to a deflationary and naturalistic analysis:

> In order for a particular species to maintain itself – and increase its power – its conception of reality must comprehend enough of what is calculable and constant for it to base a scheme of behavior on it. The *utility of preservation* – not some abstract-theoretical need not to be deceived – stands as the motive behind the development of the organs of knowledge – they develop in such a way that their observations suffice for our preservation. (KSA 13 14[122] = WP 480)

These conclusions about both self-knowledge and knowledge about the perceived world seem to leave the knowledge seeker in a bind: nothing about either our interoceptive states or our perceptual states is such that it can be a foundation of knowledge. But if we are to reject the conclusion, some shortcoming to the argument must be identified. Unfortunately, Nietzsche's hostility towards the alleged epistemological stability of reflective consciousness is the result of a fairly straightforward argument, each premise of which is probably true. If, as he affirms, the chronological order of psychological states is unknown to us, then the causal order of psychological states cannot be fixed either. And if the causal order of psychological states cannot be fixed, then there are no facts about reflective, reflexive, or other higher-order species of consciousness. But then, since there are no facts about states of these higher-order kinds of consciousness, the indubitability, incorrigibility, and infallibility allotted to them by others is an illusion and any reliance on them as foundations of knowledge is likewise illusory. Unless some other foundation is proposed, it follows directly that knowledge, if there is any, lacks indubitable, incorrigible, and infallible foundations.

It might be thought that undermining the foundations of knowledge has unfortunate consequences for Nietzsche's own optimism about physiology, for without *some* foundation of knowledge, the idea that we can have knowledge of empirical physiology, which Nietzsche thinks we can have, likewise collapses. And if empirical knowledge of physiology collapses, then so too do all of Nietzsche's speculative claims about the dynamic embodiedness and embeddedness of the human perceptual and interoceptive systems. But the argument is unsound and the threat to physiological knowledge it may be thought to pose is a fizzling fuse. If we could experience the world unmediated by cognitive categories and perceptual and affective schemata, we might then occupy a perspective against which the extent to which those categories and schemata infiltrate conscious experience might be calibrated. But such a view is, to use Thomas Nagel's phrase, a 'view from nowhere,'[10] and, as argued in Chapter 3, perspectivism entails the negation of any view from nowhere: there are no perspectiveless perspectives, and even if there were, we could never occupy them. But the hope for foundations of knowledge entails that we can occupy such a perspective. Hence, the hope for foundations of knowledge collapses. Since all perception and interoception is ineliminably embodied and embedded – that is, perspectival – our only hope is to generate knowledge that is consistent with that ineliminable embodied embeddedness.

The perspectivity of knowledge is, as has been argued, in part a consequence of the perspectivity of all of the species of consciousness, from the most basic kinds of perceptual experience to the most refined forms of self-reflection that only meditation adepts can describe. In acknowledging this perspectivity, Nietzsche's naturalism again reveals itself. He repeatedly emphasizes the role that human and biological needs play in the formation of consciousness, and he insists that even the fully conceptualized worlds of reflective and reflexive consciousness are likewise bound by this naturalized world view. He is thus one of the few pre-20th century philosophers to recognize the acidic effect that a naturalistic reorientation must have on the pretensions we have about ourselves and our capacities for reflective thought. In particular, the humble basis of consciousness as a tool for the enhancement of life suggests that the pronouncements made from the perspective of reflective consciousness are not infallibly trustworthy and are, indeed, more likely to be untrustworthy:

> The whole of *conscious* life, the mind including the soul, including the heart, including goodness, including virtue: in whose service does it work? In that of the greatest possible perfection of the means (means of nourishment, of enhancement) of the basic animal functions: above all, of the *enhancement of life*.
>
> What has been called "body" and "flesh" is unutterably more important: the remainder is just a minor accessory. The task of weaving onwards the whole rope of life, and in such a way *that the thread becomes stronger and stronger* – that is the task. But now see how heart, soul, virtue, mind quite conspire to turn this fundamental task *upside down*: as if *they* were the goals instead…The degeneration of life is essentially conditioned by consciousness's extraordinary capacity for error: consciousness is kept under control by instincts least of all, and thus *errs* longest and most thoroughly. (KSA 13 11[83])

Thus are even the far reaches of abstract consciousness brought under the umbrella of naturalism and held to the standards it establishes. On those standards, the far reaches of abstract conscious thought are more prone to long-held and deep kinds of errors than any other kinds of thought. Moreover, these errors are the most difficult to expose and eliminate, for the products of abstract reflective consciousness are so far removed from their natural roots that we are likely to forget that those natural roots are still there behind and beneath them.

Why, if 'we could think, feel, will, and remember, and we could also "act" in every sense of that word, and yet none of all this would have to "enter our consciousness"' (*GS* 354), do we need reflective consciousness at all and how did it emerge? Nietzsche has at least four different answers to these questions, all of them speculative. What is first required is a particular natural function that might be attributed to reflective consciousness. In a *Nachlass* passage, he suggests that reflective consciousness evolves out of our relations to the extra-organismic environment world and then comes to support our need to communicate:

> *The role of "consciousness"* – It is essential that one should not make a mistake over the role of "consciousness": it is our relation with the "outer world" that evolved it. ... Usually, one takes consciousness itself as the general sensorium and supreme court; nonetheless, it is only a means of communication: it is evolved through social intercourse and with a view to the interests of social intercourse – "Intercourse" here understood to include the influences of the outer world and the reaction they compel on our side; also our effect upon the outer world. It is not the directing again, but an organ of the directing agent. (KSA 13 11[145] = WP 524)

This view is expanded upon in *Gay Science* 354, where he claims not only that reflective consciousness has come to serve a need to communicate, but also – and more specifically than what is claimed in KSA 13 11[145] – that it evolved only under the pressure of a need for survival. Humans were for eons the most endangered animal and we needed our conspecifics' protection from natural enemies. As a result, we needed to express our needs and make ourselves understood to others *via* spoken communication. This in turn required that we ourselves know what those needs are and how we feel about them, and knowing these matters entails development of a reflective capacity to form attitudes about psychological states:

> [I] surmise that consciousness has developed only under the pressure of the need for communication; that from the start it was needed and useful only between human beings (particularly between those who commanded and those who obeyed); and that it also developed only in proportion to the degree of this utility. Consciousness is really only a net of communication between human beings; it is only as such that it had to develop; a solitary human being who lived like a beast of prey would not have needed it. That our actions, thoughts, feelings, and movements enter our own consciousness – at least a part of them – that is the result of a "must" that for a terribly long time lorded it over man. As the most endangered animal, he needed help and protection, he needed his peers, he had to learn to express his distress and to make himself understood; and for all of this he needed "consciousness" first of all ...

Third, in *Daybreak,* he suggests the distinct hypothesis that a particular subset of needs that arose in our competitive interaction with
other conspecifics is what most required communication: 'As soon as
one animal sees another it measures itself against it in its mind, and
men in barbarous ages did likewise. From this it follows that every
man comes to know himself almost solely in regard to his powers
of defense and attack' (*D* 212). Here Nietzsche suggests that reflective and reflexive consciousness arose as a result of the very particular need to calibrate ourselves against those human and non-human
others surrounding us.

In *Genealogy of Morals,* Nietzsche supplements these three hypotheses
with another. On this fourth hypothesis, reflective consciousness first
emerged as a result of the 'internalization' of the drives (see GM II 16),
that fateful event when our drives re-directed their objects away from
others and inward onto ourselves. As interesting as it may be, the internalization hypothesis does not answer the following question: why did
reflective consciousness emerge as the end result of internalization?
We can grant that the redirection of drives whose objects were originally external generates new internal objects against which to struggle.
But drives whose objects are external events need not be reflectively
or reflexively conscious, as is made clear by the presence of species
whose internal milieu is not characterized by our self-laceration and
self-overcoming. Why must those drives whose objects are internal be
such that they help generate reflective consciousness? An answer to
this question has either to say that all drives with internal objects are
reflectively conscious or that all drives with internal objects provide
the necessary conditions for the generation of reflective consciousness. The former will not work since there are non-conscious drives
with internal objects, such as those connected with the body's autonomic functions. Unfortunately, Nietzsche never explains the second
alternative.

Suffice it to say, the world of phenomena is what we assume for purposes
of communication. As Nietzsche notes: 'the world of "phenomena" is the
arranged [*zurechtgemacht*] world that we *feel is real*' (KSA 12 9[106] = WP
569) and that we assume in communicating with one another. That this is
so provides one plausible interpretation of Nietzsche's somewhat cryptic
claim that reflective consciousness is a kind of 'net of communication' (GS
354). On the proposed interpretation, the contents of reflective consciousness are outside each of us but not outside the set of humans who need to
communicate with one another. The contents of reflective consciousness
exist suspended in a shared logical and conceptual space between each of

us so that we may have a common set of objects and events to refer to and so that we may have a common set of concepts to use when we communicate our needs to one another. Thus, reflective consciousness is (in as substantive sense as can be attributed to it), a common, shared, possession across humans. Of course, that shared possession is a 'surface- and sign-world' (GS 354), a world that 'does not really belong to man's individual existence but rather to his social or herd nature' (GS 354).

III   The epiphenomenality of reflective consciousness

If reflective, reflexive, and other higher-order kinds of conscious states are, as Nietzsche argues, phenomenal and prone to mis-sequencing, then some of what we assume to be true and exalted about consciousness is instead mistaken and degenerate. In particular, reflective and other higher-order conscious states, because they are the products of multiple unconscious processes, and because some of them are additionally mediated by the constraints imposed by communication and language, are unlikely to provide what many in the philosophical tradition hoped they would as foundations of knowledge.

This somber conclusion becomes part of Nietzsche's most devastating criticism of consciousness, *viz.*, that it is an epiphenomenon, where an epiphenomenon is a state that is caused but has no causal consequences of its own. On more than one occasion in the *Nachlass*, Nietzsche argues that reflective and reflexive conscious states – whether cognitive thought states or affective pleasure and pain states – are terminal phenomena (KSA 13 14[152] = WP 478). He therefore rejects any claim that reflective and reflexive conscious states are causally connected in the way we think they are: '[w]e believe that thoughts as they succeed one another in our minds stand in some kind of causal relation: the logician especially, who actually speaks of nothing but instances which never occur in reality, has grown accustomed to the prejudice that thoughts *cause* thoughts –' (KSA 13 14[152] = WP 478). Again: '"Thinking," as epistemologists conceive it, simply does not occur: it is a quite arbitrary fiction, arrived at by selecting one element from the process and eliminating all the rest' (KSA 13 11[113] = WP 477).

Rather, between any two reflective conscious thoughts 'all kinds of affects play their game' (KSA 13 11[113] = WP 477). If so, then what the philosopher and the logician assert to be a clean sequence of reflective conscious thoughts each linked to the next by tidy logical relations does not exist. Similarly, although '[w]e believe...that pleasure and pain are causes of reactions...' (KSA 13 14[152] = WP 478), we should instead 'concede that everything would have taken the same course, according to exactly the same sequence of causes and effects, if these states "pleasure and displeasure" had been absent' (KSA 13 14[152] = WP 478). Pleasure and pain are 'epiphenomena with a quite different object than to evoke reactions; they are themselves effects within the instituted process of reaction' (KSA 13 14[152] = WP 478).[11] He then generalizes these claims to make the point about all conscious states: 'everything of which we become conscious is a terminal phenomenon, an end – and causes nothing; every successive phenomenon in consciousness is completely atomistic' (KSA 13 14[152] = WP 478).

That every reflective, reflexive, or other higher-order conscious state is epiphenomenal is disturbing enough, as will be seen. But it is important to remind ourselves that, typically at least, Nietzsche does not think that all psychological states, events, and processes are epiphenomenal even if they are phenomenal. He is right to hold this view, for even if phenomenalism of the psychological is true, epiphenomenalism of the psychological would be hard to reconcile with how we and Nietzsche conceive of ourselves. It is hard to imagine that sexual pleasures cannot cause desires for more of them, that the desire to repeat those pleasures never yields consequences, that memories of past sexual encounters never cause grins, laughter, and, sometimes, embarrassment. For that matter, it is hard to imagine that being tossed from a horse and breaking your back does not cause moans of distress, that we never intentionally cross the street, or that we never look in the cupboard for something to eat because we're hungry. And at more abstract levels, the consequences are just as unbelievable. If epiphenomenalism of the psychological were globally true, we would be massively wrong about ourselves, and our being wrong about ourselves would be undiscoverable, since every psychological state would be a terminal phenomenon. We could never reach the level of reflection required to assess our beliefs or determine that we have made a mistake about anything, including our being wrong about the causal efficacy of conscious thoughts.

Perhaps worst of all for Nietzsche, epiphenomenalism of the psychological would undermine many of his most precious undertakings. His complaints about the perverting consequences of *ressentiment* and the liberating consequences of the new philosopher's skeptical turn would be no more significant than the breezes blowing through trees; the bad conscience would not be a disease; distinguishing between kinds of morality on the basis of their cultivation of psychological health would be without purchase; ranking individuals according to psychological type would be a waste of time; describing certain kinds of psychological health would be no more informative than describing the psychology of minerals; and advocating emotional discipline would be as effective as suggesting to squirrels that they collect only the acorns they actually need. All of these larger humanitarian projects would be ill-conceived and delusional from the start.

Even if Nietzsche does not commit himself to the mistaken claim that all psychological states are epiphenomenal, his confidence that reflective conscious psychological states are epiphenomenal is sufficiently disturbing as to warrant closer scrutiny. Can it really be true that reflectively conscious states are 'terminal phenomena' that 'cause nothing' (KSA 13 14[152] = WP 478)? As it turns out, Nietzsche cannot make up his mind about an answer. His various arguments about the causal connections between reflective conscious states are ambiguous between at least two views. According to the first, *strong* form of epiphenomenalism, reflective, reflexive, and other higher-order conscious states (emotions, affects, passions, instincts) are caused by first-order basic conscious states, subconscious states, and unconscious states but themselves cause nothing subsequent to their occurrence. According to the second, *modest* form of epiphenomenalism, reflective, reflexive, and other higher-order states are caused by first-order basic states, subconscious states, and unconscious states and themselves have some causal consequences subsequent to their occurrence, even if their causal consequences are never reflective, reflexive, or other higher-order states.

Call two successive *reflective conscious* states RC_n and RC_{n+1}, where the subscripts denote temporal indices. We can say, with strong epiphenomenalism, that RC_n and RC_{n+1} are states caused by temporally prior *basic drives* (conscious, subconscious, and unconscious) BD_n and BD_{n+1}, and that RC_n and RC_{n+1} do no further causal work of any kind – they do not cause any other reflective thoughts, and nor do they cause any other basic conscious, subconscious, or unconscious drives. Each successive higher-order state is a dead end, both cognitively and affectively, a complete epiphenomenon. Diagramming the situation, where t_n is a time, RC_n is a reflective thought at t_n, and BD_n is a basic conscious, subconscious, or unconscious drive at t_n, we have:

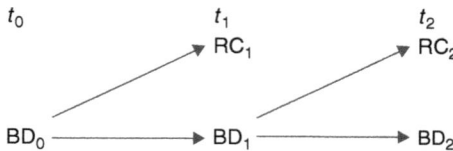

Figure 5.1   Strong epiphenomenalism of reflective consciousness

Alternatively, we can say, with moderate epiphenomenalism, that reflective states are caused by temporally prior basic conscious, subconscious, and unconscious states and reflective states turn cause temporally succeeding basic conscious, subconscious, and unconscious states, but no reflective state causes any temporally succeeding reflective state. So, reflective states are not individually epiphenomenal but members of causal sequences containing nodes not typically acknowledged. Diagrammatically:

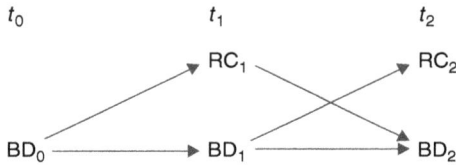

t_0 t_1 t_2

RC_1 RC_2

BD_0 BD_1 BD_2

Figure 5.2 Modest epiphenomenalism of reflective consciousness

On this view, reflective states are *cognitively* but not *affectively* epiphenomenal. Nevertheless, this too is a kind of epiphenomenalism, for no reflective states ever causes another reflective state without the intrusion of an intervening basic conscious, subconscious, or unconscious drive.

One of these two alternatives is surely the best interpretation of Nietzsche's thoughts about the epiphenomenality of reflective consciousness. Arguments for both are found in the texts. One already quoted *Nachlass* note is consistent only with strong epiphenomenalism of reflective consciousness: 'everything of which we become conscious is a terminal phenomenon, an end – and causes nothing; every successive phenomenon in consciousness is completely atomistic – ' (KSA 13 14[152] = WP 478). Another note suggests instead moderate epiphenomenalism of reflective consciousness: 'between two thoughts all kinds of affects play their game...."Thinking," as epistemologists conceive it, simply does not occur: it is a quite arbitrary fiction, arrived at by selecting one element form the process and subtracting all the rest' (KSA 13 11[113] = WP 477). According to the first passage, reflective states have no causal consequences of any kind, while according to the second passage, reflective states do have causal consequences, but, contrary to what logicians and epistemologists claim, reflective states never directly cause any other reflective states. Instead, between any two reflective states, basic conscious, subconscious, and unconscious drives and affects 'play their game.'

Given that textual evidence for both interpretations can be found, is one preferable to the other, and, if so, which is preferable? To answer

these questions, recall that Nietzsche thinks that all species of psychological states are species of the genus drive. If so, then reflective states
are likewise a kind of drive. Drives are, as already established, the basic
category of causal explanation in Nietzsche's metapsychology. But
strong epiphenomenalism of reflective thought suggests that reflective
states have no properties of any kind in virtue of which they are causally
efficacious. Even if this understanding is an immediately obvious one, it
is an unduly strong reading of Nietzsche, for it debars a reflective state
from having any properties other than those by which we specify it as
a reflective conscious state. It seems much more likely that reflective
states have multiple properties, some of which – their reflective properties – do not equip them with causal potency, while some – those
other than their reflective conscious properties – can equip them with
causal potency. The point can be put a little more rigorously as follows:
no psychological state can cause a psychological or non-psychological
state in virtue of its reflective conscious properties, even if there is some
other property that a psychological state has in virtue of which it can
cause another psychological or non-psychological state. Modest epiphenomenalism of reflective consciousness can then be understood as a
conjunction of claims: all psychological states cause other psychological
and non-psychological states in virtue of their non-reflective conscious
properties and no psychological state causes a psychological or non-psychological state in virtue of its reflective conscious properties.

Nietzsche's insistence that reflective consciousness is epiphenomenal
may thus be a little more palatable than it initially appears. On the modest
view under consideration, even reflective states have properties in virtue
of which they are causally potent and properties in virtue of which they
are not causally potent. It just so happens that none of a drive's reflective properties are among the causally potent properties. Such a view
folds in unproblematically with his claims that all reflective properties
are accidental properties of basic conscious states that also happen to
have certain qualitative character or affective valence properties that are
causally potent. If he is serious about reducing reflective states to drives,
then he should allow that reflective states are causally potent because
their drive properties or their affective properties are causally potent. Of
course, he may not be serious about reducing reflective states to drives.
On occasion, he appears to think that reflective states and other higher-
order states are exempt from reduction to drives. On this non-reductionist
alternative, there is a class of psychological states that is not reducible to
drives. Reflective states thus understood are still epiphenomenal, for their
epiphenomenality may be a direct consequence of not being reducible to

drives. Of the two alternatives, the reductionist view is recommended as the preferred interpretation, primarily because it fits more comfortably with his other claims about reflective consciousness and his analysis of psychological states as drives. But even the non-reductionist view may be defended. Indeed, both alternatives are versions of long-standing candidates in the philosophical tradition of non-reductive explanations of the mind-body relation. The former is a kind of epiphenomenalism of non-reducible reflective *properties*, the latter a kind of epiphenomenalism of non-reducible reflective *particulars*.

Since epiphenomenalism of non-reducible reflective properties is more congenial with Nietzsche's overall argumentative preferences than epiphenomenalism of non-reducible reflective particulars, the former is preferable to the latter. Of course, the former can come in a strong form or in a modest form. Here is the modest form, which is that proposed on Nietzsche's behalf:

Modest epiphenomenalism of non-reducible reflective properties

1. all reflective psychological particulars are drives; and
2. the reflective properties in virtue of which a particular drive is specified as a reflectively conscious state RC_1 do not cause reflective properties to be instantiated by any temporally subsequent reflectively conscious state RC_2; and
3. the reflective properties in virtue of which a particular drive is specified as a reflectively conscious state RC_1 may cause affective properties to be instantiated by a temporally subsequent basic conscious state BD_2.[12]

One general reason to think that modest epiphenomenalism of non-reducible properties is the best interpretation of Nietzsche's views is his claim at *Gay Science* 357 that reflective consciousness is an accidental property of experience. If that is correct, it should be expected that psychological states – that is, drives – are not causally efficacious in virtue of their being reflective conscious. However, psychological states that happen to instantiate reflective properties certainly may cause other psychological states in virtue of their being also, and at the same time, drives or instincts. This is enough to salvage the causal potency of the psychological and even the causal potency of basic conscious states while still maintaining the epiphenomenality of reflective conscious states.

An interesting question is, of course, this: is modest epiphenomenalism of non-reducible reflective properties correct? This question is actually two questions. First, is it good interpretation of what Nietzsche says? And, second, if it is, is Nietzsche right that no reflective conscious state can cause another reflective conscious property to be instantiated but can cause an affective property to be instantiated? The recommended answer to the first question is 'yes.' Modest epiphenomenalism of non-reducible reflective properties is consistent with the vast majority of passages in which he discusses reflectively conscious states even if it is inconsistent with his most stridently epiphenomenalist complaints against reflectively conscious states. The answer to the second question is more delicate. If he cannot explain how a reflective state can have affective consequences and yet cannot have reflective consequences, then, if modest epiphenomenalism of non-reducible reflective properties is a good interpretation of Nietzsche, then hewing close to him on this matter is mistaken. However, Nietzsche suggests a distinction that explains how the needed causal efficacy can be ascribed to reflective properties. Luckily for him, the distinction also allows him to defend the claim that the needed causal efficacy he ascribes to reflective properties is not equivalent to the kind of causal efficacy ascribed to reflective properties by typical defenders of reflective causal efficacy.

In *Gay Science*, Nietzsche distinguishes between *directing* and *driving* causes. Here is how he puts it: 'people are accustomed to consider the goal (purposes, vocations, etc.) as the *driving force*, in keeping with a very ancient error; but it is merely the *directing* force – one has mistaken the helmsman for the steam' (GS 360). Suppose we identify goals (purposes, vocations, etc.) as a kind of reflective property and say of all of the members of the class what Nietzsche says here about goals. Then we may infer that he would concur that all reflective properties are directing rather than driving causes. Directing causes constrain and shape drives that would otherwise attempt to realize power even were such constraining and shaping not to occur. If so, then Nietzsche may reject strong epiphenomenalism of non-reducible reflective properties. Indeed, if the distinction is otherwise consistent with his views, he *must* reject strong epiphenomenalism of non-reducible reflective properties, for otherwise these properties can provide no direction for cultivating drives along certain routes rather than others. Hence, if the distinction between helmsman and steam can be defended, even reflective properties can, as moderate epiphenomenalism of non-reducible reflective properties says, have some causal consequences, even if they are not the causal consequences others claim on their behalf. This will become crucial in the next chapter, where discussion turns to the will. There the distinction will be expanded upon and defended against criticism.

Here it may be noted in conclusion that, appearances to the contrary, it is possible to work through the thicket of Nietzsche's claims about reflective consciousness and its alleged epiphenomenalism without getting lost, without going down too many philosophical garden paths, without hitting dead-ends, and without abandoning some role for it in our psychology, even if that role is pretty limited. In the next chapter, we discuss, among other things, whether the role he is prepared to give reflective consciousness can bear the weight which some of his other commitments demand that it bear. In particular, we must come to grips with his claims about reflectively conscious purposes and goals – intentions – and the role that he appears to give them in explanations of human action. For, while Nietzsche's naturalism provides the resources required to eliminate intentionalist interpretations of drives, the very availability of those resources suggests that his frequent use of goals and purposes in explaining human action may likewise be eliminable. If all of Nietzsche's uses of goals, purposes, and intentions in explanations of human action and psychological phenomena are reductively interpreted as naturalized functions, then all of his talk about reflectively conscious goals, purposes, and intentions at use in his explanations of human action and psychological phenomena must likewise be eliminated and replaced with non-intentional explanations that appeal only to naturalized functions. If so, then all of his talk about self-discipline, self-control, promise-making, and self-overcoming is just empty blather.

Nietzsche can escape the conclusion of this argument. Although many goals, purposes, and intentions can be eliminated and replaced with naturalized functions, reflectively conscious goals, purposes, and intentions need not be included in the set of superfluous purposes and goals. In this chapter, we have seen that it is not the case that all reflectively conscious states are strongly epiphenomenal. Thus, so long as reflectively conscious goals, purposes and intentions play a role in the explanation of human action and psychological phenomena and so long as that role is consistent with modest epiphenomenalism, then some goals, purposes, and intentions may be irreducible to naturalized functions. The distinction just introduced between directing and driving causes will be crucial for this defense. As will also be seen, however, even if the distinction helps Nietzsche escape reductive eliminativism, he ends up having to confront a more formidable argument, which purports to demonstrate that, if consciousness or the self are emergent, then they must be epiphenomenal.

6
Self, Will, Power

Nietzsche is fascinated by all of the different kinds of selves there are and by the variety of psychological training programs we subject ourselves to in order to achieve them. The most superficial examination of his mature works reveals his astonishment at the self-directed tortures we are prepared to pursue in order to achieve internal organization and his bewilderment at our willingness to be convinced by philosophers and religious advocates that the best selves are those organized around pure reason, moral goodness, and asceticism. Across *Daybreak, Beyond Good and Evil, The Gay Science, Genealogy of Morals, Twilight of the Idols,* and *Anti-Christ,* he distinguishes *dozens* of regimens of psychological self-reorganization, most affiliated with moral codes and religious demands. To gauge how deep his interest in these matters is, consider only regimens associated with the ascetic ideal and mentioned in *Genealogy of Morals.* Here, he identifies at least twenty distinct self-training programs: self-denial and self-sacrifice (Preface 5); self-hypnotism (I 6); abstinence, dieting, self-abasement, self-depreciation (I 11); self-deception (I 14); self-torture (II 8, 22); self-consciousness (II 10, III 9)), self-tyranny (II 18); self-negation and self-elimination (III 3); self-mortification, self-martyrdom, self-misunderstanding (III 10); self-contempt and self-annihilation (III 17); and self-belittling and self-critique (III 25). These programs and their associated curricula turn us against ourselves and into kinds of selves that are sick, decadent, and resentful. Nietzsche denounces the religious peddlers who are their advocates, and he criticizes all of the colluding philosophers and scientists who provide domains of entities over which the programs range and species of causal intercourse that operate only within those domains.

Yet for all of his antipathy towards the ascetic ideal and its marketers, Nietzsche readily grants that the self-reorganization that decadent ideals, ascetic ideals, the bad conscience, and *ressentiment* introduce into our psyches also makes possible self-discipline, self-control, self-surveillance, self-mastery, and self-overcoming. When undertaken for purposes other than the decadent and *ressentiment*ful ones they are typically enlisted on behalf of and designed for, he has high praise for the results they can produce (GM III 16, III 27), for they are what make we humans interesting (GM III 16, GM III 27; AC 14). The intellectual project of gaining a better understanding of our ways of being a self in the world, 'the range of inner human experiences reached so far, the heights, depths, and distances of these experiences, the whole history of the soul so far and its as yet unexhausted possibilities – that is the predestined hunting ground for a born psychologist and lover of the "great hunt"' (BGE 45). Part of that better self-understanding consists in giving shape to the logical space for understanding a kind of naturalized self that is both robust enough to be the subject of such self-reorganization projects and yet not so full-bodied as to re-admit all of the nonsense found in religious and moral thinking about the self. That is the topic of Section I.

An example of psychological nonsense is free will, a faculty routinely defended as a prerequisite psychological property of the self as moral agent. In Section II, we argue that Nietzsche is an eliminativist about the free will faculty. But he is not an eliminativist about intentional action, that is, action that is explained by having reasons. Nietzsche's challenge is thus to provide an account of intentional human action that eschews the free will faculty. He rises to the challenge by identifying a kind of causality reserved only for reflectively conscious intentions. Unfortunately, this account runs up against an argument that purports to show that if all causation is natural causation, then reflective conscious states, and, perforce, intentions, cannot be any kind of cause, that is, that reflective conscious states are epiphenomenal. It will be argued that Nietzsche's account can escape this argument's conclusion. In Section III, a descriptive sketch of the way intentions fold into his naturalized self is briefly outlined. This sketch focuses on self-discipline, self-control, and self-overcoming.

I   Physiology, psychology, and the self

Having analyzed drives and conscious states in previous chapters, a more substantive description of the structure of a self that is comprised of conscious and unconscious drives remains unfinished business. It is a strikingly different description than the kinds of descriptions of the self offered by many in the philosophical tradition. As argued in Chapter 4, a Nietzschean drive-comprised self is not, as skeptics would have it, an illusion; is not, as dualists would have it, a simple immaterial substance; and is not, as Kant would have it, a transcendental presupposition of experience. For that matter, a drive-comprised self is neither a reason-saturated moral agent who inhabits a rational kingdom of ends, nor a wholly spiritual entity whose thoughts create the world, nor an eternal, everlasting soul cared for by God. A Nietzschean self is a naturalized self, that is, it is a self consistent with science's discoveries about human physiology and psychology and a self, therefore, lacking all properties that fall outside a naturalist explanatory framework.

Nietzsche's eliminativist proclivities are never put to better use than when he argues against typical philosophical descriptions of the self and subject. He is ruthlessly eliminativist about what most philosophers have had to say about subject, souls, and selves, primarily because most such accounts smuggle in the moral commitments of the philosopher. For Nietzsche, if some spiritual or mental or psychological property cannot be explained as something natural, his immediately inference is that it is to be eliminated. As numerous and compelling as these arguments may be, we are not interested in them except as they are pertinent for under-standing Nietzsche's own positive views about the self. And they are, on occasion, pertinent, for his positive views about the self are complicated by his apparently non-naturalist claim that humans are the most pecu-liar of all animals: we are the 'interesting' animal (GM I 6), the 'manifold, mendacious, artificial, and opaque' animal (BGE 291), the 'uncanny' animal (BGE 291), the 'undetermined' animal (BGE 62), the 'fantastic' animal (GS 1), the 'mistrustful' animal (GS 33), the 'insane, laughing, weeping, miserable' animal (GS 224), the 'reverent' animal (GS 346), and the 'sick, sickly, crippled' animal (GS 352). Nietzsche's peculiar kind of naturalism must then account also for these apparently non-natural psychological and social characteristics. And he emphasizes that the category of being a self is what most needs rehabilitation as a corrective against clumsy naturalists who think that human psychology is no more intricate than that of other animals. In brief, then, he expects to articu-late a view of the self that is both eliminative as against philosophers and religious thinkers and yet non-reductive and non-eliminative as against clumsy naturalists. It is an open question whether he can achieve this goal. We suggest here that he can.

Philosophical accounts of the self or subject typically try to provide answers to three different sorts of questions. The first set of questions has to do with the *epistemology* of self-knowledge, that is, the special epistemic privilege that first-person introspective access is supposed to bestow on *de se* beliefs.[1] The second set has to do with what may, in a relaxed sense of the term, be identified as the *ontology* of the self, that is, a description of the location, structure, and composition of the self. Frequently, inquiries into the self's simplicity or complexity, its unity or disunity, its spatiality or non-spatiality, and its materiality or immateriality are conducted as purely ontological inquiries. However, these ontological inquiries are routinely informed by a third kind of consideration, which may be called the *phenomenology* of being a self. Here, relevant phenomena include: (a) being embodied and embedded in an environment; (b) being the subject of occurrent perceptual and interoceptive experiences and being the subject of occurrent thoughts, desires, memories, emotions, moods, fears, pleasures, and pains; (c) being the subject of self-involving thought experiments about future and counterfactual possibilities; (d) being able to ascribe thoughts to oneself; (e) being the author of one's thoughts; (f) being able to assent to some thoughts and reject others; and, finally, (g) being the agent of one's actions.

Phenomenological issues about experience-ownership and agency engage Nietzsche on a regular basis, and he has interesting things to say about them. In the last chapter, we took advantage of contemporary philosophical and neuroscientific work to articulate a minimal self, which, when applied to Nietzsche's work, provides him with a concept of a naturalized pre-reflective self that is embodied and embedded and robust enough to be the subject of occurrent experiences and psychological states. But even if (a) and (b) from above are thereby accounted for, (c) – (g) remain. What he says about these additional phenomenological features of being a self goes beyond being an embodied and embedded locus of subjective perspectivity. Furthermore, these additional phenomenological features bleed into his anthropological concerns about the uncanny animal that we are. Thus, this set of phenomenological issues implies that, on pain of abandoning many of these projects, Nietzsche must commit himself to a view of the self that is more robust than the minimal embodied self.

Even if it is granted that a human self must be naturalized, it does not follow that a human self's structure can be no more complex than that of a cat or a pollywog. Nothing about the naturalization of the human self requires that *all* of the unique features of our form of subjectivity – its embodiment and embeddedness, the complex subjective perspectivity of basic and higher order species of conscious experience, our being agents of actions – *must* upon acceptance of naturalism be written out as nothing but residual flotsam of discarded dualist, transcendentalist, or spiritualist modes of thinking about the self. Naturalism does however impose constraints on which properties a drive-comprised self has and what kind of structure it can have by requiring that the categories and explanation types used to defend those properties and that structure either be confirmable by empirical science, or, failing that, reducible to such confirmable categories, or failing even that, at least supervenient upon such confirmable or reducible categories. So, naturalist accounts of human psychology and the self must range over only entities, processes, states, and events that are confirmable by, reducible to, or supervenient upon, those sanctioned by biology, chemistry, physiology, and the neurosciences and psychological sciences, and their explanation types must be consistent with those found in the natural and psychological sciences. Naturalism thus supplies the logical and conceptual space for philosophical ambitions about describing the self to be considered while substantively and methodologically limiting all such ambitions.

Nietzsche has on occasion been interpreted as a Humean about the self, where to be a Humean about the self is to reduce the self to a temporal sequence of perceptual, cognitive, and affective experiences and to argue that any conception of the self more robust than that is a fiction towards which the appropriate response is scepticism.[2] If so, the ontology of the self is no more complex than that of a temporally organized bundle. Now, it is undeniable that there are strong strains of skepticism towards the self and equally strong strains of bundle thinking in Nietzsche's works. One may cite any number of passages in support of such views, but consider only *Genealogy of Morals* I 13: '[T]here is no "being" behind doing, effecting, becoming; "the doer" is merely a fiction added to the deed – the deed is everything' (see also TI '"Reason" in Philosophy' 5; TI 'Four Great Errors' 3; KSA 10 8[23] = WP 372; KSA 12 2[152] = WP 556; KSA 12 7[60] = WP 481; KSA 12 9[108] = WP 370; KSA 12 10[19] = WP 485; KSA 13 11[113] = WP 477). A skeptical conclusion about the self is an obvious implication to derive from this and similar passages. Similarly, he says things that are congruent with bundle theory on a regular basis.

However, Nietzsche himself in *Beyond Good and Evil* 12 describes a self that is neither eliminativist nor Humean. The self is, rather, a 'subjective multiplicity' or a 'social structure of the drives and affects' (see also his talk of the self as regent at KSA 11 40[21] = WP 492). Making the self a *subjective* multiplicity suggests that, despite being a complex, the self can be a subjective perspective and can be host to and author of some of its own psychological states; and making it a *social* structure of drives and affects suggests that the self is not reducible to any of its constituent drives and affects. Likewise, he elsewhere describes a kind of self that is more complex than any (obvious) version of bundle theory of the self can support and towards which he is far from being skeptical. Consider the sovereign individual described in *Genealogy of Morals*, Essay II, someone:

> who has his own independent, protracted will and the *right to make promises* – and in him a proud consciousness, quivering in every muscle, of *what* has at length been achieved and become flesh in him, a consciousness of his own power and freedom, a sensation of mankind come to completion. This emancipated individual, with the actual *right* to make promises, this master of a *free* will, this sovereign man – how should he not be aware of his superiority over all those who lack the right to make promises and stand as their own guarantors, of how much trust, how much fear, how much reverence he arouses – he *"deserves"* all three – and of how this mastery over himself also necessarily gives him mastery of circumstances, over nature, and over all more short-willed and unreliable creatures? The "free" man, the possessor of a protracted and unbreakable will, also possesses his *measure of value* ... The proud awareness of the extraordinary privilege of *responsibility*, the consciousness of this rare freedom, this power over oneself and over fate, has in his case penetrated to the profoundest depths and become instinct, the dominating instinct. (GM II 2)

Here, a robust self is described and commended as an exemplar. Since the sovereign individual is aware of its privilege of responsibility and all that flows from it, hers is a self that is, first, embodied and embedded in both a natural and a social environment. Second, the sovereign individual is conscious in a basic way of her own perceptual and interoceptive experiences and is owner of her thoughts, desires, memories, emotions, and moods. Third, fourth, and fifth, insofar as the sovereign individual has the right to make promises, she can (i) engage in self-involving future and counterfactual possibilities, (ii) identify her will and the right to make promises about the future as her own, and (iii) ascribe these and other thoughts to herself across future and counterfactual possibilities. Sixth, she is reflectively conscious of all that has been achieved by her appearance in the world and all that must still be achieved by others, which entails that she assents to some thoughts and rejects others. Finally, she is reflectively conscious of her actions.

Since laudatory descriptions of each of the sovereign individual's features are found not only in this isolated passage but in other passages in which Nietzsche discusses self-overcoming, self-discipline, self-control, and psychological health, they cannot be dismissed as unrepresentative exceptions to an otherwise consistent bundle version of reductive physicalism. So, interpreting his claims felicitously requires that we acknowledge that he is not a physical reductionist about the self and is not a typical bundle theorist about the self either. He appears instead to be open to the possibility that the human self is – or at least can – be unified in ways that most bundle views of the self just cannot countenance, and is complex in ways that reductive physicalisms cannot possibly explain.

No one would infer from the failure of simple bundle theories and reductive physicalisms that Nietzsche should be interpreted as a substance dualist, and it should likewise be common ground that he does not argue on behalf of any kind of pure mind view, according to which the self is a stream of pure conscious activity untethered to the body. Of course, the conceptual landscape of the self is not exhausted by reductive physicalism, substance dualism, and pure mind views – between these extremes are other views about what a self is, of what it is comprised, and of the manner in which it is structured. Two others that are obviously consistent with Nietzsche's naturalizing tendencies are, first, the view according to which a self is *constituted* by the body or by some part(s) of it – for instance, the distributed dynamic system of the brain and central nervous system; and, second, that according to which a self *supervenes* on and *emerges* from the body or some part(s) of it, typically from a set of relations between cortical events and processes.

The proposed interpretation is that most of what Nietzsche has to say about selves suggests a supervenience/emergence view. Note, to begin with, that naturalism about what the self is and how it is organized more or less demands the supervenience of psychological states on physical, mostly physiological, states of various kinds. Now, supervenience is one of those paradigmatic philosophical relationships that one rarely hears mentioned outside of the discipline. Nevertheless, it captures an important aspect of certain kinds of relations between levels of properties and Nietzsche avails himself of this aspect on a number of occasions. *Supervenience* is a relation between families of properties or states or events: one family of supervenient properties (states, events) S supervenes on another family of basal properties (states, events) B when there can be no changes in the supervening family without changes in the subvening basal properties (Davidson 1980). More carefully: as a matter of nomological necessity, some member of a basal property (state, event) family B is instantiated whenever some member of the supervening property (state, event) family S is instantiated, and when anything instantiates that member of the basal family B, it instantiates that member of the supervening property (state, event) family S.[3]

Excepting eliminativism, all physicalist views of the self comply with supervenience. But some views of the self are consistent with supervenience and inconsistent with physicalism. Among such views are parallelism and occasionalism, which likewise affirm that whenever a psychological or conscious property is instantiated some physical property is also instantiated and that anything else instantiating that physical property will also instantiate that psychological or conscious property. Of course, the parallelist also argues that, while co-instantiating and correlating, the psychological/conscious and the physical proceed along parallel but completely disconnected tracks. That the tracks run parallel to one another without ever crossing paths makes parallelism a kind of dualism about the self. So, since supervenience is consistent both with accepting and with rejecting physicalism, it is consistent both with accepting and rejecting reducing the psychological/conscious to something physical. Hence, something else is additionally necessary if supervenience is to be a kind of reductive physicalism. Moreover, since, as will be argued, Nietzsche is neither a reductive physicalist nor a parallelist about the self, something else is needed to square his views about the self with his avowed naturalism. He is not a reductive physicalist and claims nevertheless to be a naturalist about the self, so he must think it is possible to square the apparent circle of non-reductive naturalism.

Characterizing the additional element that, when conjoined with supervenience, successfully implies reductive physicalism is a matter of ongoing debate, some facets of which are relevant for understanding Nietzsche's views of the self.[4] Here is one way of focusing the issue. One might agree that the self supervenes on something but deny that what it supervenes on is the activity of the brain's neural pathways or the states of the central nervous system, or even the states of the embodied central nervous system. Perhaps the self supervenes instead on all of those *plus* observable behavior, or perhaps it supervenes on the embodied central nervous system, observable behavior, *plus* the embedded interaction between such an organism and (some part of) the extra-organismic environment. As can be appreciated, supervenience is consistent with an array of views about the kinds of things that are basal, and some of these views are pretty clearly physicalist only in letter and not in spirit, and some, although physicalist in letter and spirit, lend no support to reducing the self to something occurring in the brain.

At least as it is standardly deployed, supervenience has been taken to allow us to preserve the thought that the physical is more basic than the psychological and the thought that the psychological is nonethe-less explanatorily autonomous from the physical, that is, that psychological explanations cannot be reduced to physical ones. The promise of physicalism without reduction is for many the most salient attraction of supervenience: it appears to be strong enough to model covariation of the self with the physical – thus tying the self down to the physical and excluding pure minds, pure consciousnesses, pure egos, spiritual subjects, and other dualist concepts of the self – but weak enough to safeguard against reducing the self to the physical, thus preserving the domain of psychology as irreducible.[5]

Nietzsche concurs that psychological states are supervenient on some-thing and that some conscious states – the reflective ones – are super-venient on more basic conscious and unconscious states. Since for him all psychological states are drives and since drives are constituent sub-personal elements of a self, he predictably holds that the self is super-venient on drives, and that drives are supervenient on physiological conditions. The following has already been quoted:

> The body and physiology the starting point: why? – We gain the correct idea of the nature of our subject-unity, namely as regents at the head of a communality, also of the dependence of these regents upon the ruled and of an order of rank and division of labor as the conditions that make possible the whole and its parts The most important thing, however, is: that we understand that the ruler and his subjects are of the same kind, all feeling, willing, thinking – and that wherever we see or divine movement in a body, we learn to conclude that there is a subjective, invisible life appertaining to it. (KSA 11 40[21] = WP 492)

In this passage, the non-reductive supervenience of the unity of the subject on the ongoing dynamic activity of the brain and body is directly asserted. The subject, like a regent, is separately identifiable as a ruler, and so is not reducible to its constituent elements. However, the subject, again like a regent, is dependent upon and even of the same kind as those constituent elements. The unified subject supervenes on – covaries with and depends on – all of the feeling, willing, and thinking drive states (conscious and unconscious alike) that comprise our kind of animate organism even as it does not reduce to those states. The subject is, thus, 'a simplification with the object of defining the force which posits, invents, thinks, as distinct from all individual positing, inventing, thinking as such. Thus a *capacity* as distinct from what is individual – fundamentally, action collectively considered with respect to all anticipated actions (action and the probability of similar actions)' (KSA 12 2[152] = WP 556).

That Nietzsche recognizes the self's supervenience on drives is a reason for allowing that reflective consciousness may yet have a place in our psychological economy. He is anxious to emphasize that this place is that of being 'just a "tool" and nothing more – a tool in the same sense that the stomach is a tool' (KSA 11 37[4]). Downplaying reflective consciousness to this less than central causal role allows him to say that its activities pale in comparison to the 'admiration for how the human *body* has become possible; how such a prodigious alliance of living beings, each dependent and subservient and yet in a certain sense also commanding and acting out of its own will, can live, grow, and for a while prevail, as a whole' (KSA 11 37[4]). While reflective consciousness is relegated to a minor place in the self's structure, Nietzsche acknowledges that this minor role exists and uses it to preserve explanatory autonomy for psychology, sociology, genealogy, and, in some cases, even ethical evaluation (in his idiosyncratic senses of these terms). So long as the biological and the physiological are accorded causal priority in those higher-level explanations and descriptions, reflective consciousness and its products can and do also factor into psychological explanations. So his is a non-reductive supervenience-based physicalism about the psychological and the self: psychological causal explanations do not reduce to more basic physiological causal explanations and the self supervenes on some set of drives, conscious or unconscious.

Supervenience augmented with basal causal priority thus gets some of what Nietzsche says about the non-reducibility of the psychological/ conscious world and the self correct. However, supervenience only provides a constraint on our understanding of psychological causation; supervenience does not explain or describe the species of causation for which it provides that constraint. But Nietzsche is, at least on occasion, prepared to speculate about the nature of psychological, and in particular, reflectively conscious causation. As will be detailed in the next section, he identifies a unique sort of causal efficacy for supervenient reflective conscious states and for the supervenient self. If he can defend this unique sort of causal efficacy, then not everything true of reflective conscious states and not every aspect of the self can or must be described by describing only basal physiological levels alone, and that entails that we go beyond the explanatory resources available with supervenience. For in these cases, Nietzsche appears to advocate that at least certain kinds of psychological states and the self *emerge* from the conscious and unconscious drives of which we are constituted. Having emerged, they and it also make things happen.

Like supervenience, emergentism is a philosophical position about the relation between the supervenient and the subvenient, but unlike supervenience, emergentism enjoys a quite active public life outside the seminar room (even if philosophers have done the most to articulate the idea). Emergentism affirms the supervenience of the psychological and the reflectively conscious on the (neuro-) physiological and affirms also that psychological and reflectively conscious levels are casually novel as compared to the (neuro-) physiological levels from which they emerge. Emergentism thus goes farther than other supervenience-based physicalisms in explaining the irreducibility of the psychological and the reflectively conscious. Whereas supervenience labels without explaining how reflective conscious states cause anything, emergentism offers part of an explanation (this formulation follows a similar claim made in Kim 1999).

Emergentism partitions non-systemic from systemic properties; identifies emergent properties with systemic properties; and suggests, first, that systemic properties are irreducible to non-systemic properties, and, second, that there is causation between emergent systemic and basal non-systemic levels. The difference between systemic and non-systemic properties is of singular importance in most emergentist views. A *systemic property* is a property of a whole system or a whole mechanism that is distinct from the properties of any of the system's constituent elements. A *non-systemic property* is a property of a constituent element of a whole system or a whole mechanism. Recall the category of a self-organized dynamic system first introduced in Chapter 2. It will be remembered that a dynamic self-organized system is a set of entities that is in constant motion or is constantly changing, is structured so as to realize a function or maintain a particular configuration, and is such that its structure is not imposed by an external cause system. Recall also from that discussion that some self-organized dynamic systems are linear because their causal outcomes are roughly proportional to causal inputs, and that some systems are nonlinear because their causal outcomes are disproportional to causal inputs, thanks to the presence of positive and negative feedback loops. Marrying these analyses of linear and non-linear self-organized dynamic systems to the distinction between systemic and non-systemic properties of systems allows us to focus directly on the kinds of systems emergentists are most interested in and the criteria they use for distinguishing systemic from non-systemic properties.

Candidate non-linear self-organized dynamic systems include entities and events from the most basic system of all organic life, the cell, up to macro-events such as large crowds, swarms of locusts, schools of fish, flashfloods, hurricanes, tornadoes, wildfires, and avalanches (if you don't like some of the named candidates, feel free to ignore them). For no reason other than that they are vivid, consider tornadoes and wildfires. Both are dynamic, self-organizing, and nonlinear: each constantly changes from the moment of its inception to the moment of its dissolution; each maintains a particular configuration without external causes, and each is subject to positive and negative feedback loops, the activity of which makes its causal outcomes disproportional to their causal inputs, and thus nonlinear. A variety of criteria for distinguishing emergent systemic from basal non-systemic are suggested. Among them, some are epistemic, some focus on structural issues, and others focus on casual powers. Thus we may distinguish emergent systemic properties from basal non-systemic properties by claiming that emergents are novel given what is known about the basals or that emergents are unpredictable except by simulation given what is known about the basals. Alternatively, we may distinguish the classes by claiming that emergent properties are not structural resultant properties, as is, for instance, the shape of a whole composed of parts, or that they are not aggregative scalar sums of those of the basals from which they emerge, as is, for instance, the mass of a whole comprised of parts. Again, we may, following Strevens 2005, distinguish the classes by claiming that emergents are the result of particular kinds of complexity on the basals from which they emerge. Finally, we may, following Kim 1999, focus on causal powers, arguing that the causal powers of emergent properties are not vector sums of those of the basals from which they emerge, as is, for instance, engine horsepower.

According to most emergentists, the distinction between systemic and non-systemic properties is consistent with emergent systems nevertheless being physical systems. After all, the systems that have emergent properties are systems composed entirely of physical entities or parts thereof and emergent properties supervene on basal properties. According to *weak* emergentism, these systemic properties of systems of physical entities supervene on the non-systemic properties of that system's parts. *Strong* emergentism adds to weak emergentism the claim that, again at a time, a system's systemic properties are casually irreducible to basal properties.[6] Weak emergentisms are nondescript versions of reductive physicalism. On the other hand, strong emergentisms, whether synchronic or diachronic, affirm that even if emergent properties supervene on some basal properties, they are causally irreducible to those subvening basal properties.[7] Strong emergentism is obviously compatible with the dynamic embodied-embedded view of human physiology and psychology that has been our focus and is, as will be shown, the version that fits most comfortably with Nietzsche's thoughts about the self.[8]

If there are properties, states, and events at various levels and strong emergentism is true, then there must also be causal relations *at* and *between* levels, that is, there must be *intra-level* causation and *inter-level* causation. So, strong emergentism also requires both that some systemic properties are new and that intra-level casual powers are distinct from and irreducible to those of the subvenient levels of the system's components. A *basal* cause is then a basal state that causes another basal state. An *upward* cause is a basal state that causes an emergent state. An *emergent* cause is an emergent state that causes another emergent state. A *downward* cause is an emergent state that causes a basal state.

To illustrate these claims, suppose that at some time, t_1, we can ascertain all of a physical system's physical states. Call that set 'B_1' These are the basal states from which emergent states emerge. Suppose a group of physical states from B_1 at t_1 causes an emergent state at t_2. Call the emergent state 'E_2'. E_2 then emerges from B_1 and supervenes on B_2 (see Fig. 6.1). Suppose also that E_2 causes nothing subsequent to its occurrence. Where '$\rightarrow$' represents causation and '$===$' represents supervenience, we have an instance of *upward* causation:[9]

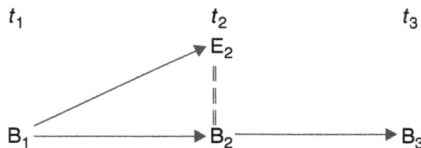

Figure 6.1   Upward causation from basal to emergent

Here, E_2 is an effect of upward causation from B_1 and supervenes on B_2. But E_2 is epiphenomenal: it is a momentary blip on the screen upwardly caused by a basal state. Suppose next that an emergent, E_3, is again generated, this time by B_2, but again causes nothing. Then we have:

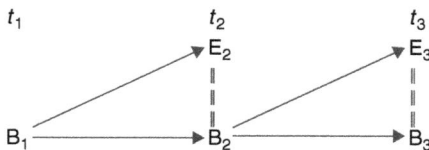

Figure 6.2   Iterated upward causation from basal to emergent

In Figure 6.2, two successive emergent states are represented as successive supervening epiphenomena upwardly caused by successive basal physical states. Suppose next that E_2 lays claim as cause of emergent state E_3. Then there will be a putative case of *emergent* causation:

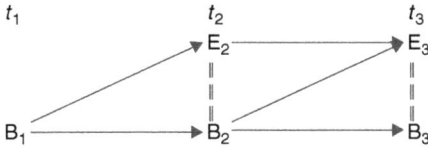

Figure 6.3   Emergent causation from emergent to emergent

If Figure 6.3 represents a possibility, some emergent causes have emergent effects. Suppose finally that E_2 claims instead to cause a basal state, B_3. Then there will be a putative case of *downward* causation:

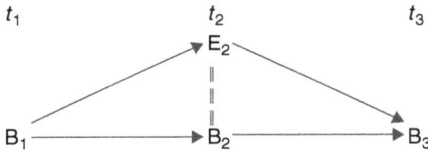

Figure 6.4   Downward causation from emergent to basal

If Figure 6.4 represents a possibility, some emergent causes have basal effects. So, if upward causation is possible, then some basal states are upward causes; if emergents are emergent causes and downward causes, then some emergents are not epiphenomenal. Strong diachronic emergentism is committed to all three kinds of causal relations.

II   Will, downward causation, and exclusion

Carving out logical space for downward causation is, it is proposed, a reasonable interpretation of Nietzsche's critical views about the will and his tempered acquiescence that reflectively conscious states, including purposes and intentions, may yet play a role in explaining human action. The following *Nachlass* note clearly suggests this view, suggesting that the will is epiphenomenal and yet that reflective purposes – or, preferably, intentions – have some causal role to play in explaining action:

> why could "a purpose" not be an epiphenomenon in the series of changes in the activating forces that bring about the purposive action – a pale image sketched in consciousness beforehand that serves to orient us concerning events, even as a symptom of events, not as their cause? – But with this we have criticized the will itself: is it not an illusion to take for a cause that which rises to consciousness as an act of will? Are not all phenomena of consciousness merely terminal phenomena, final links in a chain, but apparently conditioning one another in their succession on one level of consciousness? (KSA 12 7[1] = WP 666)

According to this passage, purposes are epiphenomena in the chain of activating states and events that implement or realize any action. For that reason, the will is itself an epiphenomenon and any thought that it is otherwise is an illusion. And yet he also acknowledges that purposes and other reflectively conscious states can "serve to orient us concerning events, even as a symptom of events." Note that 'orienting' is a causal verb, implying that reflective phenomena, while not realizing or implementing causes, do have another causal role to play in explaining action. This conjunction can, it will be argued here, be defended.

Nietzsche's reflections on the will and willing have been thoroughly discussed by others (for a good introduction, see the essays collected in Gemes and May 2007). Summarizing what increasingly appears to be a shared interpretation, we say that, at a minimum, he argues that there is no faculty of the will, much less a faculty of *free* will. His eliminative stance towards the faculty is stated baldly: 'The will no longer moves anything, hence it does not explain anything – it merely accompanies events; it can also be completely absent' (TI, 'Four Great Errors' 4, among many others). And as for free will, it is, he thinks, crucial to remember that 'the whole of the old-style psychology, the psychology of the will, has as its precondition the desire of its authors, the priests at the head of the ancient communities, to create for themselves the *right* to ordain punishments … Men were thought of as "free" so that they could become *guilty*' (TI 'Four Great Errors' 7, among many others). Explanations that invoke the will are to be eliminated and *replaced* with explanations that invoke intentions, goals, and purposes. On this view, action is undertaken if (but not only if) one has an intention that the action realizes.

Intentional action is thus a complex 'of sensation and thinking [and] above all an *affect* and specifically the affect of command' (BGE 19), or, alternatively put, a collection of different kinds of psychological and physiological states, every one of them a drive with affective/qualitative character and some with content.

One might think that Nietzsche's willingness to countenance intentional explanation in the case of human action is incompatible with his reductive analysis of superfluous goals and ends in nature, discussed in Chapter 2. It is certainly true that explaining the activity of unconscious drives and the consequences which that activity has cannot invoke goals or purposes, which, after all, are reflectively conscious. But from the absence of reflective goals and purposes – intentions – in the structure of unconscious drives it hardly follows that the structure of reflectively conscious drives must likewise be stripped of intentions. So long as intentions can be components of a reflective drive's structure and so long as their place in psychological explanations is consistent with modest epiphenomenalism (according to which every reflective conscious state that is causally efficacious is so not in virtue of being reflective but in virtue of being a drive, and every reflective conscious state has only non-conscious consequences), their place is secured against the threat of being superfluous.[10]

Nietzsche's distinction between *directing* and *driving* causes, which he considers to be one of his 'most essential steps and advances,' is precisely what is needed to accomplish the task. He thinks we must distinguish between:

> the cause of acting [and] the cause of acting in a particular way, in a particular direction, with a particular goal. The first kind of cause is a quantum of dammed-up energy that is waiting to be used up somehow, for something, while the second kind is, compared to this energy, something quite insignificant, for the most part a little accident in accordance with which this quantum "discharges" itself in one particular way – a match versus a ton of powder. Among these little accidents and "matches" I include so-called "purposes" as well as the even much more so-called "vocations": They are relatively random, arbitrary, almost indifferent in relation to the tremendous quantum of energy that presses...to be used up somehow. The usual view is different: People are accustomed to consider the goal (purposes, vocations, etc.) as the driving force, in keeping with a very ancient error; but it is merely the directing force – one has mistaken the helmsman for the steam. (GS 360)

Reflective goals and purposes may therefore be causally efficacious, not as driving or implementing causes but as directing causes. A reflective goal's causal efficacy consists in constraining, structuring, and shaping – directing – rather than being a propelling force, which, of course, no goal has. Hence, in the counterfactual absence of a particular goal, our various drives would continue to impel us to be active across the various domains over which the drive acts, although the constraining and shaping associated with that goal would not occur. Modest eiphenomenalism of reflective consciousness is, moreover, consistent with the distinction between driving and shaping causes. Even if there are some reflective conscious states that have no causal consequences at all, every reflective conscious state that is efficacious is so only on members of the set of basic conscious and unconscious states. Reflective conscious states are, of course, various and include not only purposes, intentions, plans, and goals, but also reflective thoughts, imaginings, beliefs, desires, hopes, feelings, valuations, convictions, and all the rest of the reflective contents of our psyche. If he is right about them, the causal efficacy of all of them is exhausted by their provision of direction for cultivating and developing certain drives along certain routes rather than others. Hence, they have *some* causal consequences, for they cause certain other drives to implement or realize the direction they provide. But only those other drives actually implement or realize the direction that a reflective state provides and it is not in virtue of a drive's reflective conscious properties that such implementation occurs.

The distinction between directing and driving causes appears to provide an analysis of intentional action that carves out a role for intentions as downward emergent causes shaping and constraining the ways that drives express. So, Nietzsche's views about intentions can be defended as consistent with other things that he says about reflective consciousness and drives. Still, intentions, if they are emergent, face a challenge that all emergentist views face. As Nietzsche himself recognizes, since the physical, the biological, and basic kinds of consciousness all have causal priority over reflective consciousness, they all threaten reflective conscious states – and, perforce, intentions – with epiphenomenality. The final sentences of *Gay Science* 360 raise the specter of epiphenomenality directly. Here, he openly wonders whether 'the "goal," the "purpose" [is] not often enough a beautifying pretext, a self-deception of vanity after the event that does not want to acknowledge that the ship is following the current into which it has entered accidentally? that it "wills" to go that way because it – must? that is has a direction to be sure, but – no helmsman at all?' Allow that this is often the case, that is, that we often engage in *ex post facto* rationalization of an action by providing with it with the intention required to have that action be its realization when, to the contrary, we would have performed exactly the same behavior had that intention been different or entirely absent. Yet Nietzsche acknowledges even here that this is not *always* the case and that our actions are at least sometimes best understood as the realization of some intention that provides its direction.

Reflective directing states must, if they are not to be epiphenomenal, cause changes in other psychological states – basic conscious states and unconscious states alike – that initiate a driving or implementation chain that eventually realizes the helmsman's directions. Grant that subsequent to the causal nexus between a directing intention and the initial driving cause, every causal nexus is between drives that are not reflectively conscious. But consider the causal nexus between directing and the initial implementing cause. By hypothesis, it is not a causal nexus between two driving or implementing causes. For, if it were, then there would be no distinction between directing and driving causes. If so, Nietzsche seems to commit himself to a kind of causation that occurs only between some members of the subset of reflectively conscious states and all of the others that are not reflectively conscious. Although grounded in the obvious Nietzschean need to explain how reflective thought can effect some change to our character or to the actions we perform, such a view appears to fit poorly with his attempt at analyzing all causal power in terms of drives and driving causes and all efficient causality in terms of will to power.

The problem confronted by Nietzsche's views on this matter is an instance of a general problem that any emergentist view robust enough to accommodate novel emergent causal powers must confront: any emergent that is a downward cause appears to overdetermine what it causes. Because this is a quite general problem, it appears that all downward causation, including the directing causal efficacy that Nietzsche attributes to intentions, goals, and purposes, is threatened with epiphenomenality. This argument, known as the *supervenience argument* or the *causal exclusion argument*, purports to demonstrate that any emergent that supervenes on a basal is an overdetermining cause, and is for that reason epiphenomenal. If so, then the causal independence of emergents is undermined and the explanatory autonomy of reflective consciousness is undermined.[11]

Contemporary versions of the exclusion argument proceed in a general setting. The argument typically takes two steps: the first shows that causation between emergents must be replaced by downward causation; the second shows that downward causation must be replaced by basal causation. It will be helpful to keep the following notions in mind. First, where we have E_n, B_{n+1} and E_{n+1}, E_n and B_{n+1} *overestablish* E_{n+1} whenever E_n claims to cause E_{n+1} and B_{n+1} subvenes E_{n+1}. Second, where we have B_n, E_n, and B_{n+1}, B_n and E_n *overdetermine* B_{n+1} whenever E_n and B_n both claim to cause B_{n+1} and only E_n or B_n (and not both E_n and B_n) cause B_{n+1}. The exclusion argument then relies on premises assessing the causal efficacy of overestablished emergents and overdetermined basals. These premises are the *Disqualification* premise and the *Preemption* premise:

> Disqualification: If E_n and B_{n+1} overestablish E_{n+1}, then E_n is *disqualified* as a cause of E_{n+1}.
>
> Preemption: If E_n and B_n overdetermine B_{n+1}, then E_n is *preempted* as a cause of P_{n+1}.[12]

So, if a state is either disqualified or preempted as a cause, it is *excluded* from being a cause. From exclusion, epiphenomenality may be directly inferred.

The first step of the exclusion argument re-describes causation from one emergent E_2 to another as a combination of downward causation plus supervenience. Suppose E_2 lays claim to cause E_3. Now, E_3 has a basal on which it supervenes, namely B_3, and E_3's supervenience on B_3 also guarantees E_3's instantiation. So, E_2 and B_3 overestablish E_3. That looks like one cause too many. The way to solve this problem is to say that E_2 causes not another emergent E_3 but downwardly causes B_3, on which E_3 supervenes. Hence, E_2 is disqualified as an emergent cause of E_3:

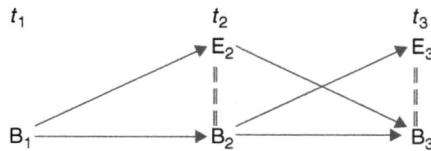

Figure 6.5 Disqualifying emergent causation

Since E_2 is *disqualified* as a cause of E_3, emergents are *excluded* from being causes of other emergents.

Look, now, at the downward causation in Figure 6.5: E_2 supervenes on B_2 but also claims to cause B_3. It appears that both B_2 and E_2 each cause B_3. Again, that looks like one cause too many, that is, B_2 and E_2 appear to overdetermine B_3. The solution just offered points the way to a solution here: downward causation from emergent to basal may be redescribed as causation between basals and supervenience of subsequent emergent on basal.

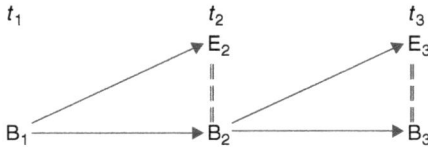

Figure 6.6 Preempting downward causation

Figure 6.6 represents the remaining causal relations once E_2 is *preempted* and thus excluded as cause of B_3. In short, emergents are disqualified as causes of other emergents and preempted as causes of basals. They are, therefore, excluded from being either emergent or downward causes. From exclusion, emergent epiphenomenality follows directly. From a causal point of view, that makes strong emergentism indistinguishable from reductive physicalism. Hence, strong emergentism fails.

The exclusion argument identifies a fundamental problem with emergent conscious states that claim to be downward causes: they appear to be causally superfluous given the physical states from which they emerge. But the exclusion argument fails if either the Disqualification premise or the Preemption premise is irrelevant or if either the Disqualification premise or the Preemption premise is false. Perhaps surprisingly, there is reason to think that both the Disqualification premise and the Preemption premise are irrelevant and false. Interestingly enough, although he does not consider the Disqualification premise, Nietzsche's perspectivism is a pretty good reason for thinking that the Preemption premise is irrelevant in a general way, and his distinction between directing and driving causes is a pretty good reason for thinking that the Preemption premise is false in the case of reflective downward causation.

Although Nietzsche doesn't consider them directly, the problems facing the Disqualification premise help us understand the nub of the issue between emergentists and reductionists in general and so help orient us to the problem confronting downward causation. Note that the reasoning employed in the exclusion argument can be reapplied to the initial assumption that there is upward causation from basals to emergents. If, in general, basal causation plus supervenience can replace emergent and downward causation, then basal causation plus supervenience can just as easily replace upward causation. That is, if B_2 is sufficient for E_2, then B_1 is redundant on B_2:

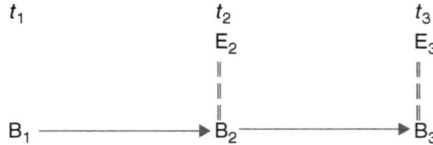

$$
\begin{array}{lll}
t_1 & t_2 & t_3 \\
 & E_2 & E_3 \\
 & \| & \| \\
 & \| & \| \\
 & \| & \| \\
B_1 \longrightarrow & B_2 \longrightarrow & B_3
\end{array}
$$

Figure 6.7   Eliminating upward causation

B_1 is thus eliminated as an upward cause of E_2. So, just as emergents are downwardly epiphenomenal, basals are *upwardly* epiphenomenal.

This extension of the exclusion argument typically goes unnoticed. There is a reason for this, but to identify that reason, two other candidate reasons must be rejected. First, note that B_2's subvenience of E_2 does not *disqualify* B_1 as an upward cause of E_2, for were B_2's subvenience of E_2 to disqualify B_1 as cause of E_2, then B_2 would have to block B_1's causal work. But then B_2 would be a cause that works backward in time, and so long as we are not prepared to defend backward causation, this answer is a nonstarter. Similarly, B_2 does not *preempt* B_1 as cause of E_2 either, for B_2 would then be a simultaneous cause, and that alternative is also a nonstarter.[13] So, although the conclusion of the exclusion argument – that basal causation plus supervenience suffices to understand emergentism – may be true in the case of upward causation, neither of the premises used against emergents and leading to that conclusion is true in the case of upward causation.

This is a curious feature of the exclusion argument, but the oddity is explained when one recognizes that the exclusion argument is really just a stalking horse for a more global worry about emergents, *viz.*, that they are not real. The exclusion argument inoculates against emergents doing any causal work once they have emerged, but inoculating them against doing causal work would be unneeded if basal causation plus supervenience in general provides all that is needed to explain emergents. Of course, as just argued, neither the Disqualification premise nor the Preemption premise can be used to explain why upward causation is bogus. But if emergents are only misleadingly spoken of as expressing or referring to extra-linguistic entities and properties, then a ready and reductive explanation of emergence is at hand. On this way of thinking about emergents, all talk of emergent *properties* is misleading and it is better to replace such talk with talk of emergent *designators* or *descriptions* instead (Kim 1998). If there is nothing more to an emergent than its description, then emergents are ersatz entities that extend no further than the predicate expressing them. That is, they are *pleonastic*. If so, there is a direct argument to emergent epiphenomenality: if they are pleonastic, emergents are washed out of all causal networks, so *any* causal claim made on their behalf is false. But note that, since the antecedent of the Disqualification premise will always be false if emergents are pleonastic, tolerating emergents long enough to disqualify them with the Disqualification premise is a moot exercise.

In the previous chapter, we investigated some Nietzschean passages that imply a similarly dismissive assessment of reflective conscious states. Recall the distinction between strong and modest epiphenomenalism of reflective conscious states. On the former, every reflective conscious state is a terminal phenomenon with no subsequent causal effects, while on the latter, every reflective conscious state is always and at the same time also a drive, and it is only in virtue of it also being a drive that it is casually efficacious. If, now, we understand reflective conscious states to be states that are not drives, then since Nietzsche routinely affirms that all psychological states *are* drives, it falls out directly that 'reflective conscious state' is an empty singular term, that is, a term that fails to refer. In this case, reflective conscious states are pleonastic entities, for their existence extends no further than a singular term. Even if we understand 'being reflectively conscious' to be a predicate that expresses a property that some drives have, we can still interpret the passages that affirm strong epiphenomenalism as implying that the property of being reflectively conscious is a pleonastic property. However, as we have also seen, these strong epiphenomenalist passages do not fit comfortably with other Nietzschean claims, which is just another way of saying again that modest epiphenomenalism + non-pleonastic reflective conscious states + non-reductive physicalism is preferable to strong epiphenomenalism + pleonastic reflective conscious states + reductive physicalism.[14]

If, now, some group of basals is an upward cause of a non-pleonastic emergent, it turns out that there is no good reason for claiming with the exclusion argument that an emergent thus caused is disqualified as a cause. For consider an emergent's supervenience on a basal: supervenience establishes a nomological covariation between emergent and basal at a time, not an instantaneous or backward causal relation between emergent and basal. If so, then an emergent's supervenience on certain basals does not entail disqualifying emergents from having distinct causal powers from those of the basals on which they supervene. Thus, supervenience alone does not entail rejecting upward, emergent, or downward causation. However, the Disqualification premise affirms just this, namely that supervenient emergents are overestablished and do not have causal powers distinct from those of the basals on which they supervene. Hence, the Disqualification premise is false. In summary, then, the situation is this: either emergents are pleonastic or they are not pleonastic. If they are pleonastic, then upward causation from basals to emergents is eliminated, there is only basal causation, and the Disqualification premise of the exclusion argument is irrelevant. If, on the other hand, emergents are not pleonastic, then basals are not disqualified as upward causes, and emergents are not disqualified as causes, and the Disqualification premise of the exclusion argument is false.

Of course, from the falsity or irrelevance of the Disqualification premise it does not follow that strong emergentism is vindicated, for the problem of overdetermination remains. Even if emergents *can* be downward causes of basals, for any given emergent claiming to cause some basal, there will always be a cotemporaneous basal that appears to compete with it. Suppose that E_2 emerges from B_1 and supervenes on B_2. So, where E_2 occurs, so too will B_2. Suppose now that E_2 claims to cause B_3. But were E_2 and B_2 both to cause B_3, then there would be two causes of B_3 where there is room only for one. That is overdetermination. Having B_2 preempt E_2 as cause of B_3 and affirming E_2's epiphenomenality looks like a good solution to the problem of overdetermination. So, even if the exclusion argument fails to show that emergents are excluded as causes, it appears to show that where emergents are candidate causes, their candidacy will never go uncontested and that they might lose every contest they enter. This dashes the strong emergentist's hopes for defending downward causation.

Yet even here appearances are deceiving. Emergentists, and, if the interpretation here is sound, Nietzsche also, have options against the Preemption premise. Emergentists like Nietzsche can try to defend one or more of the following:

a. E_2 and B_2 do not conjointly cause B_3; and E_2 and B_2 do not overdetermine B_3; so B_2 does not preempt E_2.
b. E_2 and B_2 conjointly cause B_3; and E_2 and B_2 overdetermine B_3; but overdetermination is not sufficient for preemption; or

c. E_2 and B_2 conjointly cause B_3; yet E_2 and B_2 do not overdetermine B_3; so B_2 does not preempt E_2.

Recall, now, the Preemption premise from above: if E_n and B_n overdetermine B_{n+1}, then E_n is preempted as cause of B_{n+1}. If either (a) or (c) is true, then the antecedent of the Preemption premise is false and the Preemption premise is moot. Likewise, if (b) is true, then the antecedent of the Preemption premise is true and the consequent of the Preemption premise is false, in which case the Preemption premise is false. Nietzsche does not advocate (a), but he does consider (b) in a general setting, and he affirms (c).

Although Nietzsche does not discuss (a), we do so to show why it is sub-optimal. If (a) is true, E_2 and B_2 do not conjointly cause B_3, and E_2 and B_2 do not overdetermine B_3, so B_2 does not preempt E_2. That is, although overdetermination mandates preemption, since E_2 and B_2 do not *conjointly* cause B_3, they are not guilty of overdetermination. This alternative is true in either of two cases: first, when E_2 and not B_2 causes B_3, or, second, when B_2 and not E_2 causes B_3. Emergentists think the first alternative is true; reductive physicalists think the second alternative is true. The burden falls, then, on advocates of emergentism to identify how the first is true, for it is one thing for emergents not to be disqualified as causes just because they are supervenient, but it is quite another thing to specify what, if anything, is that in virtue of which they *are* qualified as causes. Some emergentists simply assume that emergents are qualified as distinct causes, and others simply announce that emergents are qualified as causes because they have causal powers distinct from those of their subvenient basals. Since neither tacit assumption nor simple announcement are philosophically satisfying, if it turns out that Nietzsche has no option other than (a), he would be in trouble.

However, Nietzsche has options other than (a). Consider (b): on this alternative, it may be allowed that overdetermination occurs, but we deny that preemption of overdetermining causes is mandated. Before responding with a blank stare or yelling 'non-starter!' we might ask, is overdetermination really *that* bad? After all, given overdetermination, there is an embarrassment of causal riches: there will never be events popping into existence from nowhere or a slow ratcheting down to nothing.[15] If Nietzsche is prepared to defend the existence of such a causally congested world, then the Preemption premise is straightforwardly false. And he is on occasion prepared to defend the existence of such a causally congested world. He sometimes proposes certain ontological claims about the relations between will to power, causation, and perspectives that support such a view. For if all causation is, as he sometimes claims, reducible to will to power (see, for instance, BGE 36; GM I 13; KSA 10 24[14] = WP 641; KSA 10 24[9] = WP 664; KSA 13 14[79] = WP 634; KSA 13 14[121] = WP 688), and if, as he sometimes claims, will to power is ineliminably perspectival (see e.g., BGE 36; KSA 11 36[20] = WP 637; KSA 12 7[54] = WP 617; KSA 13 14[184] = WP 567), then there cannot be a fixed number of causes. Rather, there are as many causes as there are perspectives, and there are a lot of perspectives.[16]

Having to buy a causally congested world may seem an extravagance if all that needs defending is the causal efficacy of intentions. So if (c) can be defended more narrowly than committing ourselves to a controversial ontological position, it may be preferable to (b). On (c), E_2 and B_2 are not *competing* causes of B_3 but *conjoint* causes of B_3. This option is true if E_2 and B_2 are cotemporaneous causes without each of which B_3 does not occur and with both of which B_3 does occur, an exemplary case of individually necessary and conjointly sufficient causes. But then E_2 and B_2 do not *over*determine B_3 and the antecedent of the Preemption premise is false. If so, the Preemption premise does not apply to emergent downward causation in general, and does not apply to intentional action in particular. This alternative is exactly what Nietzsche thinks is the case with intentional action. His distinction between directing causes and implementing causes can be interpreted an instance of individually necessary and conjointly sufficient causes. Both reflectively conscious purposes and energetic drives are cited as causes, each necessary for actions, and, when put together, sufficient for a particular action. For a purpose or intention is analogous to a match put to the dynamite of the energetic drives. Without this particular match, the dynamite will find some other way to explode, but with this match, the dynamite finds a particular occasion to explode. Likewise, without a particular purpose or intention, the energetic drives will find some other way to express themselves, but with a particular purpose, the drives find a particular way to express themselves.

III   Achieving a self, power, and self-overcoming

If the interpretation offered here is on the right track, Nietzsche's thoughts about the self can be defended even if he affirms the existence of a fairly robust emergent self, a self that emerges from a set of drives, some of them unconscious, some of them basically conscious, some of them reflectively conscious, and some of them reflectively and reflexively conscious. The self's emergence is both synchronic and diachronic. Synchronically, the self's supervenience tethers it to the drives from which it emerges. Those drives are varied and themselves organized synchronically in supervenient hierarchies, some of them more basic than others, some of them conjunctive combinations of others, others disjunctive or conditional combinations. Diachronically, the self's supervenient emergence implies that the self is dependent and transitory, something not to be taken for granted and something that can weaken or strengthen over time depending on the state of the drives from which it emerges. Finally, since all drives, whether unconscious or conscious, have qualitative/affective character, and since all drives are dynamic, embodied, and embedded, both the felt character of experience and our experience of ourselves as causally efficacious agents in the extra-organismic environment are safeguarded against elimination or reduction.

The formal and abstract characterizations of the emergent self and the equally abstract criticisms of emergence considered thus far are admittedly remote from what makes Nietzsche the acute psychologist and critic of morality that he is. In our efforts to defend the cogency of an emergentist view of the self against philosophical criticism that would undermine it altogether, most of Nietzsche's substantive views about human psychology and his reflections on what makes thinking about selves necessary and what makes certain kinds of selves more interesting than others have been pushed down the road. But here, in the final section of the last chapter, at least some of his vibrant and textured psychological insights can be investigated by putting them onto the meta-psychological skeleton that, if the arguments above succeed, has been shown to be sound.

The complexity of our drives and affects undeniably makes us interesting. But Nietzsche thinks that if we are honest with ourselves, that complexity also makes us embarrassing almost beyond comprehension. For the sad truth is that most of us are simply bags of affects and 'contrary drives and impulses' (KSA 11 27[59] = WP 966) that go unordered and undisciplined for most of our lives. We do not know much about, and, worse, we lack what is needed to control and order, the jumble of drives, affects, and impulses that are us. As a result, we rebound from one unhappy or degrading disappointment to another, clucking and flapping our tongues at others who are just as ridiculous as we are. Some of us continue on this humiliating trajectory all of our lives, some eventually collapse, and some begin a long slow-motion emotional shutdown. Many of us fall into the arms of ascetic philosophers, priests, and 'experts' about the self. These opportunists are all too happy to diagnose the lunacy of passions and drives as the culprit of our misery and to imme-diately prescribe their 'extirpation...as a preventive measure against their stupidity and the unpleasant consequences of this stupidity' (TI 'Morality' 1). The results are all of the philosophical and religious re-or-ganization programs and methods that make us self-contradictory, self-abusing, self-hypnotizing, self-abasing, self-depreciating, self-deceived, self-torturing, self-tyrannizing, self-negating, self-eliminating, self-mortifying, self-martyring, self-misunderstanding, self-contemptuous, self-annihilating, self-belittling, and self-critiquing. But these ascetic programs are one and all decadent (in Nietzsche's idiosyncratic sense of 'decadent' as being against life) and thus far from optimal. As he acidly observes, these decadent regimens 'strike us as merely another acute form of stupidity. We no longer admire dentists who "pluck out" teeth so that they will not hurt any more' (TI 'Morality' 1). For trying to ease the suffering that passions and drives cause by eliminating them altogether is contrary to life: 'an attack on the roots of passion means an attack on the roots of life' (TI 'Morality' I).

A few of us – certain saints, some artists, a few political and cultural figures, occasional philosophers and scientists scattered across the centuries – come in for Nietzsche's praise because they escape the almost universally decadent consequences of these self re-organization programs. Despite coming equipped as the majority of us are, and despite being subjected to the same decadent curricula that others are, and despite re-organizing themselves at least in part in accord with those decadent curricula, these individuals manage to become interesting exemplars who provide insight into what we all might become. For their flourishing lives display what humans are capable of: self-control, self-discipline, and even self-overcoming. They thus reveal just how uncanny, how much a lucky throw of the dice pregnant with a future (GM II 16), we really are.

Flourishing individuals have several cognitive and affective qualities in common. They are, Nietzsche thinks, composed of as many strong and conflicting drives and affects as can be brought together into some kind of unified whole. But the sheer number of strong drives and affects is not what makes a flourishing individual powerful; it is their capacity to synthesize drives and affects into a coherent unity that their power consists in. Compare two individuals, both from the same cultural setting. Each of them, like all of us, 'have in their bodies the heritage of multiple origins, that is, opposite, and often not merely opposite, drives and value standards that fight each other and rarely permit each other any rest' (BGE 200). These inherited and embodied drives and affects, whether consonant with one another or not, dynamically self-organize into various other drive/affect complexes that, in turn, are causally coupled with the surrounding environment, forming feedback and feed-forward loops that sometimes reinforce and augment, and sometimes battle and destroy, those elements and the complexes formed therefrom. The weaker individual wants nothing more than that this dynamic battle of conflicting drives and affects come to an end:

> Happiness appears to [him], in agreement with a tranquilizing (e.g., Epicurean or Christian) medicine and way of thought, pre-eminently as the happiness of resting, of not being disturbed, of satiety, of finally attained unity, as a "sabbath of sabbaths," to speak with the holy rhetorician Augustine who was himself such a human being. (BGE 200)

For the stronger individual, on the other hand, the internal conflict across the drives and affects is itself a goad and incentive to master the internal warzone, to give one's drives and affects shape and structure:

> But when the opposition and war in such a nature have the effect of one more charm and incentive of life – and if, moreover, in addition to his powerful and irreconcilable drives a real mastery and subtlety in waging war against oneself, in other words, self- control, self-out-witting, has been inherited or cultivated, too – then those magical, incomprehensible, and unfathomable ones arise, those enigmatic men predestined for victory and seduction. (BGE 200)

Strong individuals eschew the ascetic recommendation that drives and affects be subjected to 'weakening and extirpation,' preferring instead to put them 'into service: which may also mean subjecting them to a protracted tyranny,' so that 'at last they are confidently granted freedom again: they love us as good servants and go voluntarily wherever our best interests lie' (KSA 12 1[122] = WP 384).

One of the few who exemplifies this kind of flourishing is Goethe, for he is one of the few of whom the following – 'only this should be called greatness: the ability to be just as multiple as whole, just as wide as full' (BGE 212) – is true. Goethe first conceived and then re-organized his drives, his affects, and even his physical health and perceptual experience in so many ways that he eventually became someone who is 'highly educated, skilful in all bodily matters, self-controlled, reverent toward himself, and who might dare to afford the whole range and wealth of being natural' (TI 'Skirmishes' 49). For such a person, 'there is no longer anything that is forbidden – unless it be weakness, whether called vice or virtue' (TI 'Skirmishes' 49). Since the internal conflicts between the various drives, between the various affects, and between sets of drives and affects are in him ordered, structured, and controlled, he sometimes presents as an enigma and can provoke questioning, even hostile, reactions in those unlike him. For such a one, nothing is forbidden, not because he is morally exceptional but because his successful self re-organization excuses him from moral prescriptions altogether. His self-re-organization accomplishes such a thorough re-structuring of drives and affects that he no longer falls within the scope of moral prescription. He is beyond good and evil.

While evocative, these descriptions of psychological strength present numerous difficulties, not the least of which is that it appears to presuppose a conception of the self more substantial than that available to Nietzsche. Recall the minimal self from Chapter 5. If what has been argued there is sound, the only self that can start such a self-reorganization program is the minimal self that emerges as a transitory systemic state from a set of subjectively perspectival interoceptive and perceptual states and drives and affects that are, by hypothesis, disordered. On pain of internal inconsistency, Nietzsche cannot avail himself of any kind of substantial or transcendental self that adopts a panoptic perspective on its own drives and affects or that can be the starting point for such a self-reorganization project to get off the ground. Nor does a substantial or transcendental self ever emerge at any stage during a re-organization project, nor even as its end-stage. Every kind of re-organization regimen that Nietzsche advocates must be consistent with a minimal self that at initial stages, and indeed at many subsequent stages as well, is little more than a gossamer-thin and ephemeral emergent state occasionally spit out by complex and disordered systems of subconscious, preconscious, and unconscious drives, basically conscious perceptions, interoceptions, drives and affects, and the odd coherent thought.

In such a minimal self, reflective conscious states are initially only momentary flashes. But in most of us, the basal conditions required for their occurrence stabilize and reflective conscious states become recurring phenomena. When that occurs, a requirement for self re-organization is accomplished. For the minimal self must be able, as Nietzsche puts it, to *conceive* of a future counterfactual self whose currently conflicting drives and affects are re-structured in some more coherent fashion. Of course, it cannot be a requirement that one be capable of imagining that fully realized end-product; indeed, it is almost certain that whatever future self one imagines at the beginning of self-reorganization will be corrupted by the current 'multitude and disgregation of impulses and the lack of any systematic order among them' (KSA 13 14[219] = WP 46). All that is required is that the drives and affects be not so disorganized that an imaginary and counterfactual thought experiment cannot be conducted (of course, for some even the thought experiment is impossible – think of an addict in the grip of his addiction or an individual suffering from severe psychological disorders).

Note that the thought experiment entertained by the minimal self is a reflectively conscious state. Hence, it appears that self-reorganization cannot get very far without the kind of conscious state that, if strong epiphenomenalism were true, would be ruled out as having any causal consequences. Modest epiphenomenalism, on the other hand, at least provides Nietzsche with a model of what is happening. The contents of such imaginary thought experiments can, perhaps in conjunction with other reflective states such as intentions and reflectively deliberative states, serve as downward directing causes that help orient the drives and affects to different possible organizations and structures. Of course, even without the downward causes from reflective states, all of the drives would continue to find opportunities for expression, would continue to enlist affects, would continue to evaluate the world in light of their characteristic functions, and would continue to enlist other drives in their campaigns to appropriate and assimilate. Yet once reflective downward causes are thrown into the crucible of drives and affects, some of them can find new occasional satisfaction objects, some of them can enlist different affects and can, in virtue of those differences, conjoin into different complexes over time. So reflective states as directing or orienting causes and drives and affects as driving or implementing causes, each kind individually necessary and conjointly sufficient, work together to undertake the constitutive stages of a dynamic and, if all goes well, increasingly self-organizing process of self re-organization.

Unfortunately, more than a few things do not go well for the vast majority of us. Threats to self re-organization regimens are numerous, some of them internal, others external. Nietzsche recognizes that successful self re-organization projects are exceedingly rare (the glorious humans he actually deigns to mention in his books *may* add up to two dozen). Failure in this regard is the lot of most humans. Some of them are like orchids, requiring such specific psychological nourishment and such particular social environments that they wilt before ever realizing what their early growth patterns promised. Others, although they are less fastidious in their psychological eating habits and make fewer and easier-to-satisfy demands on the larger environment, nevertheless grow up dishevelled or misshapen, with odd exaggerations or gnarled burls in their character. It is depressingly difficult to exercise the self-mastery and discipline required to organize the drives or to structure the affects in ways that are both life-affirming and engender psychological health. For most of us, some deeply embedded, strong, and perversely opaque set of drives never relinquishes its hold on us and proves to be our undoing. However, for the exceptional – the strong and powerful – self re-organization results in a robust self who rejects nothing and affirms everything.

Notes

1 Naturalism, Science, Positivism

1. The distinction between substantive and methodological naturalisms is commonly made in contemporary philosophy of mind and philosophy of science. The distinction goes back at least to W.V.O. Quine, who advocates both in his work. See, for example, Quine 1953 and Quine 1969a. For more on the distinction between substantive and methodological naturalism in Nietzsche's work, see Leiter 2002 and Leiter 2013. Leiter's distinction is generally consistent with, but not implied by, the distinction between ontological naturalism and methodological naturalism defended by David Papineau in, for example, Papineau 1993 and Papineau 2009. Others who interpret Nietzsche as advocating some kind of naturalism include Schacht 1983 and Schacht 2012; Clark 1990; Richardson 1996; Cox 1999; Hales and Welshon 2000, Moore 2002; Welshon 2004; and Kail 2009.
2. We will, in Chapter 6, attribute to Nietzsche a supervenience-based diachronic emergentism about psychological states and the self, views that entail rejecting the reduction of psychological states and the self to anything physiological. Any view of psychology and the self that is supervenience-based is a species of naturalism, and any view of psychology and the self that is emergentist and non-reductionist is, it will be argued, a species of liberal (or relaxed) naturalism rather than strict or strong naturalism. The contrast between liberal and strict naturalisms is Strawson's; that between relaxed and strong naturalisms is McDowell's. See Strawson 1985 and McDowell 2008.
3. Contemporary philosophy of science does not make the distinction in the same way. There are now dynamical mechanistic explanations. See, for example, Bechtel and Abrahamsen 2005.
4. For discussion of Boskovich's argument on behalf of this conclusion and further details concerning his influence on Nietzsche, see Poellner 1995, especially chapter 2, and Anderson 2013, note 20. For discussion of Nietzsche's dynamicist power ontology, see Poellner 1995, Richardson 1996, and Welshon 2004.
5. Stack 1983, p.4, suggests that Nietzsche was 'more thoroughly influenced by, and impressed by, this single work than by anything else he ever read.' A bit hyperbolic, but probably not far from the truth. See also Salaquarda 1978.
6. It is noteworthy, for example, that Nietzsche does not discuss the views of physicists not discussed at length in Lange. As a result, Nietzsche ignores Joseph-Louis Lagrange, whose mathematical work on Newtonian equations simplified mechanics by showing how the concept of force can be avoided altogether. Nietzsche likewise appears not to have read the work of James Clerk Maxwell, whose 1867 article 'On Governors' lays out a mathematical framework for describing the behavior of dynamic mechanical controlling devices such as Watt governors.

7. Nietzsche also argues that mechanism and its mathematical models trivialize the world:

> Do we really want to permit existence to be degraded for us like this – reduced to a mere exercise for a calculator and an indoor diversion for mathematicians? Above all, one should not wish to divest existence of its *rich ambiguity*: that is a dictate of good taste, gentlemen, the taste of reverence for everything that lies beyond your horizon… an interpretation that permits counting, calculating, weighing, seeing, and touching, an nothing more–that is a crudity and naivete, assuming that it is not a mental illness, an idiocy (GS 373).

   To the extent that Nietzsche's criticism is directed only against mechanistic science it misses against contemporary science, which has for the most part abandoned the kind of mechanistic analyses that he targets.

8. It is in part because Nietzsche thinks this is the function of science that he recommends that we think of ourselves as scientific experiments: 'But we, we others who thirst after reason, are determined to scrutinize our experiences as severely as a scientific experiment – hour after hour, day after day. We ourselves wish to be our experiments and guinea pigs' (GS 319).

9. Quine 1969b and Quine 1953 both make the point.

10. For defense of the claim that Nietzsche may be so interpreted, see Hussain 2004a and Hussain 2004b. For doubts about the interpretation, see Clark and Dudrick 2004.

11. Of course, to the extent that one can saddle Nietzsche with a truth-conditional semantics, to that extent does (5) reduce to (3). For our purposes, nothing hangs on this issue, so the semantic claim may remain distinct from the alethic claim.

12. These points are implications of general features of the necessity and knowledge operators. In general, if it is necessary that not-p, then it is not possible that-p. Likewise, if it is known that not-p, then it cannot be known that-p. On the other hand, even if it is not necessary that-p, it does not follow that it is necessary that not-p. Similarly, even if it is not known that-p, it does not follow that it is known that not-p. This is just to say that the claim in which knowledge has scope over the proposition about the real world is *stronger* than the *weaker* claim in which knowledge does not have scope over the proposition about the real world. So, (a) implies (b) and (b) fails to imply (a).

13. Nietzsche's claims here are similar to Colin McGinn's claims about epistemic closure. See McGinn 2000. Occasionally, Nietzsche derives a solipsistic conclusion from the unknowability of the thing-in-itself. One example is KSA 12 9[106] = WP 569:

> Questions, what things "in-themselves" may be like, apart from our sense receptivity and the activity of our understanding, must be rebutted with the question: how could we know that things exist? "Thingness" was first created by us. The question is whether there could not be many othe ways of creating such an apparent world – and whether this creating, logicizing, adapting, falsifying is not itself the best-guaranteed reality; in short, whether that which "posits things" is not the sole reality; and whether the "effect of the external world upon us" is not also only the result of such active subjects – The other "entities" act upon us; our adapted apparent

world is an adaptation and overpowering of their actions; a kind of defensive measure. The subject alone is demonstrable; hypothesis that only subjects exist – that "object" is only a kind of effect produced by a subject upon a subject – a *modus* of *the subject.*

It is impossible to square this passage with most of the other things he writes, including a note written no more than a few months earlier. KSA 12 9[91] = WP 552 says that 'When one has grasped that the "subject" is not something that creates effects, but only a fiction, much follows.' Other passages, published and unpublished, imply that the preponderance of evidence is on the 'no subject' side of the fence (see, for example, KSA 11 35[35]), so it is safe to infer that Nietzsche was experimenting in KSA 12 9[106]. It is another question which conclusion – subject-as-only-thing or subject-as-nothing – is the correct inference given his premises. In Chapter 6, we argue that neither is correct.

14. The passage quoted here – KSA 12 10[202] = WP 558 – distinguishes monadic properties from dyadic relations. Other passages – e.g. KSA 12 2[85] = WP 557 – *reduce* even monadic properties to relations. There, Nietzsche writes: 'The properties of a thing are effects on other "things": if one removes other "things," then a thing has no properties; i.e., there is not thing without other things, i.e. there is no "thing-in-itself".' If so, this is a distinct criticism of the thing-in-itself: since all monadic properties are instead at least dyadic relations, then no individual x exists without at least one other individual y; hence, there is no thing-in-itself. One cannot help wondering whether this alternative criticism capitalizes on an ambiguity in 'thing-in-itself.' On the one hand, a thing-in-itself is, according to Kant, an unknowable thing x devoid of all of the intuitional forms and cognitive categories we supply required for sensory experience to occur; on the other hand, a thing-in-itself is, according to one reading of KSA 12 2[85], a thing x devoid of all of the relations it bears to other things. This difficulty can be eased by including among the relations that co-comprise things epistemic relations such as perspective-taking and interpretation. Then the former reading is consistent with the latter reading because the intuitional forms and cognitive categories we supply are included in the set of relations that 'things' bear to one another. Issues here are murky; for further discussion, see Hales and Welshon 2000 and Welshon 2004.

15. The modal 'possible' is needed to avoid the conclusion that existence is co-extensive with what is *actually* sensed, a view typically associated with Bishop Berkeley, who was roundly criticized for advocating it.

16. Hence, I agree with Clark and Dudrick 2012, 98–103. They likewise claim that Nietzsche's argument here is valid, and disagree with Hussain 2004b, who argues that Nietzsche's argument is invalid. However, I do not concur with one aspect of Clark and Dudrick's argument against Hussain. They claim that Hussain's conclusion that Nietzsche's BGE 15 argument is invalid rests on the false premise that physiology must philosophically justify all knowledge. They then reject Hussain's premise on the ground that Nietzsche rejects philosophical conceptions of justification (p.104). But while Nietzsche rejects foundationalist accounts of justification, it does not follow that he rejects all philosophical accounts of justification. If we attribute to him a kind of perspectival contextualist position, Hussain's premise can be rejected

without abandoning all philosophical accounts of justification. For details, see Welshon 1999.

17. For more detailed analyses of Nietzsche's sensualism, see in particular Anderson 2002 and Riccardi 2011.

18. Of course, 'rarely' does not imply 'never,' and it is to be admitted that Nietzsche occasionally advocates genetic empiricism, as, for example, at KSA 12 9[98](1887) = WP 488: 'All our *categories of reason* have sensual origins: read off from the empirical world.' However, most of the passages in which he discusses genetic empiricism advocate the regulative claim and not the dogmatic claim. More discussion of this issue occurs in Chapter 2.

19. Small 1999; the quote is from p.78.

20. Another version of the same argument type works from premises that assume a representationalist theory of the mind to the conclusion that epistemological empiricism is true. Representationalist theories of the mind are characterized by the claim that psychological states are content-bearing states that refer to but are distinct from that to which they refer. Hussain 2004a, p.123, presents a representationalist version of the argument. We start with the premise that, according to physiology, the sense organs causally generate an internal world of representations. If so, and if the sense organs aren't showing us accurately what the external world is like, then our term 'sense organs' refers only to certain representations in the internal world. But, again according to physiology, these representations in the internal world are effects, not causes. So, the sense organs can't just be representations. But then the sense organs must indeed be showing me accurately what the external world is like. This is a version of epistemolological empiricism.

2 Embodiedness, Embeddedness, Teleology

1. Difficult, but not impossible – Clark (1990) argues that BGE 36 does not represent Nietzsche's considered views about causation and will to power. Hales and Welshon (2000) argue against this interpretation.

2. See, for example, Schacht 1983; Clark 1990; Poellner 1995; Richardson 1996; Hales and Welshon 2000.

3. An example of a *static* self-organized system is a magnetized hunk of iron. Molecules composing the hunk are all little magnets – spins – each with a north and a south pole. At high temperatures, spins move anarchically, repelling and attracting each other. As the hunk's temperature lowers, a spontaneous alignment appears and the spins all line up in a single orientation, south-north-south-north and so on, creating a strong magnetic field across the hunk. This self-organization is an emergent global organization of the system of iron molecules that compose the piece of iron: it is the hunk of iron as a whole that is magnetized with a north and a south pole. The north and south poles of the individual molecules do not disappear when the hunk magnetizes, and the hunk's poles would not be as they are were the molecules' poles not as they are, but the *hunk's* poles are not the aggregate of the *molecules'* poles. An example of a dynamic self-organized system is the Bénard phenomenon, in which a liquid evenly heated from below will, after an initial state of disorganization, self-organize into a series of columnar rolls,

with ascending hot water on one side of a roll and descending cold water on the other side of a roll. The liquid's molecules are in constant motion, competing and cooperating with one another, leading to self-amplifying constellations of motion that subserve the emergent roll pattern.

4. Throwing a baseball is a linear process: if you throw the baseball with a given level of force, it will go, say, thirty feet; if you double the force, it will go about twice as far. Were throwing a baseball nonlinear, on the other hand, there would be a point where an incremental increase in the force with which the baseball is thrown would result in it going, say, 5,000 feet.

5. Hence, homeostatic equilibrium is *not* the primary function of healthy organisms. Hence, Nietzsche's views about drives are incompatible with 20th century drive theory, as is found, for example, in the work of Clark Hull. For argument on behalf of the inconsistency, see Chapter 4.

6. Some interpreters – e.g. Moore 2002 and Poellner 1995 – think Nietzsche's considered views cannot be stated without appeal to pan-psychist teleological principles. Others – e.g. Richardson 2004 – think they can. I agree with both sides of this dispute: some of his views do not escape pan-psychist teleological elements; others do escape those elements. However, Nietzsche's views can be made consistent by arguing that non-conscious goals and intentions can be re-described as functions and that reflectively conscious goals and intentions can be described as directing rather than driving causes. That conjunction is defended in Chapters 5 and 6.

7. The view developed here relies on Richardson's deflationary analysis of Nietzsche's thoughts about ends, developed in Richardson 2004, especially Chapter 1. See also Ibañez-Noe 1997, who argues that Nietzsche was working on a critique of teleology before *Birth of Tragedy*. Johnson 2010 and Johnson 2013 argue that the view developed here is incomplete because it ignores Nietzsche's larger context of a criticism of Christian morality and the role it plays in his appeal to, and ultimate rejection of, Darwinian thinking. For those who consider understanding the larger context necessary before understanding Nietzsche's naturalizing proposal about ends and goals is even possible, it may be suggested that the details of the naturalizing proposal can be set out independently of the larger context so long as the larger context is acknowledged. Consider it acknowledged. See Chapter 6 for further, albeit brief, discussion.

8. 'Fitness' refers to an organism's survivability to reproductive age; 'selection' refers to the mechanism of culling out of unfit organisms.

9. The implications of these views for Nietzsche's perspectivism and what is known as the *falsification thesis* (so-named by Maudemarie Clark in Clark 1990), are discussed in greater detail in Chapter 3.

10. See Poellner 1995, 138–162, for further developments of the issue. Poellner's analysis is considerably more generous to Nietzsche than the analysis here. We return to these matters in Chapter 3, where distinct arguments for the falsification claim are considered.

11. After Gould and Lewontin 1979. For more details on Nietzsche's development of these ideas, see Forber 2013.

12. For some of the various ways that Nietzsche caricatures and misunderstands Darwin's views and evolution, see Richardson 2004.

13. For discussion of Nietzsche's alleged Lamarckism, see Schacht 2013 and Clark 2013.
14. Recent work on non-genetic evolutionary mechanisms, including epigenetic plasticity and acquired phenotype inheritance mechanisms, has rekindled interest in some of Lamarck's claims. For more on these recent developments, see Jablonka, Lamb, and Zeligowski 2006, Gissis and Jablonka 2011, and Pigliucci and Müller 2010.
15. On these points, I concur with Clark 2013 and disagree with Schacht 2013. In addition to BGE 262, Schacht and Clark consider GS 99; BGE 264; GM II 2 – 4 and GM II 16; TI 'Improvers' 2 and 3; and TI 'Expeditions' 47. Clark shows that none of these passages is committed to Lamarckian inheritance mechanisms of epigenetic phenotypes and that each can instead be interpreted as requiring social and cultural transmission mechanisms for epigenetic phenotypes.

3 Perception, Perspectivism, Falsification

1. Dream sleep is an interesting state, of course, because while we dream, arousal is dissociated from qualitatively endowed, intentional, and perspectival experience: we are not responsive to stimuli but experience dream content. Coma and stupor are distinct from *vegetative state*, a superficially similar disorder characterized by preservation of the sleep–waking cycle and the absence of higher-order mental activity.
2. The distinction is due to Block; for more details, see the essays collected in Block 2007b. Access and qualitative character can come apart but are typically bound together in occurrent conscious processes, states, and events. Certain neuropsychological disorders show how the two properties come apart.
3. For helpful details concerning the influences from then-current perceptual physiology science on Nietzsche's thinking, see Riccardi 2011. Riccardi shows that Maximillian Drossbach's criticisms of Kant's theory of perception had a significant impact on Nietzsche's thinking about these matters. See also Schmidt 1988.
4. Just as Nietzsche's writings contain passages that are easily read as presupposing Lamarkism, so too some passages are easily read as presupposing homuncularism. The issues that homuncularism raise for his views are discussed in greater detail in Chapter 4. There it will be argued that the vast majority of his claims can be understood without saddling him with homuncularism.
5. That Nietzsche's views are in several significant respects similar to Kant's is common ground across a large number of scholars. See, among others, Anderson 1999, Green 2002, Schacht 1983.
6. The phylogenetic side of the story has been more influential than the ontogenetic side of the story.
7. The period known as the 'exuberant period,' during which synapses are added in enormous numbers (sometimes as many as a million per second) typically lasts from the age of three to the age of 11 or 12, sometimes later and then typically more often in males than in females. No long-term functional differences are implied by this gender-linked ontogenetic scheduling difference.

8. Other theories of consciousness that rely on the dynamic core have been developed. See, among others, Tononi 2004 and Tononi and Sporns 2005.

9. Edelman's notion of higher-order consciousness is distinct from David Rosenthal's higher-order theory of consciousness. Rosenthal's higher-order representationalism is a theory about the nature of consciousness. According to it, a necessary condition of any psychological state being conscious at all is that it be an awareness of another psychological state. This awareness is then analyzed either as a particular perceptual kind of relation or as a particular cognitive kind of relation (for details, see, for example, Rosenthal 2002). For Rosenthal, the *genus* of conscious psychological states is delimited from the genus of non-conscious psychological states by the fact that conscious psychological states are one and all states that possess this complex higher-order structure. For Edelman, on the other hand, higher-order consciousness is just one *species* of the larger genus of conscious psychological states, all of which are qualitatively endowed, egocentrically perspectival, and widely accessible to other neural states and processes. For reasons that will become clear, Nietzsche also marks a distinction between higher-order and first-order conscious states. Nietzsche's lack of clarity on this score is at the root of some of the apparent inconsistencies between passages in which he discusses consciousness.

10. Neuropsychological disorders accompany each of these species of binding. Some *agnosiacs* have conscious experience that is part *un*bound. For example, they may see the parts of a telephone as a scattered collection: the receiver here, the cord there, and the push buttons strewn around like candy. For someone with this disorder the world is visually experienced as composed of objects that have fallen apart all on their own. Again, some individuals – *amnesiacs* and *Balint's syndrome* patients – have conscious experience that is temporally *un*bound (see Tonkonogy and Puente 2009). Balint's syndrome patients' visual experience is of a world presented in snapshots. They cannot drive because they experience cars as frozen at a location at a time that suddenly and discontinuously jump to a much closer location a moment later, without having moved through intervening space. Amnesiacs live in sequential bubbles of a few minutes, each bubble disconnected from the past and future bubble by a lapse of memory across them. Finally, there are neurological disorders that compromise synchronic subjective perspectivity. *Asomatognosiacs*, for example, deny that certain of their body parts are their body parts; *somatoparaphreniacs* not only deny that certain of their body parts are theirs, they also affirm that those body parts are someone else's (see Feinberg *et al.* 2009). *Autoscopiacs* experience a duplicate of their body in extrapersonal space; *heautoscopiacs* experience two bodies, one real, one autoscopic from a perspective ambiguous between the two. In a related disorder, in *out-of-body experience*, individuals experience their body from a distinct, autoscopic perspective (see Metzinger 2009; see also Welshon 2011; Welshon 2013).

11. The issues implicated in the cognitive and affective penetration of perceptual experience are not obviously those implicated in disputes about the theory-ladenness of observation. For details, see Lyons 2011.

12. See Clark 1990.

13. See, among other passages, GM III 12 (discussed below); TI 'How the Real World at Last Became a Myth' (discussed in Chapter 1); KSA 12 5[22] = WP 522; KSA 12 9[38] = WP 507; KSA 12 9[106] = WP 569; KSA 12 9[144] = WP 521; KSA 13 14[93] = WP 568; KSA 13 14[105] = WP 514; KSA 13 14[152] = WP 515; KSA 13 14[184] = WP 567.

14. Hales and Welshon 2000 and Welshon 2004 discuss the warrant claim in greater detail; Welshon 2009 discusses the alethic claim and its alleged self-defeating nature. As an epistemological doctrine, perspectivism is a competitor to empiricism and positivism as understood in the Chapter 1, specifically, a competitor to the first three claims of empiricism. If perspectivism is correct, then each of the following is false:

    1. All beliefs are *generated* either immediately or eventually from sensory experience – the causal genetic claim. This claim is false because sensory experience is not the only immediate source of beliefs and does not exhaust the building blocks of all beliefs.
    2. All beliefs are *justified* either immediately or eventually by sensory experience – the warrant claim. This claim is false because warrant is always indexed to perspective and perspectives are not, as will be argued shortly, reducible to sensory perspectives.
    3. All beliefs are such that their *truth or falsity is determined* either immediately or eventually by sensory experience – the alethic claim. This claim is false because the truth of propositions is always indexed to perspective and perspectives are, again, not reducible to sensory perspectives.

15. Since they are likely to occur to the reader, a pair of ontological temptations and another, related, issue may be addressed here in a footnote. The first temptation is to attribute to Nietzsche the view that the world is exhausted by what our perceptual conscious experience displays, or, if that's too limited, by what our perceptual conscious experience displays plus what we discover through cognition. The second is to attribute to him the view since the human perspective is limited, there has to be a set of extra-perspectival entities behind what our perceptual conscious experience (plus cognition) shows. Both temptations are to be resisted. Against the first: what *we* consciously experience and think about is a function of our perspective, but every other organic entity has *its* perspective, so its experience is different from ours. Hence, even when human perspectives are subtracted, what remains is as wrapped up in perspectival interdependence as what was subtracted. Against the second: if there is at least one perspective other than the human perspective, Nietzsche may deny that a real world is entailed without that denial relapsing into a mutant form of what he denies. If even the non-human balance is perspectival through and through, any argument from some *other* perspective on behalf of an extra-perspectival real world also collapses, for the distinction between, on the one hand, objects that really exist and, on the other, those that exist only from some perspective finds no purchase.

    It is also germane to note that Nietzsche's perspectivism is not anthropomorphic. Were he to claim that the characteristics of our experience of the apparent world are criterial for all experience, then the charge might stick. However, Nietzsche is bester understood as saying not that everything is perspectival because human experience is, but rather that human experience is perspectival because everything else is. One might argue that although he might be exonerated at the first level, he cannot be exonerated at a meta-level, for he presumes to have overcome the human perspective enough to speak on behalf of what the world is like outside of that perspective, and that is itself anthropomorphic. After all, if we cannot know anything beyond the human perspective, then we cannot know that every other species introduces its own perspective or, if it does, what the nature of that perspective is. We simply cannot get enough epistemological distance from the human perspective to say that either there is a perspective other than ours or that, if there is, what it is like. Nietzsche anticipates this objection and adroitly defuses it: he thinks it is a 'ridiculous immodesty' to decree 'from our corner that perspectives are permitted only from this corner' (GS 374). He does not have to say that there are perspectives other than ours or that they have this or that content. It is enough, as he notes, that 'we cannot reject the possibility that [the world] *may include infinite interpretations*' (GS 374).

16. The following is sometimes true, depending on what substitutes for '*p*':

   (3) $\neg\Diamond Kp \rightarrow \Diamond K\neg p$

   That is, if it's not possible to know that-*p*, then it's possible to know that not-*p*. Some instances of this sentence are true on standard analyses of knowledge and standard possible worlds analyses of necessity and possibility. If it's not the case that there's a possible world where it is known that-*p*, then there certainly can be a possible world where it is known that not-*p*. No matter where in the domain of possible worlds you go, you will never land in a possible world where it is known that-*p*. But never landing in a possible world where it is known that-*p* is consistent with at least one possible world being one in which it is known that not-*p*. Hence, the sentence is true in some possible worlds, even if not in all.

   Similarly, the following is true not only in some possible worlds but in all possible worlds:

   (4) $\neg\Diamond Kp \rightarrow \Diamond\neg Kp$

   That is, if it's not possible to know that-*p*, then it is possible not to know that-*p*. This is true on any standard analysis of knowledge and any standard possible worlds analysis of necessity. For the sentence says nothing more than that if it's not the case that there's a possible world where it is known that-*p*, then there is a possible world where it is not known that-*p*. That is, no matter where you go in the domain of possible worlds, you will never land in a possible world where it is known that-*p*. But never landing in a possible world where it is known that-*p* is consistent with landing in some possible world where it is not known that-*p*, so the sentence is true. Indeed, since there are no possible worlds where it is known that-*p*, it turns out that in every possible world it is not known that-*p*.

4   Drive, Affect, Thought

1. See, among others, Cox 1997; Davey 1987a; Guay 2006; Nehamas 1985.
2. I assume that 'soul', 'ego', 'the I', and 'subject' are co-referential; see KSA 12 10[19] = WP 485, KSA 12 9[98] = WP 488, KSA 11 36 [35, 36] = WP 659.
3. For Nietzsche's relations to Hume, see, among others, Beam 1996, Davey 1987b, Kail 2009.

4. For discussion of those who may have influenced Nietzsche's thinking about drives, see Brobjer 2004; Moore 2002; and Katsafanas 2013.
5. Conceptualizing drives as dispositions is suggested by Schacht 1983. Hales and Welshon 2000 develop the view in (a little) greater detail. Katsafanas 2013 defends and enlarges the view more comprehensively and persuasively than either Schacht or Hales and Welshon.
6. Think of Dr Seuss's Little Cats in *The Cat and the Hat Comes Back,* and you'll have a pretty good idea of the problem. The Cat in the Hat has a smaller cat, Little Cat A, in his hat; Little Cat A has in his hat a still smaller cat, Little Cat B, who has in his hat a still smaller cat, Little Cat C ... and so on and so forth for every letter in the alphabet. Of course, Dr Seuss stops the iteration with Little Cat Z, the smallest of the little cats, who, although too small to see, nevertheless is the most powerful of all the little cats. He *must* be the most powerful – since he's the smallest, his causal powers have to underwrite those of all the other Little Cats.
7. Dudrick and Clark 2012, pp.195–200, opt for a homuncular interpretation of Nietzsche and think that, properly understood, it is unobjectionable; Poellner 1995 thinks homuncularism is objectionable but does not see how Nietzsche's views can avoid it; Katsafanas 2013 thinks homuncularism is objectionable but tries to defuse the threat it poses to Nietzsche's views. I think, with Katsafanas, that most of the homuncular accusations against Nietzsche can be avoided, although my reasons for thinking so differ from his.
8. See, for example, Leiter 2013.
9. See Cox 1997, especially 284, for more on supra-individual drives.
10. My thinking on the contours of affect reflects the influence of a number of interpreters, most notably Richardson 1996; Poellner 2007, 2009; Janaway, 2009; Anderson 2012; and Katsafanas 2013.
11. Human disgust responses are correlated with activity in cortical regions that are phylogenetically ancient and widely shared across mammalian species. That is one of the reasons that it is an interesting affective response: it is prompted by the same kinds of environmental input and produces the same kinds of autonomic and behavioral responses across many species, and neither its prompts nor its characteristic behavioral responses have changed much in us over our phylogenetic run. It also implies an explanation of Nietzsche's choice to use disgust to describe his response to ascetic and decadent self-organization regimens: just as disgust is prompted in all of us by decomposing flesh, so too his disgust is prompted by decadent psyches.
12. Most of what I have said here about affects merely restates and condenses points that others (see references in note 10 above) make more fully and with much greater insight and sensitivity to the texts. This area of Nietzsche scholarship is quite exciting, and much more remains to be said about the affects than has been said here.
13. Classical computationalism of the kind under discussion here may be distinguished from a generic form of computationalism that is not committed to certain of the theses that make classical computationalism problematic as a model of cognition. According to generic computationalism, cognition is the activity of processing representational vehicles and their representational features, whether symbolic or not, according to rules, whether algorithmic or

not. Space precludes further discussion of this kind of generic computation-alism or its relevance for understanding Nietzsche's claims about cognition. For those interested in the arguments on behalf of distinguishing generic from classical computationalism, see Mirolli 2012, Piccinini and Scarantino 2010, and Piccinini and Scarantino 2011.

14. One interesting question is whether symbolic representations as a category of cognitive explanation survive the transition from a classical computation-alist to a dynamic embodied-embedded view. For if all cognitive activity is causally coupled with embodied events and embedded circumstances, it may appear that none of the properties of symbolic representation are instanti-ated by what actually occurs in the neural networks of the brain. This is an ongoing debate, with no immediate resolution in sight.

5 Reflective Consciousness, Phenomenalism, Epiphenomenalism

1. If we wish to commit ourselves to a representationalist theory of conscious-ness, the distinction between basic conscious states, reflective conscious states, and reflexive conscious states can be stated in representationalist terms. A psychological state α is basically conscious if and only if α represents some-thing. A psychological state β is reflectively conscious iff β represents that α represents something. And a psychological state γ is a reflexive conscious state iff γ is a reflective conscious state β and the self is disclosed as a relatum of β.

2. Speaking of four species of consciousness is a little misleading, since it suggests that these are four distinct kinds. However, typically, access and phenom-enological conscious states are one and the same (see Block [1995]2007b, [2003]2007b, 2007a). Likewise, reflective conscious states and self-conscious states are usually access conscious and have phenomenal character. It is more accurate to speak instead of clusters of conscious properties of psychological states: the properties of being accessible, having qualitative character, and being reflective. In earlier work (Hales and Welshon 2000), I used 'moni-toring' instead of 'reflective', but I now concur with Anderson (2002) that this is a mistake.

3. Despite being of inherent interest, some issues raised by the apparent commitment to conceptualization inherent in the particularity/generality distinction will be passed over here, as will the relation between conceptuali-zation and language. See Katsafansas 2005 for further details..

4. In addition, apperception is necessary but not sufficient for consciousness of the subject of thought. Apperceptions make such consciousness of the subject possible, but must be conjoined with something else to yield self-con-sciousness. In Leibniz, that additional factor is what he calls a 'Reflective Act,' in which the subject of thought is encountered directly as an entity without qualities. For more details, see Anderson 2002. Note that '*Vorstellung*' is here translated, consistent with Kaufmann, as 'experience' and not as 'representa-tion'. I prefer the former to the latter because the latter immediately entails commitment to a representationalist theory of the mind, the attribution of which to Nietzsche is problematic (see Clark 1990; Riccardi 2007). Luckily, for the points developed herein, either translation is as comfortable as the

other. However, given that either is acceptable, there is no need to saddle him with a representationalist theory of the mind if it is unneeded.

5. Note again that I follow Kaufmann by translating '*Vorstellung*,' as 'experience' rather than as 'representation'. Reading the passage as affirming that consciousness is a property of representational phenomena rather than a property of all kinds of psychological experience does not materially affect the points being made here. For on either translation, consciousness, since it cannot exist independently of the psychological states of which it is a reflective exegesis, is not a thing, much less a thing-in-itself. Rather, it is a dependent and reflective phenomenon if it is a phenomenon of any kind. Hence, consciousness must have some ontological status different from the status of a thing or thing-in-itself.

Another issue may be mentioned here. One might insist, with Peter Poellner (Poellner 1995, 219), that '... it is difficult to understand the meaning of the assertion that an idea exists or occurs *qua* idea (rather than as, say, a series of events in a physiological substratum) without it, or more precisely its *content*, being contemplated, perceived, or attended to by anyone. How can a *Vorstellung* exist without it being *gestellt vor* – present to – a consciousness to which it displays a certain array of phenomenal properties?' Poellner's criticism of this notion is two-fold. First, he thinks it is nonsensical to attribute representational properties to unconscious drives and affects, feelings, and intentions. Second, he also thinks it is nonsensical to say that a psychological event's qualitative/affective character can exist without being contemplated, perceived, or attended to by a person. But what sense of 'unconscious' is being attributed to Nietzsche when he is taken to affirm that there are unconscious mental events? We have argued that Nietzsche's use of 'conscious' is ambiguous between those basic states that have content, qualitative/affective character, and are accessible, and those that are reflective and, perhaps, reflexive. Distinguishing between the species of consciousness helps defuse the concerns Poellner raises. It is certainly true that there can be reflectively unconscious states: any state that is a basic conscious state without also being a reflectively conscious state is an example of a reflectively unconscious state. Of course, the real problem cases are basic conscious states. It is Nietzsche's commitment to the existence of content-bearing but otherwise basically unconscious states that appears to be nonsensical. Grant that Nietzsche commits himself to such states. Are they indeed nonsensical? Well, a basically unconscious representational state is an otherwise basic conscious state whose content is not immediately available for subsequent reasoning, emotional response, and control of action. I fail to see that the existence of such states is nonsensical. Many states with content are, for one reason or another, not immediately available for subsequent reasoning, emotional response, and action direction. Something slips my mind, I forget something right now but remember it a moment later, I need to be cued to recall something, I search my mind for something and eventually find it. Such states have content but are not immediately accessible.

6. Neuroscientific research characterizes the minimal self as being an integrated and spatio-temporally located system interoceptively, affectively, perceptually, and cognitively embedded in and engaged with an environment (Vogeley and Fink 2003; Longo *et al.* 2008, 2009; Vosgerau 2009). Whatever

else is required for geometrically perspectival information to become owner-ship unified, it is not a self concept. Were ownership unity to entail posses-sion of a self concept as a condition of instantiation, then experience would be unconscious far more frequently than it actually is. Conscious experi-ence does not cease to be conscious when a self concept is not a constituent element of that experience. A self concept is a sophisticated accomplishment that presupposes simpler subjectively perspectival conscious events. So, while possession of a self concept may be required for and may be a constituent of many species of monitoring, self-reflection, and self-consciousness, it is not a pre-requisite for the sense of ownership found in non-reflective conscious experience (Burge [2006]2007 makes the same point commenting on Kant; see also Schlicht, et. al. 2009; Vosgerau 2009).

7. It turns out that much of this tracking is accomplished by the perceptual pathways, which contribute to the minimal self by embedding an organism in an environment at a particular spatial location and as interacting with its environment from that location. For instance, families of neurons in certain cortical regions present visual information from a head-centered and egocentric perspective, while certain other families of neurons in certain other cortical regions present visual information from a non-head-centered and allocentric perspective. Thus, even before visual states become conscious states, they are already perspectivally structured as from a particular spatial position in the environment. Interoceptive processes are equally important, as Tsakiris' work on interoception and his reflections on the Rubber Hand Illusion show; see Tsakiris, Schütz-Bosbach, and Gallagher 2008; Longo et al. 2008, 2009; Tsakaris 2010. Critchley also emphasizes the importance of inte-roceptive neural processes; see Critchley 2005, 2009; Medford and Critchley 2010; Singer, Critchley and Preuschoff 2009. For more on the neuroscientific details, see, among many others, Welshon 2013.

8. The genesis of this view may be in Nietzsche's reflections at *Human, All Too Human* 13 about sensory after-images. He notes there that the figures and shapes that reason and the mind conform the formless colors into when our eyes are closed are taken to be the cause of the colors. As he puts it there: 'the imagination keeps pushing images upon the mind, using in their production the visual impressions of the day ... That is, the supposed cause is deduced from the effect and imagined after the effect. All this with an extraordi-nary speed, so that, as with a conjurer, judgment becomes confused, and a sequence can appear to be a synchronism, or even a reversed sequence.'

9. This passage actually states a stronger view, viz., that all psychological phenomena are causally opaque and that the causal explanation of any psychological phenomenon – conscious or unconscious, perceptual, intero-ceptive, affective, or cognitive – must replace psychological causes with other, here unspecified, causes. This appears to be a quite global form of epiphe-nomenalism of the psychological. In section III, an argument is presented that global epiphenomenalism of the psychological is too strong.

10. Nagel 1989.

11. We consider pleasure and pain in greater detail in Chapter 6.

12. Strong epiphenomenalism of non-reducible reflective properties agrees with modest epiphenomenalism of non-reducible reflective properties on clauses (i) and (ii), but rejects the modest form's clause (iii). To wit:

    i. all reflective psychological particulars are drives; and

    ii. the reflective properties in virtue of which a particular drive is specified as a reflectively conscious state RC_1 do not cause reflective properties to be instantiated by any temporally subsequent reflectively conscious state RC_2; and

    iii. the reflective properties in virtue of which a particular drive is specified as a reflectively conscious state RC1 do not cause affective properties to be instantiated by a temporally subsequent basic conscious state BD2.

Strong epiphenomenalism of non-reducible reflective properties is consistent with (KSA 13 14[152] = WP 478); moderate epiphenomenalism of non-reducible reflective properties is consistent with (KSA 13 11[113] = WP 477).

6   Self, Will, Power

1. Since Nietzsche's suspicions about philosophers' epistemological presumptions concerning *de se* self-knowledge were discussed in the last chapter, we consider them no further here.

2. Leiter 2002, 2009; Knobe and Leiter 2007; Risse 2007. Hales and Welshon 2000 also attribute to Nietzsche a pretty basic bundle theorist of the self. I now think that the view as stated there is too sparse to be persuasive, either as Nietzsche interpretation or as a philosophical position.

3. Where '$X_s x$' represents supervening properties and '$Y_B x$' subvening or basal properties, we can state this in the following formula:

$$\Box_N (\forall x)[X_S x \to (\exists Y_B)(Y_B x \land (\forall y)(Y_B y \to X_S y))]$$

This version of supervenience is *weak* supervenience (Kim 1993). *Strong* supervenience asserts in addition that whenever there is a supervening property instantiated by some event, there will be a subvening basal property also instantiated by that event and that *as a matter of scientific law*, any other event that has that subvening basal property will also have the supervening property. Both weak and strong supervenience state a kind of 1–1 co-variation from one family of properties to another family of properties, the supervening family and the subvening family. Note that the 1–1 function from supervening to subvening does *not* imply that there is a 1–1 function from the subvening to the supervening families of properties. In fact, members of a subvening family of properties do not map 1–1 to members of supervening families. That there is not a 1–1 function from subvening to supervening is one of the ways that supervenience is distinct from identity. Identity is 1–1 and onto, so it is bidirectional; supervenience is 1–1 but not onto, so it is unidirectional.

4. Horgan 1993 is particularly good on this matter. That supervenience must be amended if it is to result in reduction may be appreciated by remembering that supervenience is asymmetric and reflexive, whereas reduction is asymmetric and irreflexive. If *x* supervenes on *y*, then it's not the case that *y* supervenes on *x*, and *x* supervenes on itself. Asymmetry makes supervenience look kind of like determination, but its reflexivity entails that it really cannot be. Determination is also asymmetric – if *x* is determined by *y*, then it's not the case that *y* determines *x* – but determination is irreflexive – nothing determines

itself. An example makes the point. Consider the determination relation of *composition*, as when a material object's shape is composed of the shapes of its parts standing in a particular set of structural relations. Composition is a supervenience relation since the properties of the composed object supervene on its composition base properties. But the asymmetric covariance that supervenience describes is not what establishes the ontological primacy that composition models for the subvenient composition base. Rather, determination of a supervenient property by its subvening property pair comes from the causal powers of the supervenient property being no other than those of its subvening property pair. These causal powers establish the direction of determination from the subvenient base to the supervenient and, as will be seen shortly, the direction of reduction from the supervenient to the subvenient composition base.

5. It is not always appreciated that supervenience is neither a causal relation nor a determination relation. Suppose there is a family of conscious states C and a family of neural states N. Then supervenience of C states on N states guarantees that anytime a C state occurs, an N state occurs and any other N state will also covary with that C state. Still, this covariation doesn't guarantee that C is nothing but N. Supervenience models a nomological covariation between conscious and neural properties of attention, but that is *all* that it models; see Burge [1986a]2007 and Kim 1997; however, Kim 2003 expresses an opposing view. Nomological covariation is, thus, neutral on causation and determination. Supervenience does not imply that a supervening state *cannot* or *must* be a cause, does not imply that a subvening state is the *only* cause, and does not imply that the causal powers of a supervening state are *nothing other* than those of its subvening state pair. One might think otherwise if one reads the conditionals in statements of supervenience as expressing causal relations. But the conditionals in statements of supervenience are truth-functional conditionals. The right-facing arrow between two terms 'p' and 'q' ('$p \rightarrow q$') means that the sentence '$p \rightarrow q$' is true whenever both 'p' and 'q' are true or 'p' is false, and false otherwise. The absurdity of taking the arrows to represent causes is exposed by trying to read a statement of supervenience off as such: any C state causes an N state and any other N state causes that C state. It doesn't even make sense.

6. Stephan 1999.

7. The world's phenomena are thus organized into various levels according to the systemic properties instantiated at a level. Different sciences investigate the phenomena fixed by property level. There are (among others) microphysical, atomic-physical, chemical, biological, biochemical, neurological, computational, psychological, and sociological kinds of properties; see Block 2003; Bontly 2002; Emmeche *et al.* 2000; Kim 2003; Oppenheim & Putnam 1958.

8. The strong/weak emergentism distinction cross-classifies with the static/dynamic distinction. There are weakly emergent dynamic systems and strongly emergent static systems.

9. If the diagrams in this section look familiar, that's because similar diagrams were introduced in Chapter 5 to describe the relation between reflective consciousness and the basic drives that cause them. The parallel is anything but accidental, as will be argued in the next section.

10. The more I think about modest epiphenomenalism, the more I think that Nietzsche is wrong that one emergent reflective conscious state cannot cause another emergent reflective conscious state. There seems no reason even for Nietzsche to require that between every reflective conscious state there *must* be some intervening basic conscious state, drive, or affect. Of course, if the point is instead that *beneath* every reflective conscious state, there must be some intervening basic conscious state, drive, or affect, then that is just a variant statement of the supervenient emergence view currently under discussion.

11. Kim 1992, 1998, 2000, 2003.

12. The term 'preemption' actually refers to two distinct phenomena. First, as discussed here, members from one family of properties may trump members from another family of properties. Preemption of one family by another then entails replacement of the former by the latter. Second, one event's occurrence at an earlier time than another's occurrence may make a mess of the latter's claim to cause anything because counterfactual dependency fails. We do not discuss the second sense. For those interested, see Collins 2000; Lewis 1979, 1986, 2000; Paul 1998.

13. Huemer and Kovitz 2003, among others, argue that there are simultaneous causes. They cite examples such as a lead ball causing an indentation in a cushion on which it is placed, lowering one end of a seesaw causing the other end of the seesaw to elevate, and the high temperature of an iron bar causing it to glow red. Each candidate can be reinterpreted as a case of diachronic causation or as not a case of causation at all.

14. In general, non-reductionists about the psychological tolerate upward causation from basals to non-pleonastic emergents because it provides some set of basals from which emergents have to emerge. One consequence is that some basals cause both basal and emergent effects, so some causes have more than one effect. A corollary is that some basals have both supervenient and subvenient effects. Both are acceptable consequences; see Lewis 1986.

15. Coady 2004; Sider 2003.

16. For details, see Hales and Welshon 2000, Chapters 3 and 4.

Bibliography

Andersen, P. B., C. Emmeche, N. O. Finnemann, and P. V. Christiansen, eds, 2000. *Downwards Causation*. Aarhus, Netherlands: Aarhus University Press.

Anderson, R. L. 1999. "Nietzsche's Views on Truth and the Kantian Background of His Epistemology." In *Nietzsche, Epistemology, and Philosophy of Science: Nietzsche and the Sciences II*, edited by B. Babich, 47–59. London: Kluwer.

Anderson, R. L. 2002. "Sensualism and Unconscious Representations in Nietzsche's Account of Knowledge." *International Studies in Philosophy* 34 (3): 95–117.

Anderson, R. L. 2005. "Nietzsche on Truth, Illusion, and Redemption." *The European Journal of Philosophy* 13: 185–225.

Anderson, R. L. 2012. "What is a Nietzschean Self?" In *Nietzsche, Naturalism, and Normativity*, edited by C. Janaway, and S. Robertson, 202–233. NY: Oxford University Press.

Beam, C. 1996. "Hume and Nietzsche: Naturalists, Ethicists, Anti-Christians." *Hume Studies* 22 (2): 299–324.

Bechtel, W. 1998. "Representations and Cognitive Explanation: Assessing the Dynamicist's Challenge in Cognitive Science." *Cognitive Science* 22: 295–318.

Bechtel, W. 2009. "Mechanism, Modularity, and Situated Cognition." In *The Cambridge Handbook of Situated Cognition*, edited by P. Robbins, and M. Aydede, 155–70. NY: Cambridge University Press.

Bechtel, W., and A. Abrahemsen. 2005. "Explanation: A Mechanist Alternative." *Studies in History and Philosophy of Biological and Biomedical Sciences* 36: 421–441.

Bechtel, W., and R. Richardson. 1993. *Discovering Complexity: Decomposition and Localization as Strategies in Scientific Research*. NY: Princeton University Press.

Bermúdez, J. 1998. *The Paradox of Self-Consciousness*. Cambridge, MA: MIT Press.

Blanke, O., and T. Metzinger. 2009. "Full-body Illusions and Minimal Phenomenal Selfhood." *Trends in Cognitive Sciences* 13 (1): 7–13.

Block, N. [1995] 2007b. "On a Confusion about a Function of Consciousness." In Block (2007b), 159–213.

Block, N. 2003. "Do Causal Powers Drain Away?" *Philosophy and Phenomenological Research* 67: 110–127.

Block, N. [2003] 2007b. "Mental Paint." See Block (2007b), 533–570.

Block, N. 2007a. "Consciousness, Accessibility, and the Mesh between Psychology and Neuroscience." *Behavioral and Brain Sciences* 30: 481–548.

Block, N. 2007b. *Consciousness, Function, and Representation: Collected Papers*, vol. I. Cambridge, MA: MIT Press.

Bontly, T. 2002. "The Supervenience Argument Generalizes." *Philosophical Studies* 109: 75–96.

Brobjer, T. 2004. "Nietzsche's Reading and Knowledge of Natural Science: An Overview." In *Nietzsche and Science*, edited by G. Moore, and T. Brobjer, 21–50. Aldershot: Ashgate.

Brown, R. S. G. 2004. "Nietzsche: 'That Profound Physiologist.'" In *Nietzsche and Science*, edited by G. Moore, and T. Brobjer, 51–70. Aldershot: Ashgate.

Burge, T. [1986] 2007. "Individualism and Psychology." In Burge (2007), 221–253.
Burge, T. [1993] 2007. "Mind–body Causation and Explanatory Practice." In Burge (2007), 344–362.
Burge, T. [1995] 2007. "Intentional Properties and Causation." In Burge (2007), 334–343.
Burge, T. [2006] 2007. "Reflections on Two Kinds of Consciousness." In Burge (2007), 392–419.
Burge, T. 2007. *Foundations of Mind: Philosophical Essays*, vol. 2. Oxford University Press.
Clark, M. 1990. *Nietzsche on Truth and Philosophy*. NY: Cambridge University Press.
Clark, M. 2013. "Nietzsche was No Lamarckian." *Journal of Nietzsche Studies* 44 (2): 282–296.
Clark, M., and D. Dudrick. 2009. "Nietzsche's Post-Positivism." *European Journal of Philosophy* 12 (3): 369–285.
Clark, M., and D. Dudrick. 2012. *The Soul of Nietzsche's Beyond Good and Evil*. NY: Cambridge University Press.
Coady, D. 2004. "Preempting Preemption." In *Causation and Counterfactuals*, edited by J. Collins, N. Hall, and L. Paul, 325–340. Cambridge, MA: MIT Press.
Collins, J. 2000. "Preemptive Prevention." *Journal of Philosophy* 97: 223–34.
Cox, C. 1997. "The "Subject" of Nietzsche's Perspectivism." *Journal of the History of Philosophy* 35 (2): 269–291.
Cox, C. 1999. *Nietzsche: Naturalism and Interpretation*. Berkeley: University of California Press.
Critchley, H. 2005. "Neural Mechanisms of Autonomic, Affective, and Cognitive Integration." *The Journal of Comparative Neurology* 493: 154–166.
Critchley, H. 2009. "Psychophysiology of Neural, Cognitive and Affective integration: fMRI and Autonomic Indicants." *International Journal of Psychophysiology* 73: 88–94.
Darwin, C. [1859] 2003. *On the Origin of Species*. London: Signet.
Davey, N. 1987a. "Nietzsche, the Self, and Hermenuetic Theory." *Journal of the British Society for Phenomenology* 18 (3): 272–284.
Davey, N. 1987b. "Nietzsche and Hume on Self and Identity." *Journal of the British Society for Phenomenology* 18(1): 14–29.
Delk, J. L., and S. Fillenbaum. 1965. "Differences in Perceived Colour as a Function of Characteristic Colour." *The American Journal of Psychology* 78 (2): 290–293.
Drossbach, M. 1884. *Über die scheinbaren und die wirklichen Ursachen des Geschehens in der Welt*. Halle: Pfeffer.
Dudrick, D., and M. Clark. 2009. "Nietzsche on the Will: An Analysis of BGE 19." In *Nietzsche on Freedom and Autonomy*, edited by K. Gemes, and S. May, 247–268. NY: Oxford University Press.
Edelman, G. 1987. *Neural Darwinism: The Theory of Neuronal Group Selection*. NY: Basic Books.
Edelman, G. 2003. "Naturalizing Consciousness: A Theoretical Framework." *Proceedings of the National Academy of Sciences* 100: 5520–5524.
Edelman, G., and G. Tononi. 2000. *A Universe of Consciousness: How Matter Becomes Imagination*. NY: Basic Books.
Emmeche, C., S. Køppe, and F. Stjernfelt. 2000. "Levels of Emergence, and Three Versions of Downwards Causation." In *Downwards Causation*, edited by P.

B. Andersen, C. Emmeche, N. O. Finnemann, and P.V. Christiansen, 13–34. Aarhus, Netherlands: Aarhus University Press.

Feinberg, T., M. Venneri, A. Simone, Y. Fan, and G. Northoff. 2009. "The Neuroanatomy of Asomatognosia and Somatoparaphrenia." *Journal of Neurology, Neurosurgery, and Psychiatry*, published online 24 September 2009, doi:10.1136/jnnp.2009.188946.

Forber, P. 2013. "Biological Inheritance and Cultural Evolution in Nietzsche's Genealogy." *Journal of Nietzsche Studies* 44 (2): 329–341.

Gallagher, S. 2005. *How the Body Shapes the Mind*. New York: Oxford University Press.

Gemes. K. 2001. "Postmodernism's Use and Abuse of Nietzsche." *Philosophy and Phenomenological Research* 62(2): 327–360.

Gemes, K. and C. Janaway. 2005. "Naturalism and Value in Nietzsche." *Philosophy and Phenomenological Research* 71(3): 729–740.

Gemes, K., and S. May, eds, 2009. *Nietzsche on Freedom and Autonomy*. NY: Oxford University Press.

Gissis, S., E. Jablonka, and A Zeligowski, eds, 2011. *Transformations of Larmarckism: From Subtle Fluids to Molecular Biology*. Cambridge, MA: MIT Press.

Gould, S. J., and R. Lewontin. 1979. "The Spandrels of San Marco and the Panglossian Paradigm: A Critique of the Adaptationist Programme." *Proceedings of the Royal Society, Series B, Biological Sciences* 205: 581–598.

Green, M. 2002. *Nietzsche and the Transcendental Tradition*. Urbana, IL: University of Illinois Press

Guay, R. 2006. "The 'I's have it: Nietzsche on subjectivity." *Inquiry* 49 (3): 218–224.

Hales, S., and R. Welshon. 2000. *Nietzsche's Perspectivism*. Urbana, IL: University of Illinois Press.

Haugeland, J. [1991] 1998. "Representational Genera." In his *Having Thought: Essays in the Metaphysics of Mind*, 171–208. Cambridge, MA: Harvard University Press.

Horgan, T. 1993. "From Supervenience to Superdupervenience: Meeting the Demands of a Material World." *Mind* 102: 555–86

Huemer, M., and B. Kovitz. 2003. "Causation as Simultaneous and Continuous." *Philosophical Quarterly* 53: 556–65.

Hull, C. 1943. *Principles of Behavior*. NY: Appleton-Century-Crofts.

Hussain, N. J. Z. 2004a. "Reading Nietzsche through Ernst Mach." In *Nietzsche and Science*, edited by G. Moore and T. Brobjer, 111–129. Aldershot, UK: Ashgate Publishing.

Hussain, N. J. Z. 2004b. "Nietzsche's Positivism." *European Journal of Philosophy* 12 (3): 326–368.

Ibanez-Noe, J. 1997. "Nietzsche and the Problem of Teleology." *International Studies in Philosophy* 29 (3): 37–48.

Jablonka, E., M. Lamb, and A. Zeligowski (2006). *Evolution in Four Dimensions: Genetic, Epigenetic, Behavioral, and Symbolic Variation in the History of Life*. Cambridge, MA: MIT Press, A Bradford Book.

Janaway, C. 2009. "Autonomy, Affect, and the Self in Nietzsche's Project of Genealogy." In *Nietzsche on Freedom and Autonomy*, edited by K. Gemes, and S. May, 51–68. NY: Oxford University Press.

Janaway, C., and S. Robertson, eds, 2012. *Nietzsche, Naturalism, and Normativity*. NY: Oxford University Press.

Johnson, D. 2010. *Nietzsche's Anti-Darwinism*. NY: Cambridge University Press.

Johnson, D. 2013. "Reassessing the Nietzsche–Darwin Relationship." *Journal of Nietzsche Studies* 44 (2): 342–353.

Kail, P. 2009. "Nietzsche and Hume: Naturalism and Explanation." *Journal of Nietzsche Studies* 37: 5–22.

Kant, I. [1787]1965. *Critique of Pure Reason*. Translated by N. K. Smith. NY: St. Martin's Press.

Katsafanas, P. 2005. "Nietzsche's Theory of Mind: Consciousness and Conceptualization." *European Journal of Philosophy* 13 (1): 1–31.

Katsfanas, P. 2013. "Nietzsche's Philosophical Psychology." In *Oxford Handbook of Nietzsche*, edited by K. Gemes, and J. Richardson, 727–755. NY: Oxford University Press.

Kaufmann, W. 1975. *Nietzsche: Philosopher, Psychologist, Antichrist*, 4th edition. NY: Princeton University Press.

Kim, J. 1992. "'Downwards Causation' in Emergentism and Nonreductive Physicalism." In *Emergence or Reduction*, edited by A. Beckermann, H. Flohr, and J. Kim, 119–138. Berlin: De Gruyter.

Kim, J. 1993. *Supervenience and Mind*. New York: Cambridge University Press.

Kim, J. 1997. "Supervenience, Emergence, and Realization in the Philosophy of Mind." In *Mindscapes: Philosophy, Science, and the Mind*, edited by M. Carrier and P. Machamer, 271–293. Pittsburgh: Pittsburgh University Press.

Kim, J. 1998. *Mind in a Physical World*. Cambridge, MA: MIT Press.

Kim, J. 1999. "Making Sense of Emergence." *Philosophical Studies* 95: 3–36.

Kim, J. 2000. "Making Sense of Downward Causation." In *Downwards Causation*, edited by P. B. Andersen, C. Emmeche, N. O. Finnemann, and P. V. Christiansen, 305–321. Aarhus, Netherlands: Aarhus University Press.

Kim, J. 2003. "Blocking Causal Drainage and Other Maintenance Chores with Mental Causation." *Philosophy and Phenomenological Research* 67: 128–153.

Knobe, J., and B. Leiter. 2007. "The Case for Nietzschean Moral Psychology." In *Nietzsche and Morality*, edited by B. Leiter, and N. Sinhababu, 83–109. NY: Oxford University Press.

Kriegel, U. 2006. "The Same-order Monitoring Theory of Consciousness." In *Self-representational Approaches to Consciousness*, edited by U. Kriegel, and K. Williford, 143–170. Cambridge, MA: MIT Press.

Kriegel, U. 2009. "Self–representationalism and Phenomenology." *Philosophical Studies* 143: 357–381.

Kriegel, U., and K. Williford, eds. 2006. *Self-representational Approaches to Consciousness*. Cambridge, MA: MIT Press.

Leibniz, G. [1765]1981. *New Essays on Human Understanding*. Translated by P. Remnant, and J. Bennett. NY: Cambridge University Press.

Leiter, B. 2002. *Nietzsche on Morality*. NY: Routledge.

Leiter, B. 2009. "Nietzsche's Theory of the Will." In *Nietzsche on Freedom and Autonomy*, edited by K. Gemes, and S. May, 107–126. NY: Oxford University Press.

Leiter, B. 2013. "Nietzsche's Naturalism Reconsidered." In *The Oxford Handbook of Nietzsche*, edited by K. Gemes, and J. Richardson, 576–598. Oxford: Oxford University Press.

Leiter, B., and N. Sinhababu, eds, 2007. *Nietzsche and Morality*. NY: Oxford University Press.

Lewis, D. 1979. "Counterfactual Dependence and Time's Arrow." *Noûs* 13: 455–476.

Lewis, D. 1983. "Extrinsic Properties." *Philosophical Studies* 44: 197–200.

Lewis, D. 1986. "Causation." In his *Philosophical Papers*, vol. 2, 159–213. Oxford: Oxford University Press.

Lewis, D. 2000. "Causation as Influence." *Journal of Philosophy* 97: 182–197.

Longo, M., Schüür, F., Kammers, M., Tsakiris, M., and Haggard, P. 2008. "What is Embodiment? A Psychometric Approach." *Cognition* 107: 978–998.

Longo, M., Schüür, F., Kammers, M., Tsakiris, M., and Haggard, P. 2009. "Self-Awareness and the Body Image." *Acta Psychologica* 132: 166–172.

Lyons, J. 2011. "Circularity, Reliability, and the Cognitive Penetrability of Perception." *Philosophical Issues 21: The Epistemology of Perception*: 289–311.

MacPherson, F. 2012. "Cognitive Penetration of Colour Experience: Rethinking the Issue in Light of an Indirect Mechanism." *Philosophy and Phenomenological Research* 84 (1): 24–62.

McDowell, J. 2008. "Naturalism in the Philosophy of Mind." In *Naturalism in Question*, edited by M. De Caro, and D. Macarthur, 91–105. Cambridge, MA: Harvard University Press.

McGinn, C. (2000). *The Mysterious Flame*. NY: Basic Books.

Medford, N., and Critchley, H. 2010. "Conjoint Activity of Anterior Insular and Anterior Cingulate Cortex: Awareness and Response." *Brain Structure and Function* 214: 535–549.

Metzinger, T. 2003. *Being No-One*. Cambridge, MA: MIT Press.

Metzinger, T. 2009. "Why Are Out-of-Body Experiences Interesting for Philosophers? The Theoretical Relevance of OBE Research." *Cortex* 45: 256–258.

Mirolli, M. 2012. "Representations in Dynamical Embodied Agents: Re-Analyzing a Minimally Cognitive Model Agent." *Cognitive Science* 36: 870–895.

Moore, G. 2002. *Nietzsche, Biology and Metaphor*. NY: Cambridge University Press.

Moore, G. 2004. "Nietzsche, Medicine and Meteorology." In *Nietzsche and Science*, edited by G. Moore, and T. Brobjer, 71–90. Aldershot: Ashgate.

Müller-Lauter, W. 1978. "Der Organismus als Innerer Kampf. Der Einfluss von Willhelm Roux und Friedrich Nietzsche." *Nietzsche-Studien* 7: 189–235.

Nagel, T. 1989. *The View from Nowhere*. NY: Oxford University Press.

Nehamas, A. 1985. *Nietzsche: Life as Literature*. Cambridge, MA: Harvard University Press.

Nietzsche, F. 1968. *The Antichrist*, translated by W. Kaufmann, in *The Portable Nietzsche*, ed. Walter Kaufmann. NY: Viking Press.

Nietzsche, F. 1966. *Beyond Good and Evil*, translated by W. Kaufmann. NY: Random House.

Nietzsche, F. 1967. *The Birth of Tragedy*, translated by W. Kaufmann, in *The Birth of Tragedy and The Case of Wagner*. NY: Random House.

Nietzsche, F. 1982. *Daybreak: Thoughts on the Prejudices of Morality*, translated by R. J. Hollingdale. Cambridge: Cambridge University Press.

Nietzsche, F. 1967. *Ecce Homo: How One Becomes What One Is*, translated by W. Kaufmann, in *On the Genealogy of Morals and Ecce Homo*. NY: Random House.

Nietzsche, F. 1974. *The Gay Science, with a Prelude of Rhymes and an Appendix of Songs*, translated by W. Kaufmann. NY: Random House.

Nietzsche, F. 1986. *Human, All Too Human: A Book for Free Spirits*, translated by R. J. Hollingdale. Cambridge: Cambridge University Press.

Nietzsche, F. 1967. *On the Genealogy of Morals*, translated by W. Kaufmann, and R.J. Hollingdale, in *On the Genealogy of Morals and Ecce Homo*. NY: Random House.

Nietzsche, F. 1968. *Twilight of the Idols*, translated by W. Kaufmann, in *The Portable Nietzsche*. NY: Viking Press.

Nietzsche, F. 1967. *The Will to Power*, translated by W. Kaufmann. NY: Random House.

Nietzsche, F. 1988. *Kritische Studienausgabe*, 14 volumes, edited by G. Colli, and M. Montinari. Berlin: de Gruyter.

O'Connor, T. (1994). "Emergent Properties." *American Philosophical Quarterly* 31: 91–104.

Oppenheim, P., and H. Putnam. 1958. "The Unity of Science as a Working Hypothesis." In *Minnesota Studies in the Philosophy of Science*, vol. 2, edited by H. Feigl, M. Scriven, and G. Maxwell, 3–36. Minneapolis: Minnesota University Press.

Papineau. D. 1993. *Philosophical Naturalism*. NY: Oxford University Press.

Papineau, D. 2009. "Naturalism." *The Stanford Encyclopedia of Philosophy*, edited by E. Zalta. URL = http://plato.stanford.edu/archives/spr2009/entries/ naturalism/.

Paul, L. 1998. "Problems with Late Preemption." *Analysis* 58: 48–53.

Peirce, C. S. 1976. *The New Elements of Mathematics by Charles S. Peirce*, 4 volumes, edited by C. Eisele, 20–1. The Hague, Netherlands: Mouton.

Piccinini, G., and A. Scarantino 2010. "Computation vs. Information Processing: Why Their Difference Matters to Cognitive Science." *Studies in the History and Philosophy of Science* 41: 237–246.

Piccinini, G., and A. Scarantino 2011. "Information Processing, Computation, and Cognition." *Journal of Biological Physics* 37: 1–38.

Pigliucci, M., and G. Müller, eds, 2010. *Evolution: The Extended Synthesis*. Cambridge, MA: MIT Press.

Poellner, P. 1995. *Nietzsche and Metaphysics*. NY: Oxford University Press.

Poellner, P. 2007. "Affect, Value and Objectivity." In *Nietzsche and Morality*, edited by B. Leiter, and N. Sinhababu, 227–261. NY: Oxford University Press.

Poellner, P. 2009. "Nietzschean Freedom." In *Nietzsche on Freedom and Autonomy*, edited by K. Gemes, and S. May, 151–180. NY: Oxford University Press.

Quine, W. V. O. 1953a. "Two Dogmas of Empiricism." In his *From a Logical Point of View*, 20–46. Cambridge, MA: Harvard University Press.

Quine, W. V. O. 1953b. "On What There Is." In his *From a Logical Point of View*, 1–19. Cambridge, MA: Harvard University Press.

Quine, W. V. O. 1969b. "Epistemology Naturalized." In his *Ontological Relativity and Other Essays*, 69–90. NY: Columbia University Press.

Raftopoulos, A., ed. 2005. *Cognitive Penetrability of Perception: Attention, Action, Strategies, and Bottom-up Constraints*. NY: Nova Science.

Raftapoulos, A. 2009. *Cognition and Perception: How do Psychology and Neural Science Inform Philosophy?* Cambridge, MA: MIT Press.

Riccardi, M. "Nietzsche's Sensualism." *European Journal of Philosophy* 21 (2): 219–257.

Richardson, J. 1996. *Nietzsche's System*. NY: Oxford University Press.

Richardson, J. 2004. *Nietzsche's New Darwinism*. NY: Oxford University Press.

Risse, M. 2007. "Nietzschean 'Animal Psychology' versus Kantian Ethics." In *Nietzsche and Morality*, edited by B. Leiter, and N. Sinhababu, 57–82. NY: Oxford University Press.

Rosenthal, D. 1997. "A Theory of Consciousness." In *The Nature of Consciousness* edited by N. Block, N. Flanagan, and G. Güzeldere, 729–754. Cambridge, MA: MIT Press.

Rosenthal, D. 2002. "Explaining Consciousness." In *Philosophy of Mind: Classical and Contemporary Readings*, edited by D. Chalmers, 406–421. NY: Oxford University Press.

Rosciglione, C. "A Non-Reductionist Physioligism: Nietzsche on Body, Mind, and Consciousness." *Prolegomena* 12 (1): 43–60.

Salaquarda, J. 1978. "Nietzsche und Lange." *Nietzsche-Studien* 7: 230–260.

Sartre, J.-P. [1936]1962. *The Transcendence of the Ego*, translated by F. Williams and R. Kirkpatrick. New York: Noonday Press.

Schacht, R. 1983. *Nietzsche: The Arguments of the Philosophers*. NY: Routledge.

Schacht, R. 2012. "Nietzsche's Naturalism." *Journal of Nietzsche Studies* 43 (2): 185–212.

Schacht, R. 2013. "Nietzsche and Lamarckism." *Journal of Nietzsche Studies* 44 (2): 264–281.

Schmidt, R. 1988. "Nietzsches Drossbach-Lektüre." *Nietzsche-Studien* 17: 465–477.

Sider, T. 2003. "What's So Bad about Overdetermination?" *Philosophy and Phenomenological Research* 67: 719–726.

Singer, W. 2001. "Consciousness and the Binding Problem." *Annals of the New York Academy of Sciences* 929: 123–146.

Singer, T., Critchley, H., and Preuschoff, K. 2009. "A Common Role of Insula in Feelings, Empathy and Uncertainty." *Trends in Cognitive Science* 13 (8): 334–340.

Small, R. 1999. "We Sensualists." in *Nietzsche, Epistemology, and Philosophy of Science*, volume 2, edited by B. Babich, and R. Cohen, 73–89. Dordrecht: Kluwer.

Smith, C. U. M. 1986. "Friedrich Nietzsche's Biological Epistemics." *Journal of Social and Biological Structures* 9: 375–388.

Sosa, E. 2002. "Privileged Access." In *Consciousness: New Philosophical Perspectives*, edited by Q. Smith, and A. Jokic, 273–294. New York, NY: Oxford University Press.

Stack, G. 1983. *Lange and Nietzsche*. Berlin: De Gruyter.

Stephan, A. 1999. "Varieties of Emergentism." *Evolution and Cognition* 5: 49–59.

Strawson, P. F. 1985. *Skepticism and Naturalism: Some Varieties*. NY: Columbia University Press.

Strevens, M. 2005. "How are the Sciences of Complex Systems Possible?" *Philosophy of Science* 72: 531–556.

Tonkonogy, J., and A. Puente. 2009. *Localization of Clinical Syndromes in Neuropsychology and Neuroscience*. New York: Springer.

Tononi, G. 2004. "An Information Integration Theory of Consciousness." *BMC Neuroscience* 5 (42): 1–22.

Tononi, G., and O. Sporns. 2003. "Measuring Information Integration." *BMC Neuroscience* 4 (31): 1–20.

Treisman, A. 1996. "The Binding Problem." *Current Opinion in Neurobiology* 6: 171–178.

Tsakiris, M., Schütz-Bsobach, S., and Gallagher, S. 2007. "On Agency and Body-ownership: Phenomenological and Neurocognitive Reflections." *Consciousness and Cognition* 16: 645–660.

Tsakiris, M. 2010. "*My* body in the Brain: A Neurocognitive Model of Body-Ownership." *Neuropsychologia* 48: 703–712.

Van Gelder, T. 1995. "What Might Cognition Be, If Not Computation?" *Journal of Philosophy* 91: 345–382.

Vogeley, K., and G. Fink. 2003. "Neural Correlates of the First-person Perspective." *Trends in Cognitive Science* 7 (1): 38–42.

Vosgerau, G. (2009). *Mental Representation and Self-Consciousness: From Basic Self-Representation to Self-Related Cognition*. Paderborn, Germany: Mentis.

Welshon, R. 2004. *The Philosophy of Nietzsche*. Chesham: Acumen.

Welshon, R. 2011. *Philosophy, Neuroscience, and Consciousness*. Chesham: Acumen.

Welshon, R. 1999. "Perspectivist ontology and *de re* knowledge." In *Nietzsche, Epistemology, and Philosophy of Science*, volume 2, edited by B. Babich, and R. Cohen, 39–47. Dordrecht: Kluwer.

Welshon, R. 2013. "Searching for the Neural Realizers of Ownership Unity." *Philosophical Psychology* 26 (6): 839–862.

Zahavi, D. 2008. *Subjectivity and Selfhood: Investigating the First-Person Perspective*. Cambridge, MA: MIT Press.

Index

9 781349 338030